C000212515

20th Century
American Literature

Andrew Blades

Longman
is an imprint of

York Press

Harlow, England • London • New York • Boston • San Francisco • Toronto
Sydney • Tokyo • Singapore • Hong Kong • Seoul • Taipei • New Delhi
Cape Town • Madrid • Mexico City • Amsterdam • Munich • Paris • Milan

YORK PRESS
322 Old Brompton Road
London
SW5 9JH

PEARSON EDUCATION LIMITED
Edinburgh Gate, Harlow CM20 2JE. United Kingdom
Tel: +44 (0)1279 623623 Fax: +44 (0)1279 431059
Website: www.pearsoned.co.uk

First edition published in Great Britain in 2011

© Librairie du Liban *Publishers* 2011

The right of Andrew Blades to be identified as Author of this Work has been
asserted by him in accordance with the Copyright, Designs and Patents Act 1988.

ISBN 978–1–4082–6664–9

British Library Cataloguing in Publication Data
A CIP catalogue record for this book can be obtained from the British Library

Library of Congress Cataloging in Publication Data
Blades, Andrew, 1980-
  20th century American literature / Andrew Blades.
      p. cm. -- (York notes companions)
  Includes bibliographical references and index.
  ISBN 978-1-4082-6664-9 (pbk.)
  1. American literature--20th century--History and criticism. I. Title. III. Series.

PS221.B48 2011
810.9'005--dc22
                              2011006469

10 9 8 7 6 5 4 3 2 1
14 13 12 11

Phototypeset by Pantek Arts Ltd, Maidstone
Printed in Malaysia (CTP-VP)

Contents

Contents

Part One
Introduction

In February 1941, some eleven months before the Japanese attack on Pearl Harbour that would kick-start American involvement in the Second World War, Henry Luce wrote an article for *Life* magazine called 'The American Century' in which he sounded a note of caution. He was concerned about the USA's reluctance to engage in international politics; instead of opting out of world affairs, he urged his people to involve themselves and exercise an influence.[1] On 7 December 1941, the USA was plunged into war with Japan; on 11 December, Germany and Italy declared war on America, and involvement in the Second World War began. The chain of events that followed – the atomic bomb, the Cold War and the emergence of the United States as one of two international superpowers – proved beyond doubt that the twentieth century was indeed the 'American century'.* By the turn of the millennium, the USA was the only remaining economic and cultural superpower, its presence at the negotiating table a diplomatic necessity, its president the 'leader of the free world'.

Nevertheless, America continued to debate its position in the wider world, not least because it was still in the process of defining itself to its

---

* A superpower is a dominant force in international politics, particularly one that can claim to act on behalf of, or in the interests of, lesser powers. The term was popularised by W. T. R. Fox in his book *The Super-Powers: The United States, Britain, and the Soviet Union – Their Responsibility for Peace* (New York: Harcourt Brace, 1944).

own citizens; in 1900, the union was barely one hundred years old, and still very much a work in progress.* The national self-image showed all the telltale signs of youth, from boundless, even naive optimism, to identity crises and outbreaks of self-doubt. These growing pains were frequently compounded by the demands of an international community both half in love with the promise of America and half afraid of its seemingly limitless potential. The story of the USA in the twentieth century, then, is one of a Janus-faced nation, selling itself in far-flung corners of the globe, while at the same time policing its own privacy and exercising its right to unilateralism, individualism or even isolationism. Much of the literature of the 'American century' enacts this duality on some level, between the inward and the outward, the public and the private, between freedom and responsibility. In doing so, it expresses the anxieties of a country whose supreme self-confidence is constantly held in check by fears of degeneration and implosion.

In 1923, the British novelist D. H. Lawrence published *Studies in Classic American Literature*. It is a gambit in the critical debate about twentieth-century American letters, written from the standpoint of an outsider both intoxicated and repulsed by the USA. He opens on a tone of sarcastic mockery:

> Listen to the States asserting: 'The hour has struck! Americans shall be American. The U.S.A. is now grown up artistically. It is time we ceased to hang on to the skirts of Europe, or to behave like schoolboys let loose from European schoolmasters.'
>
> All right, Americans, let's see you set about it. Go on then, let the precious cat out of the bag. If you're sure he's in.[2]

Lawrence does acknowledge that many nineteenth-century American writers, such as Walt Whitman, Herman Melville and Nathaniel Hawthorne, were more 'extreme' and original than many of his own

* Only forty-five states of the current fifty were officially part of the union at the turn of the century. Oklahoma (1907), New Mexico (1912), Arizona (1912), Alaska (1959) and Hawaii (1959) were yet to become official states.

contemporaries, but he is sceptical about the turn towards naturalism and 'safe' forms and styles in the first few decades of the twentieth century. However, nobody could accuse post-1923 American writers of hiding behind European models or theories. Only France has won more Nobel Prizes for literature over the last century; the list of American Nobel laureates tells its own story of diversity, ranging from the African-American Toni Morrison to the social realist Sinclair Lewis, from the Mississippi modernist William Faulkner to chroniclers of Jewish life such as Saul Bellow and Isaac Bashevis Singer. Such variety is perhaps understandable in a nation composed of other nations; indeed, some of the greatest 'American' writers of the last century, including W. H. Auden, Vladimir Nabokov and Joseph Brodsky, were actually born elsewhere, and became US citizens by necessity or choice. The breadth of American literature can also be explained by the fact that there are more Americas than there are states in the union; in a society that valorises individual freedoms and achievements, it could even be argued that there are as many Americas as there are Americans.

This volume reflects the plethora of Americas available to the writers of the twentieth and early twenty-first centuries. Some of these Americas will be more familiar than others; *York Notes Companions* are built around some of the more recognisably canonical poets, novelists and dramatists, but they encourage new readings by connecting them to lesser-known contemporaries, kindred spirits and competitors. The Cultural Overview section that follows this introduction brings together disparate and diverse voices by placing them within both their socio-historical and artistic context. It is not intended to constitute a seamless narrative of the nation and its literary history; critical thinking from the 1970s onwards (an era considered to be 'postmodern', as discussed in Part Two) has often emphasised that 'history' can only be understood as a collection of individual 'histories', and the Overview acknowledges this by focusing on particularly important and influential literary trends that illuminate and are illuminated by the political and social upheavals of their time.

Many of the figures featured in the Overview are explored in more detail in Part Three, which discusses the work of eighteen writers over six chapters. Each of these chapters groups together three writers, whose works are either connected by genre, period, setting or reference to each other. The American canon is still forming; indeed, if it did not change, it would be inadequate to the turbulence of twentieth-century American experience. Part Three reflects this by juxtaposing writers of consistent reputation with those whose public and critical reception has either wavered or only grown strong in recent years. For example, the chapter on the American short story includes two acknowledged masters of the form, John Cheever and Raymond Carver, alongside the lesser-known Grace Paley. While Paley is far from neglected, her work has arguably not yet achieved the recognition it deserves, and may be beyond the purview of many undergraduate courses; nevertheless, the brief coverage of her short stories in this volume shows that her observations of New York life can be usefully analysed alongside those of Cheever, and indeed of any New York writer. James Merrill, studied here alongside Marianne Moore and Elizabeth Bishop, is also sometimes overlooked in surveys of post-war American poetry, because his work does not sit easily among any of the literary 'schools' with which it is contemporaneous (for example, Language Poetry, the 'Black Mountain Poets' or the 'confessionals'). While the Cultural Overview traces kinships between writers of particular 'movements' or shared sensibilities, it also stresses that much American literature is individualistic and singular, in keeping with the ethos of independence and liberty so essential to national constitution and self-construction. A writer such as Merrill embodies this resistance to literary fashion, and this is a key reason for his inclusion. The three writers in the chapter on the American South (Faulkner, McCullers and O'Connor) express this resistance even more strongly. All they have in common is geography and a mistrust of the mythologies that surround it.

This mistrust is a challenge to received opinions and ideas, American non-conformism on a grand scale; but it also marks a scepticism towards fixity. The USA was still defining its international role in the twentieth century, and was thus in a constant state of flux. Some American authors attempted to pin it down in their writing, but a remarkable number sought, rather paradoxically, to capture its elusiveness. Much twentieth-century American literature, then, can be anything but conformist; as the USA remade much of the Western world in its image, so did representations of it within art and culture establish the cutting edge or vanguard that others would follow, as a litany of cultural phenomena from imagism to pop art to beat writing would suggest. This push and pull between ostensibly opposing forces – the need to define America, and the desire to escape definition – is explored most fully in Part Four, which comprises four essays on themes that have sparked ongoing critical debate. The consideration of literary attitudes to the home is particularly illuminative here. As the chapter establishes, American writers have constantly needed to tame and domesticate the wide open spaces of the national landscape, and the 'home' therefore carries an air of achievement against the odds. However, the home achieved is a place to flee, in order to regain the fantasy of freedom that has underpinned so much American literature from its very beginnings. The other chapters – on American masculinities, representations of the city, and the writing of African-American experience – all explore similar conflicts between fixed identities and meanings, and those that are shifting and contingent. The multitude of texts under discussion in these chapters trace a history of reading, as well as outlining key critical terms and suggesting further directions.

Even the most cursory glance at the timeline in Part Five will reconfirm the extraordinary tumult and trauma of 'the American century', and the astonishing range of literary texts that strive to make sense of it. If the nineteenth century saw the USA finding its literary voice, then the twentieth century arguably witnessed that voice dominating the world of Anglophone literature, and this volume outlines its progress. While focusing on a necessarily selective but significant range of writers and texts, it marks a departure point for the student eager to traverse the 'dark fields of the republic' of letters.[3]

Andrew Blades

Notes

1   See Alan Brinkley, *The Publisher: Henry Luce and his American Century* (New York: Alfred A. Knopf, 2010).

2   D. H. Lawrence, 'Foreword', *Studies in Classic American Literature* (1923. London: Penguin, 1971), pp. 3–4 (3).

3   F. Scott Fitzgerald, *The Great Gatsby* (1925. London: Penguin, 1994), p. 188.

Part Two
A Cultural Overview

At the turn of the twentieth century, the population of the USA underwent a period of rapid expansion. It had already become the most productive economy in the world, and the flow of new settlers to the continent was both cause and consequence. After the bloodletting of the Civil War (1861–5) and the period of reconstruction that followed, America enjoyed what Mark Twain famously called 'The Gilded Age'.[1] Though this was checked by an economic recession in the mid-1890s, the America that emerged in the 1900s was the wealthiest nation in the world in terms of per capita income. As GDP figures climbed inexorably upwards, so did the architecture of America's burgeoning cities. William Le Baron Jenney revealed Chicago's Home Insurance Building to the world in 1885, and Charles B. Atwood's Reliance Building followed in the mid-1890s. These grand structures expressed a newfound American independence from the architectural styles of the Old World, the skyscraper being one of the more recognisable symbols of the USA's cultural influence in the twentieth century. The individualism implied in such architecture was offset in part by the universities, hospitals, schools and concert halls that continue to bear the names of so many late nineteenth and early twentieth-century industrialists; the extremely wealthy Andrew Carnegies and John D. Rockefellers may have been 'robber barons' to some critics, but they endowed much of their wealth to institutions, believing that affluence necessitated philanthropy.* Nevertheless, it seemed that this emerging universe of high buildings and grand railroad terminals was one in which the individual triumphed over the collective, where the ambition and adventurousness that had motivated so much of the early settling of the United States and the frontier pioneering of the nineteenth century found their next expression. The difference, perhaps, was only that the frontier was now vertical, rather than horizontal.

Manifest Destiny?

In this sense, the thinking behind urban America was a continuation of the principle of 'manifest destiny' that was used to justify much of the nineteenth century's zealous colonising. Manifest destiny is the belief that the people of the United States were destined to progress across the continent from east to west; it lay behind many of the popular 'dime novels' of the early twentieth century which related the adventures of cowboys and ranchers to a readership hungry for tales of the 'Old West'. However, even Frederick Jackson Turner's influential 'The Significance of the Frontier in American History' (1893), which posited the threshold between wilderness and civilisation as the site that defined the American national character, began with the observation that by 1880 there was barely a 'frontier line' to speak of, the wilds having long been settled.[2] The cities, by contrast, were a source of seemingly limitless opportunity, where rural peasants and agrarian yeomen could reinvent themselves as possible tycoons, or immigrants anchor and make their own attempts at life, liberty and the pursuit of happiness.

There was, of course, another story, which in various ways defines many of America's most important works of art and literature in the twentieth century: the gulf between the ideal of the country and the often disappointing reality of a nation falling short of its own

* The term 'robber baron' is often used of unscrupulous industrial magnates, such as railroad entrepreneurs, and was popularised by the journalist Matthew Josephson (1899–1978) in his book *The Robber Barons: The Great American Capitalists 1861–1901* (New York: Harcourt, Brace & Co., 1934).

wondrous rhetoric. Sinclair Lewis (1885–1951) queries 'boosterism', the deliberate overselling of a town or company's reputation through extravagant claims of potential, in his novel *Babbitt* (1922). Its eponymous character is an estate agent in the fictional town of Zenith, a town whose very name satirises the inflationary promotion of boosterism. Other early twentieth-century novelists sounded notes of caution about the price of progress. In the South, the 'Agrarian' school of writers that included John Crowe Ransom (1888–1974) and Robert Penn Warren (1905–1989) sought to record and restore the region's rural heritage in the wake of ever-increasing industrialisation. In the Midwest, too, there was great ambivalence about urban expansion; in Sherwood Anderson's novel *Poor White* (1920), the rurally raised Hugh McVey goes through a period of evangelism for 'growth' only to see it eventually as a 'disease of thinking'.[3] Meanwhile, the original wealthy elite of the urban centres were losing out to the new, adrenalised capitalism of self-made entrepreneurs, a social transformation lamented by the patrician novelist Booth Tarkington (1869–1946) in *The Magnificent Ambersons* (1918) and Edith Wharton (1862–1937), whose studies of 'Old New York', however sceptical about its mores and hypocrisies, nevertheless betray a nostalgia for the world in which the writer was raised.

Understandably, many were left behind by the booster speculators and metropolitan magnates. 'Muckraking' journalists and novelists, so-called because they used aggressive investigative tactics to criticise unfair business practices, acted as America's social conscience during what was known as the Progressive Era; novels such as Frank Norris's *The Octopus* (1901), about the wheat-growing industry, and Upton Sinclair's exposé of Chicago meatpacking, *The Jungle* (1906), caused minor sensations. The Progressive Era aimed to redress the inequalities of the Gilded Age, applying the latest in scientific and philosophical thought to a series of reforms. For example, in works such as *Democracy and Education* (1916), the philosopher John Dewey (1859–1952) argued for child-led learning in schools. He also suggested that educational establishments were social institutions, and as such could be used to effect social change through education; it was in the classroom that America could become the model democracy it desired to be. Nevertheless, despite these ideals, inequalities continued to grow, not least within the African-American ghettoes that began to appear in the Northern cities as black Southerners moved to escape the bigotry and poor prospects of their hometowns.

The Progressive Era also led to the prohibition of alcohol through the 1920s. The bootlegger, immortalised in the central character of F. Scott Fitzgerald's *The Great Gatsby* (1925), became a new American anti-hero, and the 'jazz age' speakeasies embodied the spirit of a new stateside bohemia. In Manhattan especially, racial, sexual and social boundaries were challenged in the novels and poems of the writers of the Harlem Renaissance.* As well as launching the career of F. Scott Fitzgerald, 'flapper' culture, with its emphasis on hedonism and witty repartee, made stars of the *New Yorker* regular Dorothy Parker (1893–1967) and the novelist Anita Loos (1888–1981), whose *Gentlemen Prefer Blondes* (1925) became a runaway success.

Experimentalists

However, much American art and literature happened overseas in the 1920s. Many of the great figures of the modernist movement in the United States either travelled regularly to Europe or relocated to the Old World entirely. Visual artists such as Man Ray (1890–1976) flocked to France. The novelist Gertrude Stein (1874–1946) claimed that 'Paris was where the twentieth century was';[4] other American writers such as Djuna Barnes (1892–1982) and Natalie Barney (1876–1972) followed suit, setting up connections to European modernists and establishing literary salons. Barnes's novel *Nightwood* (1936) was championed by T. S. Eliot (1888–1965), who along with Ezra Pound (1885–1972) and H. D. (Hilda Doolittle, 1886–1961), had already moved to London to realise his poetic ambitions. It seemed, rather paradoxically, that American modernism was the province of the French and British, making figures such as the avant-garde

---

* See Part Four: 'African-American Writing' for a detailed discussion of the Harlem Renaissance.

Southern writer William Faulkner (1897–1962) or Wallace Stevens (1879–1955), an insurance lawyer who penned oblique and highly influential experimental poetry, all the more remarkable. Nevertheless even some of Stevens's poetry was a response to European surrealism.

In some ways, it might seem strange that so many American modernists left for Europe in the 1920s. The United States was almost synonymous with modernity, particularly in its economic and business affairs. Nevertheless, the forward march of technological innovation often appeared antithetical to historical continuity, and it was this disconnect that many European and American modernists feared. In his essay 'Tradition and the Individual Talent' (1919), T. S. Eliot urges writers to cultivate a 'historical sense' which might consider works of literature within a continuum of artistic endeavour.[5] His opinion in 'Tradition' is informed by his time in Europe; he argues that a knowledge of such tradition comes through great 'labour'. This, of course, is the work of the mind rather than the hands, the perceived contrast between a Europe of almost leisurely decadence and a United States of utilitarian sweat though a convenient caricature, certainly had some grounding in fact. In *The Protestant Ethic and the Spirit of Capitalism* (1905), the German sociologist Max Weber (1864–1920) argued that a puritan frugality lay behind the success of Western capitalism in Northern Europe and especially in the United States. Modern America was initially settled, after all, by Puritans seeking religious freedom in the New World.

This 'puritan' or 'protestant' work ethic was also behind America's most successful industrial innovation: mass production. The 'assembly line', requiring unskilled labourers to piece together individual parts along a conveyor belt, was pioneered in the 1910s by Henry Ford (1863–1947). As a mode of production it was extremely influential; from the 1920s on, Ford's methods were adopted throughout the industrialised world. Fordism, as it came to be known, resulted in a striking upturn in efficiency, which increased wages, drove down production costs and gave birth to a consumer boom in relatively cheap Model T automobiles. This was modernity at its brightest and shiniest, but it caused alarm among many observing America from a distance.

In 1932, the British novelist Aldous Huxley (1894–1963) published a novel, *Brave New World*, in which Fordism finds its satirical analogue in the 'World State' of the future. Anno Domini has been replaced by 'the year of our Ford', and apparently happy workers relinquish identity and difference for the sake of sexual freedom and consumer purchasing power. The United States may indeed have been a 'brave New World' at the time of the Founding Fathers, but the new world emerging in the early twentieth century seemed to require bravery in the face of a potentially frightening futurism.

Other European writers of the time were both allured and terrified by the America of the 1920s. In 1913, Franz Kafka (1883–1924) wrote an episode called 'The Stoker' that would form the basis of his unfinished novel *America* (published posthumously in 1927). For Kafka, who never travelled further than Central Europe, America was an imagined space, one which served as the ultimate emblem of modernist disconnection. The New York encountered by Karl, who is banished to America as a punishment for sexual misdemeanours back in the Old World, is chaotic and vertiginous, an 'inextricable confusion, for ever newly improvised, of foreshortened human figures', with the light angling over the buildings 'as if a glass roof stretched over the street were being violently smashed into fragments at every moment'.[6] Perspective is constantly deconstructed and reconstructed; the city is in a continual state of violent becoming. This New York is recognisable in the work of American modernist writers too, in the novels of John Dos Passos (1896–1970) or the poetry of Hart Crane (1899–1932). However, America, unlike 1920s France or England, had little longstanding heritage to help it make sense of itself. Furthermore, the 1920s modernism of Europe was in many ways a consequence of the First World War, a literature attempting to piece together the debris of a fractured civilisation. By contrast, the USA's involvement in the war was a distant adventure to the majority of its citizens; they came late to conflict, and saw little to no direct impact upon the geography and economy of America itself.

The Lost and the Left

A wave of American writers experienced Europe through their involvement in the First World War, and returned to Europe during the 1920s as a means of escape from their homeland. This group of artists were known as the 'Lost Generation', as stated in the epigraph to Ernest Hemingway's novel *Fiesta: The Sun Also Rises* (1926). In Hemingway's novel, American expatriates in Paris are both restless and enervated. Jake Barnes 'would rather have been in America', yet he feels alienated from the dominant American thinking of the time; when he tells his friend Bill that he doesn't dream, Bill is incredulous: 'You ought to dream ... All our biggest business men have been dreamers. Look at Ford.'[7] Bill's view is at odds with many of those around him. American writers chose to leave for Europe partly because they wanted to escape 'organised stupidity', in the words of Malcolm Cowley (1898–1989). In *Exile's Return* (1934), he claims that artists fled the production line and eschewed commercialism, being wary of writing novels 'in which salesmen were the romantic heroes'.[8] Paris was 'a great machine for stimulating the nerves and sharpening the senses', in contrast to New York, whose life was 'expressed in terms of geometry and mechanics' and whose people were 'coefficients' with a 'purely numerical function' (p. 202); this migration from America is figured as an anti-capitalist, anti-consumerist statement. For Cowley, this necessitated a resistance to the new and a return to the old: 'Plato was a symbol of escape: to read him was not to understand the innateness of the Idea, but merely to place oneself at a distance of four thousand miles and half as many years from Broadway' (p. 203). F. Scott Fitzgerald also idolised European culture, sometimes indulging in a romantic nostalgia; even in the Manhattan of *The Great Gatsby* (1925), arguably the greatest American novel of the 1920s, Fitzgerald is primarily concerned with the protagonist's determination to turn back the clock. These glances over the shoulder and fetishes for old Europe, however, would come to seem irresponsibly distant in the wake of the 1929 Wall Street Crash, which plunged the American economy into turbulence and dramatically altered the direction of its social policy.

The Depression that followed the Crash and arguably constituted the USA's severest national trauma since the Civil War caused a turn to the Left in mainstream American politics. Franklin D. Roosevelt's 'New Deal' government prioritised payouts to bust businesses, welfare for the unemployed and destitute, and reforms to the financial sector; state intervention was considered vital to recovery. This period coincided with a surge of left-wing literary activity. The works of John Steinbeck are perhaps the most widely known of the Depression era, often emphasising community strength over precarious individualism. In *The Grapes of Wrath* (1939), a type of collective organisation develops among displaced migrant workers in makeshift camps, almost implying that the survival instinct has a distinctly socialist bent; the Associated Farmers of California subsequently railed against what they believed to be communist propaganda, resulting in multiple bans and book burnings. *Yonnondio* (1974), the only novel by early feminist writer Tillie Olsen (1912–2007) also ends on a note of hope; the Holbrook family have been forced into a semi-itinerant existence by the Depression, but Anna senses that 'the air's changin'' by its close.[9] The Depression novels of Erskine Caldwell (1903–87) are less immediately sympathetic but in their day marked a new, almost savage realism, while *Let Us Now Praise Famous Men* (1941), a unique hybrid of documentary reportage, densely poetic prose and poignant images by the writer James Agee (1909–55) and photographer Walker Evans (1903–75), married quasi-modernist experimentation to the political expedients of the time. The plight of the poor had never been explored from so many different angles.

Other figures of the period emphasised community values over individualism. Thornton Wilder's play *Our Town* (1938), often revived by amateur dramatics companies, centres around a stage manager putting together a New England neighbourhood for his audience. With minimal staging and props, the play attempts to reconnect drama to the common man, and implicitly critiques the ways in which industrialisation has impacted upon community values. The work of the playwright Clifford Odets (1906–63) is more explicitly ideological, using the theatre to agitate for left-wing reforms or explore socialist ideologies. Odets's play *Waiting for Lefty* (1935) is one of the most politically charged in the canon, dramatising debates within the trade union movement. The taxicab strike that forms its central plotline is played out among the audience, with actors positioned in the stalls. They become roused to action or speech at various junctures, as if to encourage a kind of activist involvement among those watching the play. A new generation of 'Proletarian writers' also emerged in the early 1930s, including Agnes Smedley (1892–1950), whose *Daughter of Earth* (1929) was a bestseller, and Michael Gold (1893–1967), the writer of the semi-autobiographical novel *Jews Without Money* (1930). Gold edited a Marxist periodical, *The New Masses*. An editorial from 1929, 'Go Left, Young Writers', was a clarion call to the proletarian literary movement, playing on the pioneer cliché, 'Go west, young man'; the co-opting of such a recognisably individualistic motto for socialistic ends was itself a politically subversive statement. In her 1963 novel *The Group*, Mary McCarthy (1912–89) wryly notes that this proletarian writing was 'all the rage' in the 1930s; the publisher's assistant Libby McAusland observes that at the fashionable literary magazines, 'you had to run the gauntlet of Communists before getting in to see the book editor'.[10] However, by the onset of the Second World War, leftist momentum was stalling. Intellectuals were deeply disillusioned by the gap between left-wing theory and practice, as discussed in Lionel Trilling's novel *The Middle of the Journey* (1947) and Richard Wright's *The Outsider* (1953). In any case, by the end of the Second World War, there were new reactionary forces at work in the American establishment.

Darkness Visible

The most significant date in the whole of twentieth-century history might well be 6 August 1945; it was the day on which the USA dropped the world's first atomic bomb on the Japanese city of Hiroshima. The Second World War itself certainly inspired some notable literary responses through the late 1940s and 1950s, such as Herman Wouk's *The Caine Mutiny* (1951) and Norman Mailer's

The Naked and the Dead (1948); some of the greatest American novels of the 1960s, including Joseph Heller's *Catch-22* (1961) and Kurt Vonnegut's *Slaughterhouse-Five* (1969), used almost absurdist perspectives on the war to comment on the deadly ironies of the human condition. However, the end of the Second World War was not a discrete historical event. It merely led to a new conflict, the Cold War, which lasted the best part of five decades, as the USA and the Soviet Union competed to be the dominant international superpower. This new politics of brinkmanship, mutual mistrust and nuclear paranoia arguably provided writers with even more material than the Second World War; its ideological influence was so pervasive that the boundaries between the personal and political were constantly destabilised, as even the private domestic space became analogous to the wider homeland threatened by enemies without and within.

The overwhelming implications of the bomb itself were almost beyond direct representation. Characteristically, Gertrude Stein tempered the potential for nihilism with whimsy: 'sure it will destroy a lot and kill a lot, but it's the living that are interesting not the way of killing them, because if there were not a lot left living how could there be any interest in destruction', she wrote in 'Reflections on the Atomic Bomb' in 1946.[11] However, the 1950s generation of writers could not approach the issue with such ironic detachment. Gregory Corso's infamous poem 'Bomb' (1958) is an exercise in poetic detonation. It is shaped like the mushroom cloud produced by nuclear explosion, and contains gaps between many of its short phrases, as if to suggest the fragments left behind; 'I sing thee Bomb', he writes, a latter-day Walt Whitman ironically embracing a technology that both asserts America's military supremacy and threatens the future of all who rely upon it.[12] The climate of fear that the bomb engendered inspired many such visions of apocalypse; to paraphrase the title of a long work by the Anglo-American poet W. H. Auden, it was an 'age of anxiety'. The poet Robert Lowell (1917–77) summarised this in his 1956 lecture, 'Art and Evil', warning that 'today we are all looking for darkness visible, and we know that a realistic awe of evil is a mighty valuable thing for the writer to have'.[13] Some of this horror was most effectively expressed in works of science fiction. In *The Martian Chronicles* (1950) by Ray Bradbury (1920–), for example, 'taxpayers' demand a place on Mars-bound rockets in order to escape the likelihood of atomic annihilation back on Earth. The increase in the popularity of science fiction throughout the 1950s and 1960s, which made cult classics of the works of Robert A. Heinlein (1907–88), Philip K. Dick (1928–82) and Ursula K. Le Guin (1929–), was a cultural by-product of an era in which the prognostications of such writing seemed entirely plausible. By 1960, President John F. Kennedy's bold announcement of the 'New Frontier', implying a commonality between the once-endless pull of the old West and the new, limitless horizons of space, literally included the unearthly and the alien within the language of domestic politics. Robert Lowell's poem 'For the Union Dead' (1964) reflects on this when cautioning against losing sight of history; after commenting on a photograph of Hiroshima impacted by the bomb, he argues that in fact, space is 'nearer'.[14]

While the 1950s marked a period of actual combat – America supported the efforts of the Republic of Korea against the communist Democratic People's Republic of Korea from 1950 to 1953 (a conflict known as the Korean War) – there were other frontiers in the 1950s, a good deal closer to home. Americans began to mistrust other Americans; it sometimes seemed that the USA was as much at war with itself as with communist Russia. The American Left that had been so active within the literature and art of the 1930s was now the focus of intense anxiety as the government of President Dwight D. Eisenhower sniffed out the 'red under the bed'. To a post-1950s audience or readership, the archetypal image of the era is often one of stilted suburban conformism; it is a world of white-collar workers, and white consumer goods. One of the defining snapshots of the period is a 1959 meeting between the Soviet president, Nikita Khrushchev, and the US vice-president, Richard Nixon, at an American trade exhibition in Moscow, at which they exchanged choice words about democracy and consumerism to a backdrop of the latest labour-saving kitchen appliances. Some social historians, such as Elaine Tyler May, have argued that the neat suburban ideal was in fact a domestic expression of the ideology of 'containment'; to police the picket hedge was to be part of the wider national resistance to communist contamination.[15]

On that national level, the policies of Senator Joseph McCarthy, collectively known as 'McCarthyism', became notorious; citizens were encouraged to identify and report suspected communists, while writers, actors and Hollywood directors of a left-wing bent were rounded up to testify in front of the HUAC (House Un-American Activities Committee), which held many names on its blacklist. Among those interviewed were Elia Kazan, the original director of Tennessee Williams's *A Streetcar Named Desire* on both stage and screen, and the playwright Lillian Hellman (1905–84), who was asked to reveal details of the communist affiliation of her lover, the novelist Dashiell Hammett. Arthur Miller (1915–2005) was one of McCarthyism's most high-profile victims and critics, and his 1950s plays, particularly *The Crucible* (1953) and *A View from the Bridge* (1956), make connections between Cold War paranoia and the Salem witch trials of seventeenth-century New England, or the fear of illegal immigration on the East River waterfront. Miller had always been fascinated by the limits of American tolerance, as explored in the early novel *Focus* (1945), which centres on anti-Semitism in the USA of the 1940s, a risky subject in the wake of the Holocaust. Newman, the protagonist of the novel, is mistaken for a Jewish man when he acquires a new pair of glasses, eventually leading to a racist attack and a failed marriage. The novel is later recalled by the character Ira Ringold in Philip Roth's *I Married a Communist* (1998), whose own decline is set in motion by his wife's revelations about his leftist sympathies, and it is certainly true that McCarthyism's ostensible anti-communist motivations also often carried strong undercurrents of bigotry, against Jews, homosexuals and black people, for example, who were viewed as 'fellow travellers'.

Speaking Out

Two of the most famous people to be tried for espionage during the Cold War were Julius and Ethel Rosenberg, who were sentenced to death for their crimes in 1953. Their execution became emblematic of McCarthyism at large, and has been used by various writers to reassess the legacies of 1950s anti-communism; they form the subject of *The*

Book of Daniel (1971), a novel by E. L. Doctorow (1931–), and the ghost of Ethel Rosenberg haunts her prosecution attorney, Roy Cohn, in Tony Kushner's play *Angels in America* (1991). Their spectre also looms over *The Bell Jar* (1963), Sylvia Plath's only novel, which begins ominously, 'it was a queer, sultry summer, the summer they electrocuted the Rosenbergs'.[16] In this novel, the private neuroses of the narrator Esther Greenwood are often figured in the language and symbolism of the Cold War. She explicitly connects the electroconvulsive therapy she receives for her psychological instability to the fate of the Rosenbergs; the American establishment, it would seem, is full of men in lab coats trying to neutralise the enemy within.

Alienated individuals, often with psychiatric disorders, seemed to be everywhere in mid-century America. From the 1940s on, a wave of writers such as Ralph Ellison, J. D. Salinger and Richard Wright published novels centred on lonely figures operating on the fringes of society. Many of the most notable playwrights of 1950s, in particular Tennessee Williams and William Inge, openly explored alcoholism, nymphomania and homosexual guilt, while urban demi-mondes rife with prostitution, gambling and drug addiction formed the setting for groundbreaking novels by William Burroughs (*Junky*, 1953), Nelson Algren (*A Walk on the Wild Side*, 1956) and Hubert Selby, Jr (*Last Exit to Brooklyn*, 1964). Alfred Kinsey's respective reports into sexual behaviour in males and females forced debate about the urges of the human libido in 1948 and 1953, while the absorption of psychoanalysis and psychotherapy into the mainstream brought new ways of thinking about the human subject, and there was constant talk of the conscious and subconscious, the id, ego and superego.* The alienation felt by many artists and writers, running alongside the culture of disclosure created by McCarthyism and the burgeoning psychiatric and psychotherapeutic professions, resulted in a new openness of expression known as 'confessional poetry'.

M. L. Rosenthal was the first critic to identify this movement, though it had been developing for some time. Indeed, in his article 'Poetry as Confession' (1959), Rosenthal traces the tendency all the

---

* The founder of psychoanalysis, Sigmund Freud (1856–1939) proposes in 'The Ego and the Id' (1923) that the psyche comprises three parts: the *id* (the mind's basic drives and desires), the *ego* (mediating between the id and reality outside of the mind) and the *superego* (the ideal mind and the conscience).

way back to the 1860s and the 'Calamus' poems in Walt Whitman's *Leaves of Grass*, which deal explicitly with the poet's same-sex desire. However, the 'naked' confession he locates in Robert Lowell's collection *Life Studies* (1959), which initially seems 'grotesque' to him in its candid, self-incriminatory revelations, turns out to be indicative of trouble afoot in the nation: for Rosenthal, Lowell is ultimately 'not wrong in looking at the culture through the window of psychological breakdown'.[17] Readers are often tempted to conflate the writer of a poem with its speaker. The 'confessional' poets actively encouraged such readings, embodying the breakdown between the private and the public that appeared to be happening in a self-pyschoanalysing America pervaded by hypertension, and medicated with often indiscriminately prescribed Nembutal barbiturates. Other notable poets engaging in 'soul's therapy'[18] included Theodore Roethke (1908–63), whose 'Open House' (1941) is an early prototype confessional,[19] and John Berryman (1914–72). Berryman's poetry, particularly the epic cycle of *Dream Songs* published throughout the 1960s, is allusive and difficult; the speaker, Henry, changes his identity at various stages of the sequence, sometimes masquerading as a blackface performer called Bones, and refers to himself in both the first and third person. The *Dream Songs* also includes elegies for other recognisably 'confessional' poets including Roethke, Sylvia Plath,* Randall Jarrell (1914–65) and Delmore Schwartz (1913–66), a whole generation of artists who died violent and sudden deaths in young or early middle age, or committed suicide. Berryman killed himself at the age of fifty-seven.

Many of the poets who have been considered 'confessional' were also important to other social movements and trends. Allen Ginsberg (1926–97)[†] unveiled 'Howl' in 1955 to outcries of blasphemy and obscenity; one of the most shocking aspects of the poem to those who desired its suppression was its candour about gay sex and drug use, though diligent critics heard the voice of Whitman in it. The work

---

* Sylvia Plath published most of her poetry while resident in England. For a detailed study of this work, see William May, *York Notes Companions: Postwar Literature, 1950–1990* (London: Pearson Longman & York Press, 2010).

[†] See Part Three: 'Visionary Poetry' for a detailed study of Ginsberg's work.

of Anne Sexton (1928–74) was equally frank about female sexuality, menstruation and depression, as in the poem 'In Celebration of My Uterus'. While other poets might have frowned at being termed 'confessional', Sexton seemed to relish it. Her 1960 collection, *To Bedlam and Part Way Back*, is a virtual manifesto for this type of art, even featuring a poem entitled 'Said the Poet to the Analyst'.[20] Poets such as Ginsberg and Sexton reflected a larger social transformation that would sweep through the USA in the 1950s and 1960s.

Rebels with a Cause

The cosy suburban cliché of 1950s America is counterbalanced by the archetype of the rebellious teenager, a word that first entered the language in the 1940s and became ubiquitous in the golden age of Hollywood and rock 'n' roll. The 1950s boasted an abundance of new idols, from the leather-jacketed Marlon Brando of the film *The Wild One* (1953) to Elvis Presley, whose hip swinging and lip curling was described by the Anglo-American poet Thom Gunn as a stylish expression of revolt.[21] The 'rebel without a cause' himself, James Dean, was perhaps most iconic of all. However, for the various rebellions that made the 1960s such an explosive decade in American history, causes were everywhere in abundance. From the Civil Rights and Black Power movements (analysed in detail in Part Four: 'African-American Writing'), to women's liberation and gay activism, the period from the assassination of President John F. Kennedy in 1963 to the scandal of Richard Nixon's dishonest fall in the 1974 Watergate scandal saw seismic shifts in the American public consciousness.

Sexual permissiveness, black consciousness and the continued widening of the generation gap that began in the 1950s could all be bracketed under the term 'counterculture'. The counterculture challenged the institutions and mores of the establishment. It took its cues from rock musicians such as Bob Dylan and John Lennon, and launched protest movements against the Vietnam War, which officially lasted from the early 1960s to 1975. The anti-communist war in

Vietnam remains a traumatic episode in American history. Young men were conscripted, and over fifty thousand died in action; it was also the first war to receive mass coverage on evening television, bringing the horror into the living rooms of millions of Americans. Students were galvanised into protest, and writers followed suit. The poet Denise Levertov (1923–97) published many war protest poems, while Norman Mailer (1923–2007) recounted the Washington protests of October 1967 in his experimental pseudo-novel *The Armies of the Night* (1968). In Mailer's work, the trope of the military draft is inverted as 'volunteers ... answer the call' to march on the capital; he calls on the reader to 'brood' over America, 'once a beauty of magnificence unparalleled, now a beauty with a leprous skin'.[22] Indeed, from the assassinations of presidents and civil rights leaders, to inner-city riots and Hell's Angels vigilantes, America seemed to be on fire through much of the 1960s; the sound of the guitarist and countercultural hero Jimi Hendrix playing 'The Star Spangled Banner' at the Woodstock Festival in 1969, deconstructed and smothered in electronic feedback, may be the defining artistic statement of the era.

Woodstock was a milestone in the so-called 'hippie' movement. The term 'hippie' was applied to members of the counterculture of acid-dropping youths, commune-dwellers, suburban Buddhists and long-haired, sparsely dressed 'peaceniks'. Surreal psychedelic music was the main mode of expression among the new generation; much of the literature of the period, however, is more sceptical about peace and love, sensing darkness on the horizon. Works of 'new journalism' combined the techniques of fiction and reportage to comment on hippie eccentricities. Tom Wolfe's *Electric Kool-Aid Acid Test* (1968) may have defined the genre, but the dangers of dropping out of mainstream society are more starkly conveyed by Joan Didion (1934–) in 'Slouching Towards Bethlehem' (1967). She depicts late 1960s San Francisco with understated irony, ending with the image of a young child starting a fire in a squat while his mother's oblivious friends try to retrieve 'some very good Moroccan hash' from under the floorboards.[23] In the novel *In Watermelon Sugar* (1968), Richard Brautigan (1935–84) paints an even bleaker picture of life in

a commune. The house in the countryside initially seems idyllic, but
its name 'iDEATH' holds a clue to the fate of its inhabitants; while
it spells out the death of individualism (the 'I'), it also prefigures the
suicide of the character inBOIL. If the hippie movement fantasised
about transporting Americans 'back to the garden' of Eden,[24] it was
a paradise destined to witness the repeated falls and failures of its
flower-children.

Signs and Simulacra

The various activist movements of the 1960s placed American
university campuses at the centre of the national debate; the Californian
institutions, particularly Berkeley, were associated with radical
academics and students of the 'New Left', who took their credo from
European thinkers inspired by a similarly energetic counterculture on
the continent.

Giles Goat-Boy (1966) by John Barth (1930–) successfully satirises
this academia in a style that would itself come to be keenly theorised
on campuses. This style is 'postmodern', a term notoriously hard to
define but key to any understanding of American literature since the
1960s. In Barth's own terms, postmodern writing is the 'literature
of replenishment', revitalising the novel whose forms have become
'exhausted',[25] but there have been many other postmodernisms. Some
versions are strongly associated with French theorists such as Roland
Barthes (1915–80) and Jacques Derrida (1930–2004), who used
semiotics (the study of sign systems) and 'deconstruction' (an analysis
of texts that foregrounds their internal contradictions and resistance to
fixed 'meaning') in their work. Others draw on the theories of Jean-
François Lyotard (1924–98), who proposed that postmodernism is an
'incredulity towards metanarratives', by which he means that it rejects
grand principles such as the idea of social and historical progress, or
the truth of science.[26] In Lyotard's terms, there is no such thing as
knowledge; there are only knowledges, and these are entirely dependent
on culture, geography, historical context and the position of the
person(s) who know(s).

This shift of emphasis from the 'grand narrative' to the 'situated' or particular is reflected in some of the writing of previously marginalised groups. In 1975, Maxine Hong Kingston (1940–) published *The Woman Warrior*, which is postmodern in both its writing style and its premise. Kingston is Chinese American, born in California, but in the partly autobiographical *Woman Warrior* she confides that her 'American life' 'has been such a disappointment'.[27] She reconstructs her subjectivity through the telling of Chinese folktales, interspersed with the factual and fictional to convey the complexity of the multiple identities of postmodern America. In *Tripmaster Monkey: His Fake Book* (1989), Kingston continues her experiments with form. The protagonist Wittman Ah Sing is a Chinese-American Walt Whitman, who spends much of the novel trying to reconcile his two identities, as well as puzzling over postmodern linguistic riddles, such as 'Wittman was not el pachuco loco. Proof: he could tell a figment from a table. Or a tree.'*[28] Much postmodernist thinking adapts the theories of the Swiss linguist Ferdinand de Saussure (1857–1913), who proposed there was no natural relationship between a thing (the 'signified') and the word that describes it (the 'signifier'); theorists in many postmodern-influenced fields such as feminism, postcolonialism and queer theory are involved less in analysing the 'signified' than its 'signifiers', the ways in which we represent objects, people and places. Kingston's novels are thus especially postmodern in their fascination with the gap between how identity is perceived as an object and how it is assumed by the subject.

This domain of signs, in which the way an idea or object is represented transcends its physical or essential properties, might result in there only being representations; any 'reality' behind them is inaccessible or moot. Many writers believe the USA is the most postmodern of all nations, because these 'signs' are essential to the market-led economy of a consumerist society, where the branding of a product is more important than the product itself.[29] The communication theorist Marshall McLuhan (1911–80) summarised this famously when he

---

* For further discussion of Maxine Hong Kingston, see Wendy Knepper, *York Notes Companions: Postcolonial Literature* (London: Pearson Longman & York Press, 2011).

wrote that 'the medium is the message',[30] and many writers since the 1970s have laid open this 'Megamerica', a society of 'neon, fiber glass, plexiglass'.[31] Some have sung its praises, if with a tinge of irony. The French cultural theorist Jean Baudrillard (1929–2007) eulogises it in *America* (1986); he sees it as a 'simulacrum', a place of artifice and 'perpetual simulation', because it has no real 'origin or mythical authenticity'.[32] He claims that Americans have no sense of themselves as 'simulation' because they 'have no language in which to describe it, since they themselves are the model'; a site such as Disneyland, then, is 'hyperreal', the term Baudrillard gives to a simulation that becomes more real than the original model. The novels of Don DeLillo journey across this America of billboards, endless commercials and product placement; in *White Noise* (1985), for example, Jack goes on a drive with his friend Murray to see 'the most photographed barn in the country'. The advertising rhetoric becomes self-fulfilling; Murray and Jack encounter massed ranks of telephoto lenses at the site, causing another character, Alfonse, to quip, 'once you've seen the signs about the barn, it becomes impossible to see the barn'.[33] These are not new ideas; the 1950s and 1960s 'pop art' of Andy Warhol, in which Campbell's soup cans are reduced to the two-dimensionality of their own logo on canvases in galleries, anticipated the postmodern sensibilities of later novelists and poets. However, by the 1980s, life was more 'virtual', and advertising more pervasive, than ever before; even the president himself, Ronald Reagan, was an ex-Hollywood idol, highly suited to the demands of the televisual age.

Millennial Angst

By the early 1990s, one key 'virtual' had nevertheless disappeared: with the fall of the Berlin Wall in November 1989, the Eastern Bloc of Soviet-controlled communist states began to crumble, marking the end of the Cold War and the lessening of the nuclear threat. The philosopher Francis Fukuyama (1952–) proclaimed in his book *The End of History and the Last Man* (1992) that the period of conflict between ideologies of the left and right was largely at an end in the Western world; market capitalism had triumphed over socialism. The 1990s were the decade in which the USA rose to become the only international superpower. To the world beyond its borders, it seemed more at ease with itself than in the past. In 1993, Toni Morrison (1931–) became the first African-American writer to win the Nobel Prize, while in the same year the black poet and memoirist Maya Angelou read at President Bill Clinton's inauguration. Native American writers, such as Leslie Marmon Silko (1948–) and Sherman Alexie (1966–), also published groundbreaking novels; previously underrepresented minority groups were now finding their voice and their readership. Popular movements such as the 'book club' segment of Oprah Winfrey's television talk show also increased book sales and gave several careers much needed impetus.

Nevertheless, a crop of young writers detected a malaise within American youth. The Canadian novelist Douglas Coupland (1961–) dubbed these disenchanted youngsters 'Generation X', in his 1991 novel of the same name. They worked in 'McJobs' as low-paid service industry hands, and had trouble finding anything to believe in; there were no issues left to support. His 1995 novel, *Microserfs*, is almost Baudrillard's technological 'utopia achieved', an account of everyday life in the extraordinary world of Silicon Valley, in which all of the characters work, eat, sleep and breathe computer programming. Here, the entrepreneur of the information age, Bill Gates, is almost Henry Ford updated; his distance from his workers, however, is an ironic analogue to that between those workers and the world outside their Micro-serfdom. Other writers of the period catalogue the minute and fleeting trends of popular culture with verve and sometimes macabre ingenuity; perhaps most notable are the novels of Bret Easton Ellis (1964–) and the essays, novels and short stories of David Foster Wallace (1962–2008), whose thousand-page novel *Infinite Jest* (1996) is a highpoint of late postmodern literature.

From the vantage of the last ten years, however, the relatively peaceful 1990s, with their détentes, handshakes and economic security, have come to seem like a brief period of rest between one ideological conflict and the next. On 11 September 2001, suicide bombers hijacked four commercial airliners and crashed two of these into the World

Trade Centre twin towers. The sight of these edifices of American wealth, prosperity and influence 'collapsing with malign majesty' into downtown Manhattan is the symbolic image of the decade.[34] In Lorrie Moore's novel *A Gate at the Stairs* (2010), the young Tassie Keltjin recalls the attack, not yet known as '9/11', and the 'marching poli-sci majors' announcing that 'the chickens have come home to roost'. She does not understand the grave international political implications of the attack, only contemplating the events 'as if in a craning crowd, through glass', the way that people stare 'at the *Mona Lisa* in the Louvre'.[35] Much has been made of the way in which 9/11 was represented in the media; it was arguably the first catastrophic world event to happen in a twenty-four hour news culture, and the first to be transmitted through the new technologies of the 2000s, as camera-phones turned ordinary bystanders into journalists relaying images to the networks.

It is still too early to say how the American cultural landscape has been changed by 9/11 and the subsequent 'wars on terror' implemented by President George W. Bush's Republican administration. The events sparked much literary activity; John Updike's final novel *Terrorist* (2006) and Don DeLillo's *Falling Man* (2007) were among the most high-profile, though Jonathan Safran Foer's *Extremely Loud and Incredibly Close* (2005), centring around a boy trying to piece together the details of his father's last phone call from the burning World Trade Centre, may be the most moving, and one of the first to gesture towards a more inclusive and humanist America emerging from the rubble. Neil LaBute's play *The Mercy Seat* (2002) is less optimistic. In his preface, he states that the play explores how 'selfishness can still exist during a moment of national selflessness'.[36] The lead character must balance the danger of his own extramarital affair being revealed against the possibility that his family believe him to be dead inside the twin towers; the clash between private and public that defined so much of the 'American century' remains as potent beyond the Millennium as ever. It remains to be seen how the first ten years of the new century, from 9/11 to the financial crisis of 2008 and the inauguration of the USA's first black president, Barack Obama, in 2009, will be recounted by the writers of the future. It is certain, however, that the twentieth century will be remembered not just as the American century in politics, but in culture too; and literature, as the remainder of this book shows, often had a central part to play in shaping it.

Notes

1	See Mark Twain and Charles Dudley Warner, *The Gilded Age* (1873. Oxford: Oxford University Press, 1996).

2	Frederick Jackson Turner, 'The Significance of the Frontier in American History', in *The Frontier in American History* (New York: Henry Holt and Co., 1921), pp. 1–39 (1).

3	Sherwood Anderson, *Poor White* (1920. New York: New Directions, 1993), p. 363.

4	Quoted in J. Gerald Kennedy, *Imagining Paris: Exile, Writing, and American Identity* (New Haven: Yale University Press, 1993), p. 185.

5	T. S. Eliot, 'Tradition and the Individual Talent', in *Selected Essays* (London: Faber & Faber, 1999), pp. 13–22 (p. 14).

6	Franz Kafka, *America* (1927. London: Vintage, 2005), pp. 42–3.

7	Ernest Hemingway, *Fiesta: The Sun Also Rises* (London: Arrow, 1993), pp. 9 and 104.

8	Malcolm Cowley, *Exile's Return: A Literary Odyssey of the 1920s* (London: Penguin, 1994), p. 6.

9	Tillie Olsen, *Yonnondio: From The Thirties* (London: Virago, 1980), p. 191.

10	Mary McCarthy, *The Group* (Harmondsworth: Penguin, 1975), p. 179.

11	Gertrude Stein, 'Reflection on the Atomic Bomb' (1946), reprinted in *Writings 1932–1946* (New York: Library of America, 1998), p. 823.

12	Gregory Corso, 'Bomb' (1958), *The Happy Birthday of Death* (New York: New Directions, 1960), pp. 32–3 (32).

13	Robert Lowell, 'Art and Evil', in *Collected Prose*, ed. Robert Giroux (London: Faber & Faber, 1987), pp. 129–44 (129).

14	Lowell, 'For the Union Dead', *Collected Poems*, ed. Frank Bidart and David Gewanter (London: Faber & Faber, 2003), pp. 376–8 (377).

15	See Elaine Tyler May, *Homeward Bound: American Families in the Cold War Era* (New York: Basic Books, 1988).

16	Sylvia Plath, *The Bell Jar* (London: Heinemann, 1964), p. 1.

17	M. L. Rosenthal, 'Poetry as Confession', *Our Life in Poetry: Selected Essays and Reviews* (New York: Persea, 1991), pp. 109–13 (110).

18	Rosenthal, 'Poetry as Confession', p. 109.

19 Theodore Roethke, *Selected Poems*, ed. Edward Hirsch (New York: Library of America, 2005), p. 1.

20 Anne Sexton, *Selected Poems*, ed. Diane Wood Middlebrook and Diana Hume George (London: Virago, 1991), p. 17.

21 Thom Gunn, 'Elvis Presley', *Collected Poems* (London: Faber & Faber, 1993), p. 57.

22 Norman Mailer, *The Armies of the Night* (Harmondsworth: Penguin, 1971), pp. 102 and 300.

23 Joan Didion, 'Slouching Towards Bethlehem', *Live and Learn* (London: Harper, 2005), pp. 72–103.

24 Joni Mitchell, 'Woodstock' (1969), in *Complete Poems and Lyrics* (London: Chatto & Windus, 1997), p. 58.

25 See John Barth, 'The Literature of Exhaustion', *The Friday Book: Essays and Other Nonfiction* (Baltimore: Johns Hopkins University Press, 1984), pp. 62–76; 'The Literature of Replenishment: Postmodernist Fiction', *The Friday Book*, pp. 193–206.

26 See Jean-François Lyotard, *The Postmodern Condition: A Report on Knowledge*, trans. Geoff Bennington and Brian Massumi (1979. Manchester: Manchester University Press, 1984).

27 Maxine Hong Kingston, *The Woman Warrior: Memoirs of a Girlhood Among Ghosts* (New York: Vintage, 1989), p. 45.

28 Maxine Hong Kingston, *Tripmaster Monkey: His Fake Book* (New York: Vintage, 1989), p. 3.

29 Fredric Jameson equates postmodernism with consumer-led economies in *Postmodernism, or, The Cultural Logic of Late Capitalism* (1991. London: Verso, 1993).

30 See Marshall McLuhan, *Understanding Media: The Extensions of Man* (London: Routledge, 1964).

31 Don DeLillo, *Americana* (1971. London: Penguin, 1990), p. 119.

32 Jean Baudrillard, *America*, trans. Chris Turner (1986. London: Verso, 1988), p. 76.

33 Don DeLillo, *White Noise* (1985. London: Picador, 2002), p. 12.

34 Ian McEwan, 'Only Love and Then Oblivion', *The Guardian*, 15 September, 2001.

35 Lorrie Moore, *A Gate at the Stairs* (London: Faber & Faber, 2010), p. 5.

36 Neil LaBute, *The Mercy Seat* (New York: Faber & Faber, 2003), p. x.

Part Three
Texts, Writers and Contexts

Visionary Poetry: Crane, Frank O'Hara and Ginsberg

It is possible to trace a line of poets through American literary history who consider poetry as a visionary medium, an art-form that should embody a special, almost mystical kind of 'sight'.

This sight is a part of the American pioneering spirit, and is linked to a sense of poetic adventurousness, where new verse forms are required to express an American experience different from those of European forefathers. In the nineteenth century, the American poet had to invent a new poetic 'line', in both senses: a heritage that could sever itself from the ideas and ideals of the Old World, and a means of expression that might owe little to the over-familiar, established verse-forms of Europe. One poet especially has come to embody the nineteenth-century spirit of American self-discovery: Walt Whitman (1819–92), whose voice reverberates through the twentieth century and into the present day. Those whose work breaks loose of formal stricture must at some point acknowledge the Whitman within them; the three poets discussed below – Hart Crane (1899–1932), Frank O'Hara (1926–66) and Allen Ginsberg (1926–97) – all held him in high esteem, and their careers offered various responses to his unique poetic legacy.

Whitman's Legacy

As Harold Bloom states, 'British poets swerve from their precursors, while American poets labor rather to "complete" their fathers'.[1] Though this is a generalisation, it is a very useful one. The USA is a country with clearly visible foundations, and an easily accessible written history. Furthermore, it is a country that constructed itself at a phenomenal speed, a country enthralled by the very idea of construction. Such rapidity requires ambition and a constant desire for betterment. Walt Whitman's verse would appear to extol the virtues of this individual aspiration. He is most noted for establishing the 'long line' at the heart of American poetry, which renders his verse a projection of the spirit of American freedom, unencumbered by the constraints of old structures and orders. However, the potential grandiosity of this voice is kept in check by the poet. His most famous poem, 'Song of Myself' (1855), begins 'I celebrate myself, and sing myself', and runs to over thirteen hundred lines, but though its voice is potentially egocentric, it advocates a civilisation of empowered individuals over the vision of one subject.[2] To Whitman, this grand symphony of peoples is the very definition of America, and poetry is at the heart of it. Nevertheless, he is acutely aware of the need to restate continually the collective as well as the individual; perhaps he is heedful of the warnings of the French political theorist Alexis de Tocqueville (1805–59), who stated in his seminal study, *Democracy in America* (1835–40) that democracy can be alienating, separating people from their ancestors and contemporaries through its emphasis on the rights of the individual.

The individual might defend against this outcome by absorbing and embodying the different characteristics of those around him. Whitman famously allowed for the consciousness to be both itself and the opposite of itself: 'Do I contradict myself? / Very well then I contradict myself, / (I am large, I contain multitudes)' (p. 123). In light of this, his long poetic lines seem less the pronouncements of an unchecked ego than the expression of a generous inclusivity, comprising America's unique 'multitudes'; they reflect the exceptionally vast and plural makeup of the hybrid nation in its first flush of self-confidence. In Whitman's eyes, poetry is a crucial democratic tool, and the uniqueness of America's destiny requires an equally unique poetics, as he writes:

> Stop this day and night with me and you shall possess the
> origin of all poems,
> You shall possess the good of the earth and sun, (there are
> millions of suns left,)
> You shall no longer take things at second or third hand,
> nor look through the eyes of the dead, nor feed on the
> spectres in books,
> You shall not look through my eyes either, nor take things
> from me,
> You shall listen to all sides and filter them from your self. (p. 65)

Here, Whitman strongly advises the poet to take his subject matter and style from what is immediately around him, rather than searching the ghosts of literature past, or indeed taking his cue from contemporaries. Yet this poses a problem of sorts: how can any poet after Whitman advocate a similar independence of sensibility without in some way acknowledging or invoking him, even unwittingly? This is perhaps one of his central self-contradictions: constructing himself as a channel for America's polyglot population and a believer in 'the numberless unknown heroes equal to the greatest heroes known' (p. 81), he nevertheless becomes the known and exalted hero of the many American poets who followed him in the twentieth century.

Shifting Vistas: Hart Crane

In a letter to Waldo Frank of 1926, Hart Crane wrote, 'If only America were half as worthy today to be spoken of as Whitman spoke of it fifty years ago there might be something for me to say – not that Whitman received or required any tangible proof of his intimations, but that time has shown how increasingly lonely and ineffectual his confidence stands.'³ Crane wanted to believe in Whitman's capacity to speak to the 1920s American, but history had proved the father of American poetry an idealist rather than a prophet. If America really was a fundamentally poetic subject, as Whitman and his contemporary literary pioneer Ralph Waldo Emerson (1803–82) maintained, then the poetry that came out of modernist America had to contend with its harsher realities, such as the legacy of the First World War, increasingly expanding materialism, and the dislocation of the urban individual dwarfed by ever taller buildings and alienated from other beings through technological 'advances'. Modernism was a transatlantic movement, with several epicentres, not least London and Paris; but in many ways it was the American city that most symbolised the 'modern' world, particularly New York, whose epic architecture expressed both the limitless possibilities of twentieth-century technology and its potentially disorientating effects.

In his first published collection, *White Buildings* (1926), Hart Crane hovers on the threshold between this uncertain new world and the imagined utopias of Whitman and Emerson. Many of the poems concern themselves with the trickeries of memory, which in the writings of European philosophers such as Henri Bergson (1859–1941) and European novelists such as Marcel Proust (1871–1922) and Virginia Woolf (1882–1941) already constituted a key focus of modernist enquiry. 'Emblems of Conduct' is exemplary here. It depicts a wanderer figure, who stations himself in the landscape to sketch its shady valleys.⁴ Crane's use of the word 'aureate' in this poem does not just denote the golden cast of the light; Crane also uses it in its figurative sense, to suggest rhetorical brilliance. Strong echoes of 'laureate' also connect it to poetry specifically; it is a word hinted at even further with the reference to spiritual orators later in the poem. These aureate laureates and orators all call Whitman to mind, even if he is not mentioned by name. For Crane, however, the old bard is ultimately inaccessible, for in the last stanza, Crane makes clear that his time is passed, and only memories of his great vision are left. Crane both succumbs to the seductions of memory and expresses wariness of them, as in another *White Buildings* poem,

'My Grandmother's Love Letters', in which there is profound doubt that the past can be even drawn upon for inspiration (p. 6). In several of these early poems, poetic sources and roots appear elusive and hard to pin down. For example, 'North Labrador' describes a frozen landscape that is both eternal and shifting, beyond time and the sun's rays (p. 15). Yet to Crane these absences are not necessarily negative. In 'Garden Abstract', for example, he refigures Eve's desire for the apple in Eden so that it is not original sin so much as original bliss, a state of nature, without fear, hope or memory to disturb her (p. 9). This approximates the state of mind Whitman espouses in 'Song of Myself', in which the human subject becomes his or her environment, achieving oneness with other organisms.

Crane and *The Bridge*

In 'Garden Abstract', the apple hanging on the bough is described as being suspended, and Crane plays on a double meaning here: it is both hanging ('suspended') and a transcendent object, without time and space. Another suspension would dominate his writing from the mid-1920s, the Brooklyn Bridge, which the poet could see from his apartment window. *The Bridge* (1930) is Crane's masterpiece, an attempt to write an epic celebrating contemporary American experience. The bridge is variously a symbol of connectivity, progress, spirituality and the capabilities of humankind. It is an example of what Crane called the 'logic of metaphor', which is inherent within much of his poetry; that is, a trope that may seem obscure at first but grows to express its own logic, regardless of any literal, denotative meaning. To paraphrase Whitman, it might be a metaphor that contradicts itself, and contains multitudes.

All the bridge's different meanings are explored in the proem,[*] simply titled 'To Brooklyn Bridge'. The very first image is of a gull in flight over the bay and the bridge itself (p. 43). The aspiration of the human spirit, which the bridge signifies, allows contraries to coexist,

---

[*] The proem is an introductory poem of 44 lines. The rest of *The Bridge* comprises eight other poems of varying length and metre.

as Crane describes a miraculous landscape that can contain both the chains, cables and bars of the bridge and the Statue of Liberty, the ultimate symbol of freedom, that salutes the city from Upper New York Bay. The bridge can be one thing and another, and by extension it is therefore both of man and beyond him, a monument to his tangible achievements and a thrilling symbol of those to come. At times, it is an anchor, a solid and unchanging presence that helps to root and orientate New Yorkers, and yet there is the constant promise of movement, of kinetic energy stored within its frame (p. 43). Our perception of the bridge depends upon the light in which we see it, and light is ever-shifting; despite the solidity of its girders and hoists, then, the bridge mutates. Here, by deploying a clever double meaning, Crane affirms that the bridge is both static and mobile: it will never cease being free, and cannot be tied down, but 'staying' here also refers to the 'stays' that buttress the bridge, helping to fix its foundations firmly to the land. This paradox, of being simultaneously fixed and free, invites multiple interpretations. The most optimistic might be that the bridge is an emblem of the rootedness of freedom within the American constitution; it is a symbol of how Americans are bound to liberty. However, it could be read more ambiguously, as communicating the impossibility of true freedom. Any ideology of liberty can, paradoxically, become burdensomely unachievable the moment a government attempts to enact it; legislating for freedom is a contradiction in terms.

When Crane talks of the mythical properties of the bridge, then, he is commenting as much on the wonder of investing a structure with such hope as he is of its capacity to fulfil it. Hope itself is an enabler, because it depends on a vision of the future; as his earlier poems testify, the past and memory are seductive for a writer, but they also comprise the failures and compromises of those who have gone before him. In the poems of *The Bridge*, this is sometimes communicated with a romantic longing, as in 'Van Winkle' (p. 56), but more often than not its intoxications are rejected for those of the limitless future. In 'The River', Crane moves the poetry through a sequence of geographies, propelling his verse into diverse American landscapes just as the Pullman trains he depicts shuttle through the frontiers (p. 60).* Ultimately, he settles on the Mississippi, but not for any mythological or allegorical significance. Instead, it is the river's onward compulsion that the poet celebrates (p. 61). The thrill of the river is its mindless momentum, even if this is made tortuous by the cultural histories that attend it.

Pioneers Past and Present

Where does this leave the pioneering legacy of Whitman? In another section of *The Bridge*, 'Cape Hatteras', Crane appeals to him directly, juxtaposing the spirit of the nineteenth century with the advances of the twentieth, in this case the emergence of air travel. Some of the most significant technological innovations of the modernist world came in the field of aeronautics, and Crane associates them with another great scientific discovery of the age – the atom, expressing neatly how the revelations of molecular science have both humbled and empowered humankind. This prompts him to address his literary forefather directly (p. 78).[5] He is intrigued by what the old poet–prophet might have to say about the twentieth-century understanding of space and time. Infinity, by definition, should be timeless, for it is the absence of time; yet the concept of infinity has changed as human understanding of the makeup of the universe has grown more detailed and nuanced. In this section Crane is really asking whether it is possible for Whitman's visions to speak to 1920s America. At the climax of 'Cape Hatteras', those visions certainly appear to be viable; the limitlessness of the airborne man is likened to the freed consciousness of the open road (p. 83). Nevertheless, the promise of connection, of a 'bridge' between the glorious gambits of nineteenth-century American literature and US poetry sixty or seventy years hence, is perhaps a promise unfulfilled. 'Cape Hatteras' concludes on a deeply ambiguous note. Crane suggests that he and Whitman

* The Pullman Palace Car Company was the most prominent US manufacturer of railroad cars throughout the nineteenth and early twentieth centuries.

propel themselves forward together, but their affinity falters (p. 84), the line broken by a dash, a form of punctuation Whitman seldom used.* The sequence of negatives here, 'not', 'nor', 'no' and 'never', also frustrates any intention to move upward or forward. The dashes may point towards the unknowable, inexpressible future, but even if the lines retain some degree of possibility, they mimic baby steps on the page, and proceed with caution.

This is the type of ambiguity that ultimately led Hart Crane to believe his work was doomed to failure, a conviction that might well have been a contributory factor in his suicide in 1932 (feelings of guilt about his homosexuality and alcoholism further damaged his self-esteem). *The Bridge* is now recognised as one of the most important long American poems, in spite of, or even because of its inconsistencies. In these at least, Crane pays ample tribute to the USA in all its glittering complexity, and advances the legacy of Whitman, the poet of multitudes and contradictions.

Frank O'Hara in Context

If American poets do indeed 'labour' to 'complete' the work of their predecessors, as Harold Bloom contends, we might think of poetic history in the USA as a sequence of intersecting genealogies. To some poets, the line from Walt Whitman to Hart Crane was especially significant. For Frank O'Hara (1926–66), they were two of the three most important American poets. As he wrote in 1959, 'after all, only Whitman and Crane and Williams, of the American poets, are better than the movies'.[6] Candid about his attraction to men, O'Hara found valuable precedents for writing about homoerotic desire in Whitman and Crane, but his appraisal of William Carlos Williams (1883–1963) is also crucial to our understanding of his own work. From the 1920s on,

---

* As stated earlier in this chapter, Whitman was most noted for his 'long line'. If anything, it is Emily Dickinson (1830–86) who is most associated with the dash, which she uses with great variety in her poems, sometimes to indicate an inadequacy of expression, sometimes to convey a lateral move from one idea to another.

Williams's modernist poetry contrasted sharply with that of many of his contemporaries. He rejected the densely allusive and self-conscious literariness of T. S. Eliot (1888–1965) and Ezra Pound (1885–1972), both of whom looked more to European history and experience than into their native USA for inspiration. For Williams, poetry was only vital if it recorded everyday circumstance and spoke in a voice that owed little to older, pre-American cultures. According to the Anglo-American poet Thom Gunn (1929–2004), Williams was 'in love with the bare fact of the external world, its thinginess'.[7] His was a poetry that offered few connections to what had gone before, for Williams was suspicious of the political implications of writing with one eye on the past; as he wrote in 1952, 'the old line, the medieval masterbeat, has to be broken down before it is built up anew'.[8]

Frank O'Hara took from Crane's work a sense of the possibilities of American life, and an unabashed passion for New York; from Whitman, he developed a fluency in the long line, and an emphasis on the spoken qualities of poetry over the written. However, his work rarely follows Crane in sonic luxuriance, nor does it value metaphor so highly; and while stylistically there are considerable debts to Whitman, O'Hara makes no claim to speak for the nation or to embody its diverse voices in one. For Crane and Whitman, poetry is a vital constituent in the greater narratives of history and culture, but for Williams a poem is an 'object (like a symphony or a cubist painting)' and 'it must be the purpose of the poet to make of his words a new form: to invent, that is, an object consonant with his day', and this could well have been O'Hara's manifesto too.[9]

An object 'consonant' with the artist's day was already a concept familiar to many of O'Hara's contemporaries in the world of the visual arts. O'Hara was as much involved with painters as he was writers; in the early 1960s, he was an assistant curator at the Museum of Modern Art in New York, as well as a sometime art critic and friend of 'abstract expressionists' such as Willem De Kooning (1904–97) and Joan Mitchell (1925–92). Like many movements, 'abstract expressionism' was somewhat amorphous, and many artists with quite different aesthetics came to be bracketed under the term. Its offshoot, 'action painting', was one of the most discussed cultural trends in 1950s America, not least because of the endeavours of Jackson Pollock (1912–56). Action painting accentuated the physicality of the painter. Pollock's giant canvases, onto which he would drip paint spontaneously and apparently randomly, caught the moment of painting in a way few artists had ever managed before. The subject of the painting is therefore itself – how it came to be and what it remains. It is also the painter: not the artist as a cultural type or symbol, but rather the straightforward agent in the 'act' of painting.

The poetry of Frank O'Hara should be read in the context of these developments in the visual arts, not only because of his connection to the figures involved but also because his work itself often makes use of similar techniques in a literary context. His poems do not make claims for the artist as a seer or oracle. He is only a vessel for the unfiltered energies of his surroundings. In the tongue-in-cheek proposals that comprise 'Personism: A Manifesto', O'Hara writes:

> I'm not saying that I don't have practically the most lofty ideas of anyone writing today, but what difference does that make? They're just ideas. The only good thing about it is that when I get lofty enough I've stopped thinking and that's when refreshment arrives. (p. 498)

The Poem as Object

To stop thinking is to cease interpreting images and events, and to start recording them more neutrally. One consequence of this is that the poet becomes a device; in 'Memorial Day 1950', O'Hara compares the usefulness of poetry to that of a machine (p. 18), a view O'Hara shares with William Carlos Williams, who once defined the poem as 'a machine made out of words'.[10] Machinery implies not only strict and regulated patterns but also automation, and there are plenty of poems in which it would appear that O'Hara has written the first lines to have entered his head (what might be called 'automatic writing'), before simply representing them on the page without interpretation or reorganisation; good examples are juxtapositions such as in 'Ashes on a Saturday Afternoon' or lines that are grammatically legitimate yet semantically unintelligible, like 'noose arriving tropically masterful, estimating and caught'.[11] These are almost the lexical equivalent of a Pollock canvas, words running together at random on the page; they also have the dreamy illogic of surrealism. Many of O'Hara's earlier poems experiment with these approaches, borrowed from the visual arts. However, although their effects can approximate some of the innovations of the American artists O'Hara knew and liked, they can still seem over-structured. Unlike a painting which could literally be the product of an accidental spillage onto a canvas, there is always a lag between the word as thought and the word as written or typed. A line of verse, no matter how apparently nonsensical, can never be completely haphazard. O'Hara's work is highly conscious of how difficult it is to avoid such artifice. Sometimes he revels in it, deliberately overemphasising it in order to send it up. He has a fondness for camp phrasing, most often seen in lines of pastiche in which the excesses of poetry past are mischievously lampooned: see how he enthuses in one of his many plainly titled 'Poems', as if momentarily possessed by the spirit of Wordsworth and Hollywood melodrama at the same time (p. 43).

As his art progressed, O'Hara became less drawn to disorientating or whimsical juxtapositions, instead preferring a less obviously 'poetic' voice to represent the everyday. This voice is apparent right through his oeuvre; the early poem, 'A Scene', for instance, begins with a shopping list of ordinary food items (p. 19). However, in the earlier work, these details almost mimic a still-life painting and take on a stilted quality; O'Hara is still seeking to poeticise visual modes of expression, which means that his poems are often representations of representations. Nevertheless, another early 'list' poem, 'Today', makes a kind of manifesto out of itself, name-checking random objects, which still make a poem quotidian and yet surprising and powerful (p. 15). Objects are poems waiting to be written. The chief task of the poet is to realign them for the reader in such a way that their unique properties are renewed. In recognising this,

O'Hara draws on the work of 'imagist' poets such as Ezra Pound and H. D., who formed a loose collective in the earlier decades of the twentieth century. Their poems were marked by precise descriptions of objects, and a refusal to contain them within established poetic structures or elaborate upon their 'meanings' through figurative language. A similar phenomenon took hold in the modernist visual arts, most famously in the 'readymades' of Marcel Duchamp (1887–1968), namely found objects placed in the context of a gallery, without ornamentation or explanation, such as the urinal presented as 'Fountain' in 1917. Poets responded to these too, most notably Wallace Stevens (1879–1955) in poems such as 'Anecdote of the Jar' (1919) and 'Thirteen Ways of Looking at a Blackbird' (1917). William Carlos Williams penned similar experiments, and some of his poems constitute a missing link between those poets of the 1910s and 1920s and the O'Hara of the late 1950s and early 1960s. One of Williams's most anthologised poems, 'This is Just to Say', is in its entirety an apology for having eaten some plums in the refridgerator, because 'they were so delicious'.[12] The poet takes a domestic memo and makes a poem of it. He turns an apparently banal action into art; but the inference is also that the art is already there in the action, ready for the poet merely to extract it. For O'Hara too, the poem is both an artefact and a real thing, as he termed it in 'To the Poem'. Nothing is too commonplace for it.

Poetry and 'Common Sense'

For O'Hara then, the poem itself, all too frequently a self-consciously elevated or at the very least a highly structured mediation of experience, is made ordinary. This seems far removed from the spirit of Whitman. Whilst appealing for the attention of individuals across social class and background, his work nevertheless assumes the existence of an American exceptionalism, and that the natural expression of this exceptionalism is poetry.* O'Hara, on the other hand, either evades discussion of American destiny and history or

---

* Exceptionalism is the principle that America is not like other nations; that it has a unique destiny borne of its singular history of revolution and liberty.

41

views it with a sceptical eye, as in the poem 'A Terrestrial Cuckoo', in which the speaker asks his travel partner, 'Oh Jane, is there no more frontier?' and declares that 'New York is everywhere like Paris' (pp. 62–3); Americans have colonised the land to such an extent that their country's original promise is long gone, but their culture is ubiquitous. If America can no longer claim to be fresh, then its poetry must trade pioneer rhetoric for a more commonplace voice.

O'Hara's 'lunch poems' are perhaps his most popular and recognisable, so-called by critics and readers because they document the kinds of errands and encounters that might make up a typical lunch hour; they were also often literally written in O'Hara's own work breaks, composed in his head as he walked from his office at the Museum of Modern Art into midday Manhattan, then noted down spontaneously without redrafting. 'A Step Away from Them' is the archetypal 'lunch poem', a glorious tribute to the polymorphous joys of New York in which O'Hara lists his food and drink of choice (Coca-cola, cheeseburger and a chocolate drink), ponders the death of Jackson Pollock, and admires the bodies of workmen in the sun, before winding up back at the museum (pp. 257–8). Even the portability of other people's poetry is emphasised. The poem ends with O'Hara confiding to the reader that he keeps his heart in his pocket, which is 'Poems by Pierre Reverdy'; O'Hara is not studying verse in a dusty room, but carrying it with him into the bustle of Main Street.

The accent on the everyday also throws up some surprising subjects of praise; at least three O'Hara poems pay tribute to instant coffee: 'Cambridge', 'John Button's Birthday' and the 'Poem' that begins with a line about coffee and cream.[13] This is a different kind of democratic art to Whitman's generous oratory or Crane's attempts to 'bridge' the diverse territories and peoples of America. O'Hara's vision has no vantage as the sun points out in 'A True Account of Talking to the Sun at Fire Island' (p. 307; discussed in the Extended Commentary to this chapter, below). However, to survey America with an omniscient eye, as if from above, is invariably to place the concept of the nation before the experience of it. O'Hara is not so interested in fitting his surroundings to this kind of preconceived vision. Moreover, the devices of poetry are reused and reclaimed mainly in the spirit of American pragmatism; in his 'Personism' manifesto, O'Hara wryly quips, 'As for measure and other technical apparatus, that's just common sense: if you're going to buy a pair of pants you want them to be tight enough so that everyone will want to go to bed with you' (p. 498).

This typically insouciant remark implies that the stricter the form is, the more attractive the poetry or the poet. However, its 'common sense' is also an innate comfort within one's own skin as a writer, a quality accentuated within the image of the close-fitting trousers; a poet must trust the lines and limits of his own body. Like many of O'Hara's ideas, this in part comes from the visual arts, in this case once more from action painting, in which the scale of the canvas in some way represents the scale of the artist's body. But it also extends and restates Whitman's commitment to the long line. In poems such as 'Song of Myself', Whitman's lines rise and fall with the breath of the reader; they are simultaneously bound and freed by the physical capabilities of he or she who voices them. O'Hara realigns his poetry to these capabilities, often dwelling on respiratory images. Many poems conclude with a breath or a description of somebody breathing. For example, there is the 'Ode to Tanaquil Leclercq', which imagines the world holding its breath (p. 364), and the 'Poem' which contrasts a dull lecture with the immediacy of a sleeping body, trailing off with the line that compares the body's breathing with the history lesson (p. 354). The lack of a full stop in this case visually signals the continuity of the breath. A similar trick occurs in 'The Day Lady Died', which describes how news of the jazz singer Billie Holiday's death interrupts O'Hara's daily chores; the poem finishes in mid-air with the unpunctuated comment that he stopped breathing, neatly doubling as an expression of the breathless beauty of Holiday's singing, which is playing in the background, the sudden death of the singer herself, and the shock this causes among her fans (p. 325).

In 'Song', the recurring line about the refusal to breathe is a rhetorical invitation to those who might approach the polluted and sexually charged city with prudish caution, while another simply titled 'Poem' debates what love might be, before proposing that it is like a chemical dropped on paper, spreading quietly, to which O'Hara simply responds that he is sure of nothing but this and its intensification by breathing (p. 350). However, the most telling breath of all in O'Hara's poetry is ultimately that of Whitman himself, implicitly invoked in 'Ode', which closes thus:

> I am moved by the multitudes of your intelligence
> and sometimes, returning, I become the sea –
> in love with your speed, your heaviness and breath. (p. 196)

Though the subject is not specifically named as Whitman, the 'multitudes' are hard to read without calling him to mind; it marks a momentary confluence, as the old master and the young upstart briefly breathe in tandem, and become one body.

Inspiration and Expiration: Allen Ginsberg

One of Frank O'Hara's contemporaries, Allen Ginsberg (1926–97), made breath and breathing even more central to his poetic practice. Ginsberg is famous, perhaps infamous, for many things. As one of the 'Beat Generation' of 1950s writers (which also included the poets Gregory Corso and Lawrence Ferlinghetti, and the novelists Jack Kerouac and William Burroughs), he achieved rapid recognition as one of a new literary breed, who, disaffected ('beat') with Cold War geopolitics and what they saw as the deadening conformity of 1950s America, prioritised travel, spiritual and philosophical openness, and the youth culture of jazz and drugs. Much of their work, Kerouac's novels and Ginsberg's poetry especially, yearns to rediscover the innocent, unlimited Eden that once was America, before the wrangles of international politics and the uglier aspects of human development overwrote its original promise. For Ginsberg, this America is the terrain of Whitman, and Whitman's long line must be restored to its original, visionary purpose. Ginsberg's relationship to the whiskered father of American verse was both superficial and deep. In the popular imagination, as Ginsberg himself grew more bearded and was called on for his opinions on diverse political and social questions, his status as a late twentieth-century poet–prophet seemed inevitable; but he also believed very profoundly that he was in some ways continuing Whitman's work, if not quite 'labouring to complete' him.

In a 1968 interview with Fernando Pivano, Ginsberg said that 'Whitman broke the ground, opened up the soil for first cultivation.'[14] This is, of course, not an unusual proposition, but Ginsberg restates it because he wants to plant his own seeds in that soil, and to argue that his own poetic concerns and techniques find their precursors in Whitman's verse, but flower in new ways more relevant to the age in which he is writing. In the opinion of the critic Helen Vendler, 'he is recognizably the native heir of Emerson, Whitman, and Williams [but] he was not born with their regenerative sporadic optimism'.[15] Nevertheless, it could be added that although the possibility of regeneration in the world outside the poetry is severely compromised by its *de*generation into war and self-destruction, Ginsberg's work still retains a faith in poetry's magical ability to refresh itself, and to open up previously inaccessible recesses of the human body and mind.

To communicate this, Ginsberg places great emphasis on the etymology of the word 'inspiration'. It comes from the Latin *inspirare*, which means 'to breathe in', which in turn comes from *spiritus*, 'breath'. It is easy to see how this mutated into the more metaphorical sense which is now more commonly used; for Ginsberg, however, one definition did not morph into the other; the two are concurrent, and synonymous. In a published conversation with the poet Robert Duncan, Ginsberg refutes his contemporary's opinion that inspiration cannot be taught. He argues that it can, because good breathing can be taught, and to 'inspire' is literally to breathe in.[16] This point is repeated in the poem preface to *Cosmopolitan Greetings*, 'Improvisation in

Beijing', where he makes clear that he writes poetry because he wants to breathe freely and because of the freedom Whitman gave poetic form.[17] The links between the two senses in both these instances are not merely a case of clever etymological pedantry. Ginsberg was a well-known Buddhist, and meditation was an integral part of both his life and his art. Very often his inspiration was a direct consequence of focusing on breathing. It goes without saying that spoken poetry is fundamentally dependent on the human lungs, and Ginsberg desires that this link be explicitly stated in his poetry; in this poem, the poetic verse-line effectively becomes an airway, an essential body part, and exercising it correctly can bring physical benefits, much as meditation might. Ginsberg affirms that this is possible with all worthwhile poetry. As he writes of the traditional canon:

> So you find in Blake or in any good poetry a series of vowels which if you pronounce them in proper sequence with the breathing indicated by the punctuation ... you find a yogic breathing ... that, if reproduced by the reader, following the poet's commas and exclamation points and following long long long breaths, will get you high physiologically.[18]

He detects these vowels in Wordsworth's 'Tintern Abbey', Shelley's 'Mont Blanc', Hart Crane's 'Atlantis', and, rather audaciously, in his own poem 'Howl'; he goes on to say that the buzz they deliver can equal or even exceed that of marijuana. Ginsberg is partly positioning poetry within the 1960s counterculture here, proposing that it can be useful and pleasurable to the 'hippie' generation who protested against the Vietnam War and practised Eastern mysticism; he was indeed an icon of the movement. But he is also suggesting that the poets on his list derived physical pleasure from writing and reading their own work, and expanded their consciousnesses in the process; in turn, this would stimulate the mind to further creativity, sparking a chain of inspiration sustained through individual poetic expression, and between the writers themselves through the centuries.

Paying Homage

This line of 'inspired' poets is a brotherhood to Ginsberg, in both senses of that word: a consanguinity between writers and a kind of secret society of initiates. His poetry is a perfect example of Harold Bloom's theory of influence, that a poet's inspiration issues from his or her struggle to match and better predecessors. It is an anxiety, as in 'Contest of Bards' which pitches the young poet against the old in a battle for knowledge, both jealously claiming possession of the riddle of an ancient rune of poesy; and it is also a necessity. Like Frank O'Hara, naming poetic icons such as Vladimir Mayakovsky (1893–1930) and Guillaume Apollinaire (1880–1918) explicitly throughout his poems,* Ginsberg does not hold back in paying homage. He too rates Apollinaire, as evidenced in the poem 'At Apollinaire's Grave', in which he visits the poet's resting place at Père Lachaise cemetery in Paris (p. 188).† Hart Crane is also a considerable influence. Ginsberg does not attempt to refashion Crane's style, but his status as a cult figure appeals greatly; it can be seen in 'Death to Van Gogh's Ear', in which Crane is used as a beacon of truth against what Ginsberg believes is a corrupt and mendacious federal government (p. 177). 'Kansas City to Saint Louis' takes this further. It comes in the collection *The Fall of America* (1965–71), which is concerned primarily with the Vietnam War. 'Kansas City' is one of many stops on Ginsberg's journey across the paranoid, divided USA of the late 1960s in search of a new hero, or rather an old hero renewed. Journeying across America, the figure who emerges by the end of the poem is Hart Crane. Ginsberg addresses him directly in a conscious nod to Crane's own words to Walt Whitman in the 'Cape Hatteras' section of *The Bridge*, reassuring him that all is well and that the wanderer has returned (p. 425). This Shamanic, bearded wanderer is Ginsberg himself, who wants to convince his fellow Americans that a new age is coming.

---

* The influence and significance of Mayakovsky in O'Hara's poetry is discussed in further detail below, in the Extended Commentary to this chapter.
† Père Lachaise is a cemetery on the eastern fringe of central Paris, in which many great writers are buried, including Oscar Wilde, Honoré de Balzac and Gertrude Stein.

Nevertheless, it is not the young Buddhist Beat who ultimately directs the way to this nirvana, but his predecessor. Ginsberg wishes to emulate Crane, to be beloved by the people. This is a significant piece of reclamation. Crane's reputation among poets has generally always been high, but in the critical and popular consciousness, his centrality has taken longer to emerge. Here, Ginsberg puts 'Hart' at the very 'heart' of urban American experience; he is a personal guide to enlightenment, teaching the population how to open themselves to the thousands of potential epiphanies within the landscapes and structures they take for granted. These are not merely sudden revelations; the poem charts an accumulation of ideas and possibilities, with Ginsberg's poetry the latest in the chain.

Some of Ginsberg's poems are virtual lists of poetic allegiance. 'Ignu' constructs a pantheon of divine ignoramuses who understand few of the world's pragmatic necessities, but have knowledge of the spiritual and artistic truths of the 'angel'; Whitman, Rimbaud and Coleridge, among others, are members of this fellowship (pp. 211–13). Frank O'Hara is also an occasional presence; their paths crossed in New York, and Ginsberg even mimics his voice to some extent, particularly in a poem addressed to O'Hara, 'My Sad Self' (p. 209). He also dedicates 'City Midnight Junk Strains' to O'Hara's memory, mining the dead poet's 'The Day Lady Died' for ways of writing the grief he feels at his passing. He comments on his chatty gaudiness and describes him as a prophet, while after retracing O'Hara's lunch-hour route through Manhattan, he concludes that he sees New York through O'Hara's eyes and appreciates his ear for language (p. 467).

But the two figures that haunt Ginsberg's poetry most strongly are the English visionary poet William Blake (1757–1827), and Walt Whitman. Blake is perhaps most celebrated for his *Songs of Innocence and of Experience* (1794), and for Ginsberg, it is desirable that the two are one and the same, that eternal innocence is the highest state of consciousness and understanding. Blake also wrote with deceptive simplicity, and even at his most allusive and circumlocutory, Ginsberg is a readable poet, his work full of the pith and froth of slang and street-speak. Tellingly, Blake is the only poet to be mentioned in 'Howl', the notorious poem that made Ginsberg's name and provoked censorship across the USA; he writes of university students 'hallucinating' the poet, in amongst the references to Benzedrine use, heroin addiction and gay sex. Just as Blake was visited by the spectres of Dante and Milton, so are the 'best minds' of Ginsberg's generation privy to apparitions of Blake.

Whitman's influence, though, is the greatest of all; as a homosexually inclined American of self-proclaimed genius, he is the strongest of Ginsberg's available templates. He allows the Beat poet to write of erotic encounters with sailors and bellboys while arguing for the centrality of such sexual freedom and congress to national narratives of liberty, as in 'Love Poem on Theme by Whitman', which ends on an image of companionate ghosts (p. 123), ghosts that could well make up Ginsberg's fraternity of likeminded writers. However, perhaps it is 'A Supermarket in California' that sums up the pervasiveness of Whitman in Ginsberg's work, and that of so many twentieth-century American poets at large. He encounters the 'father' of American verse in the refrigerated meats section of the supermarket, but his presence does not translate easily (p. 144). Ginsberg knows his mentor would be baffled by the orgy of materialism at work in mainstream America, the slide from the innocent promise of the nineteenth century to the cynical consumerism of the twentieth. Ginsberg gets round this by tasting all the delicacies with Whitman, but never buying anything; nevertheless, the final stanza of the poem asks searchingly about their next destination. It seems the two are on an adventure, about to traverse further, but really these are questions about the future of American civilisation. His final questions could well have been asked by Crane in *The Bridge* as he ends on an elegiac long line which cites the boatman Charon and the river Lethe (p. 144). In Greek mythology, Lethe was the river that led to the underworld. This is not the optimism of the pioneer spirit, but a jaded voice, soured by the knowledge that the so-called American Dream has turned nightmare. It is the democratic voice of Whitman, so often, that is summoned to gauge how poetry might broach and overcome this darkness, or at the very least to remind the reader that the poem can be a weapon on the side of good, a tool that the great mass of the American people might use both to record their everyday experiences and effect new perspectives.

Extended Commentary: Frank O'Hara, 'A True Account of Talking to the Sun at Fire Island' (1968)

Frank O'Hara wrote 'A True Account of Talking to the Sun at Fire Island' in 1958, but it was not published until 1968, two years after he died. Its posthumous publication seems tragically appropriate now, for Fire Island was the scene of O'Hara's untimely death from a collision with a beach buggy in 1966. Moreover, the poem is concerned with death and artistic legacy, but, characteristically, it does not agonise over these issues; instead, it approaches them with a quizzical spontaneity. Like much of O'Hara's work, 'Fire Island' is not easy to categorise. It treats the subject of poetic tradition with both reverence and irreverence, and places the figure of the artist at its centre while simultaneously deflating any potential for egocentricity with irony and whimsy.

'Fire Island' is actually one of O'Hara's many homages to the Russian poet Vladimir Mayakovsky, who is also invoked in 'Ann Arbor Variations', 'Second Avenue' and the poem 'Mayakovsky'. In this instance, O'Hara uses the Russian poet's 'An Extraordinary Adventure Which Befell Vladimir Mayakovsky in a Summer Cottage' as a loose template. In the earlier poem, the poetic subject is roused to 'anger' by the sun encroaching on his privacy.[19] However, the sun enters into direct conversation with him; the two take tea together, and by the end of the poem, Mayakovsky has resolved 'always to shine, / to shine everywhere' for 'that is my motto – / and the sun's' (p. 143). O'Hara, too, finds the sun intrusive at first, almost recalling the 'busy old fool' of John Donne's 'The Sonne Rising', but its insouciance is immediately eclipsed by O'Hara's, as it remarks to him that he is on the second poet he has deigned to speak to personally and that Mayakovsky was more prompt (p. 306). It turns out that O'Hara has slept in because he was up late the previous night, talking to his old Harvard room-mate and friend Hal Fondren, but he tries his best to apologise to the sun for being so idle.

Already, then, in the first fifteen lines or so, a dichotomy is established between O'Hara's ostensible ignorance of poetic expectation, and his actual knowledge of it. Readers of poetry might conventionally expect the sun to be eulogised, or at the very least to be addressed as a superior, but O'Hara initially speaks to it in the same, casual, good-natured tone he uses for most poetic reports of his interactions; apologising simply and without flourish. It is immediately diverted from its more usual poetic function as either a muse or a metonym for Creation. This in turn suggests O'Hara accords himself no especial status as a poet, because it appears he is either innocent of the sun's conventional figurative role, or blind to the possibility of being 'chosen' by muse or deity to practise his art for the greater good. Consequently, it is the sun, rather than the poet, who seems egocentric; and it is the sun who demands an audience, inverting O'Hara's understanding of 'personism' to turn the poet into a reader. However, O'Hara knows that poetry too often appropriates solar imagery unthinkingly; elsewhere he expresses impatience with such lazy devices (see 'Poem', p. 352); his use of it here is therefore an act of poetic subversion. 'Fire Island' is also far from unselfconscious about its potential literary significance. Despite the O'Hara within the poem being taken aback by the sun's decision to address him personally, the poet himself nevertheless claims an association with his forebears in the writing of it, seeking connection with Mayakovsky. Here, then, as in many of his greatest poems, O'Hara's apparent artlessness is itself a construction.

Once the two subjects of the poem enter into dialogue, it emerges that the sun has been keeping an eye on O'Hara; it proceeds to give him advice about how to live and write, based on the premise that the two are more alike than would appear, telling him matter-of-factly that it likes his poetry (p. 306). The tone here is almost that of a seasoned Manhattan publisher, saving a manuscript from the slush-pile with an understated endorsement. But it is also a statement of empathy;

the sun compares public ignorance of the poet to its own position, simultaneously undervalued and expected to appear constantly, with non-appearance being equated with laziness or death (p. 307). This could almost be read as an arrogance on O'Hara's part; his poetry, for all its ingenuity, is hardly as essential as the sunshine. Yet the sun is voiced so amiably that at this point it effectively becomes O'Hara, and the reader realises he is staging a dialogue with himself, working through his anxieties about the value of his art; voicing the sun is an act of ventriloquism.

This is most apparent when the sun advises O'Hara not to worry about his 'poetic' or 'natural' lineage (p. 307), which could almost be a note to self or a line from the poet's 'Personism' manifesto. The sun is really restating O'Hara's credo, that the act of writing should not be compromised by concern about posterity or renown. This is the very opposite of Harold Bloom's contention that originality is only achieved in the ongoing battle with poetic precedents. However, it also strongly suggests that for O'Hara, poetic lineage is inseparable from the poetic 'line', the metrical patterns of the verse. While the sun appears to be speaking of heritage, either 'poetic' or 'natural', it is also reminding O'Hara that it is of no consequence whether the poetic line itself mines established 'poetic' modes or is instead 'natural', faithful to lived experience and everyday speech.

The implicit opposition between the terms 'poetic' and 'natural' here poses further questions; for example, is universality in art more valuable than particularity? This question is as old as poetry itself, but O'Hara refreshes it in the light of his stated intent not to veer into 'abstraction' in his writing. The sun reassures the poet that not everyone will appreciate his poetry and that it can only be hoped that his work will find those who are inclined towards it, and vice versa (p. 307). Then there is a gentle caution, advising O'Hara to broaden his horizons beyond his beloved Manhattan. It is received wisdom that New York is a microcosm, but O'Hara is fully aware that it is not the world, and that the immediacy with which he represents it may in fact risk a level of egocentricity that he would not countenance in theory; hence the sun's emphasis on having a sense of space, where 'space' denotes objective distance from the subject as much as straightforward dimension.

Being keen to avoid any accusation of egotism, O'Hara finally suggests to the reader that the poem itself is not his own, but the sun's, which it leaves an act of farewell. O'Hara here can present himself as a mere scribe reporting the sun's dictation. Many poets have aspired to this kind of disinterested voice; it is the objective behind John Keats's 'negative capability', for example, in which the poet has the power to write what he sees in the world objectively without recourse to interpretation, prejudgement or emotional response. However, here O'Hara seems to be subverting one of America's most recognisable literary totems – the poet as prophet or oracle. This is perhaps the one legacy of Whitman's that O'Hara rejects. He plays the part of the innocent, uncertain as to the sun's motive, and he protests his status as its amanuensis. The title of the poem is highly significant here. O'Hara stresses that this is a 'true account'; it is almost reportage rather than art, and thus emphasises its own apparent impartiality. It is only at the end of the poem that Frank O'Hara properly emerges. As the sun begins to disappear, he seems to awake fully; but then, five lines later in the poem's final line, as the sun rises darkly, O'Hara writes that he slept. It is a highly ambiguous ending. It seems that the sun is being called away by 'they', but O'Hara cannot go with it to meet them; there is a strong implication that he is on the threshold of death, but his time is not yet up, and so the sun puts him back to sleep. The 'true account', then, would appear to be a dream.

Along with 'The Day Lady Died', 'Fire Island' is perhaps the best-known and most anthologised O'Hara poem. It demonstrates many of the dichotomies and ambiguities that lie not just behind O'Hara's verse, but much poetry that shuns the stylisation of European literature and seeks a more demotic language in which to comment on contemporary America.

Notes

1   Harold Bloom, *The Anxiety of Influence: A Theory of Poetry* (London: Oxford University Press, 1973), p. 68.

2   Walt Whitman, *The Complete Poems*, ed. Francis Murphy (Harmondsworth: Penguin, 1977), pp. 63–124 (63).

3   Hart Crane, *The Letters of Hart Crane: 1916–1932*, ed. Brom Weber (Garden City, NY: Anchor, 1966), pp. 261–2.

4   Hart Crane, *Complete Poems of Hart Crane*, ed. Marc Simon (New York: Liveright, 2001), p. 5.

5   'Recorders ages hence' is the opening of Walt Whitman's poem of the same name. See Whitman, 'Recorders Ages Hence', *The Complete Poems*, pp. 154–5.

6   Frank O'Hara, 'Personism: A Manifesto', *Collected Poems*, ed. Donald Allen (Berkeley: University of California Press, 1995), pp. 498–9 (498).

7   Thom Gunn, 'A New World: The Poetry of William Carlos Williams', *The Occasions of Poetry: Essays in Criticism and Autobiography* (London: Faber & Faber, 1982), pp. 21–35 (22).

8   William Carlos Williams, 'The American Spirit in Art', *Proceedings of the American Academy of Arts and Letters* 2:2 (1952), pp. 51–9 (59).

9   William Carlos Williams, *The Autobiography of William Carlos Williams* (1951. New York: New Directions, 1967), pp. 264–5.

10   William Carlos Williams, 'Introduction to *The Wedge*', *Selected Essays* (New York: New Directions), p. 256.

11   See O'Hara, 'Ashes on a Saturday Afternoon', *Collected Poems*, pp. 77–8 (77); 'Invincibility', *Collected Poems*, pp. 121–3 (122).

12   William Carlos Williams, 'This is Just to Say', *Collected Poems I: 1909–1939*, ed. A. Walton Litz and Christopher MacGowan (Manchester: Carcanet, 2000), p. 372.

13   O'Hara, *Collected Poems*, p. 239; pp. 244–5; pp. 267–8.

14   Allen Ginsberg, *Spontaneous Mind: Selected Interviews 1958–1996*, ed. David Carter (London: Penguin, 2001), pp. 103–23 (110).

15   Helen Vendler, review of 'The Fall of America', repr. in Lewis Hyde, ed., *On the Poetry of Allen Ginsberg* (Ann Arbor: University of Michigan Press, 1984), pp. 203–9 (209).

16   Allen Ginsberg, 'Advice to Youth (with Robert Duncan)', *Allen Verbatim: Lectures on Poetry, Politics, Consciousness* (New York: McGraw Hill, 1974), pp. 103–30 (109).

17 Allen Ginsberg, *Collected Poems 1947–1997* (London: Penguin, 2009), pp. 937–9 (937).

18 Ginsberg, *Allen Verbatim*, pp. 22–3.

19 Vladimir Mayakovsky, 'An Extraordinary Adventure Which Befell Vladimir Mayakovsky in a Summer Cottage', *The Bedbug and Selected Poetry*, trans. Max Hayward and George Reavey (London: Weidenfeld and Nicolson, 1961), pp. 136–43 (139).

Poetry of Revision: Moore, Bishop and Merrill

As the previous chapter of this book outlines, to say 'I' in American poetry is to evoke a complex network of connotations and associations. Whitman's 'I' is the poetic voice as a synecdoche* of the nation, both of America and equal to it, but it remains divisive. There have always been poets who recoil from his work. For Ezra Pound, he was a purveyor of 'crudity' whose poetry was 'exceedingly nauseating'; in his 1915 poem, 'A Pact', Pound admits that he 'detested' Whitman as a 'pig-headed father'.[1] For other poets, he was almost unmentionable. The post-war poet Elizabeth Bishop (1911–79) recalls meeting her mentor and friend, the modernist Marianne Moore (1887–1972) for tea in New York; on discovering that the teahouse was on the same street as the former offices of the *Brooklyn Eagle*, the newspaper for which Whitman worked, Bishop paid tribute to the bearded bard, only for Moore to exclaim, 'Elizabeth, don't speak to me about that man!'[2]

Much received opinion on American poetry of the twentieth century emphasises its adventurousness; its history is often narrated as a sequence of avant-garde movements, sometimes interlinked (such as the works of the Beat Generation and the 'Black Mountain' poets)

---

* A synecdoche describes the substitution of a part for the whole, or vice versa, i.e. 'the government rejected the bill' means 'the ministers who sit in the government building rejected the bill'.

or connected in a chain of influence. However, not all great twentieth-century American poets insisted on experimentation, nor did they claim allegiance to particular poetic 'schools'. Marianne Moore might be considered a modernist by association (she was a friend of T. S. Eliot and Ezra Pound) but her closely observed miniatures, for example, held more influence over poets who came to be considered formally conservative. These poets are sceptical of America's own self-projected image, its insistence on always being new, radical or iconoclastic. They recognise that spontaneity is often both elusive and illusive, and that the USA did not simply spring up without precedent or heritage; instead, it was and continues to be a revision, a transplanting of different cultures and heritages. This makes for a poetry that must be equally cautious of affected spontaneity.

Moore's work is almost antithetical to Whitman's in this regard. To her, America is not a poem in and of itself, and the poet cannot simply channel it in order to communicate this. One of her most anthologised poems, simply titled 'Poetry', begins with the startling line 'I, too, dislike it: there are things that are important beyond all this fiddle'.[3] It is a heavily ironic and seemingly antipoetic statement. Although she goes on to redeem poetry, finding in it 'a place for the genuine', her assumption is that readers hold it in contempt. In particular, it is the capitalised 'Poetry' of the title to which she refers: poetry as a formidable body of knowledge, as an accumulation of canons and great works, poetry that announces its own importance.

At times, Elizabeth Bishop shares Moore's scepticism about the value of poetry, though she counters a short discussion of the work of some of her favourite poets, including Moore herself, with this bold statement:

> Writing poetry is an unnatural act. It takes great skill to make it seem natural. Most of the poet's energies are really directed towards this goal: to convince himself (perhaps, with luck, eventually some readers) that what he's up to and what he's saying is really an inevitable, *only* natural way of behaving under the circumstances. (p. 207)

57

Poetry, then, is seldom truly spontaneous. The outpourings of Whitman or Ginsberg, the unmetaphorical 'objectivism' of Williams, or the casual 'lunch hour' inspirations of O'Hara are crafted to appear of the moment. This is one of poetry's magical sleights of hand, a skill that impresses Bishop and causes her to rank 'spontaneity' as one of the 'three qualities' she admires in poetry, along with 'accuracy' and 'mystery'; but this 'spontaneity' clearly comes, somewhat paradoxically, with practice.

In the context of much twentieth-century American poetry, Bishop's is a quietly daring proposition. Spontaneity was a key tenet of many movements and 'schools' of poetry. For the 'Beat' poets, including Ginsberg and his friends Gregory Corso (1930–2001) and Lawrence Ferlinghetti (1919–), this might mean writing in free, unmetred verse. For the so-called 'Black Mountain' school, a loose group of mid-twentieth-century avant-garde poets that included significant figures such as Robert Creeley (1926–2005) and Robert Duncan (1919–88), spontaneity in poetry was similarly a case of dismantling the metrical assumptions of the Western tradition; the work of Charles Olson (1910–70), a Black Mountain figurehead, argued for a 'projective verse' in which the unit of breath determines the poetic 'utterance'.[4] Artlessness was also key to a very different movement – that of the 'confessional' poets who achieved fame in the early 1960s, such as John Berryman (1914–72), Robert Lowell (1917–77), and Sylvia Plath (1932–63). Although all of these movements stressed their own newness, the drive for spontaneity in verse is not unique to the post-war period, nor is it necessarily peculiar to America. In a key manifesto, the 'Preface' to *Lyrical Ballads*, the English Romantic poet William Wordsworth (1770–1830) describes 'all good poetry' as 'the spontaneous overflow of powerful feelings'.[5] The artistic credos of Romantic poetry – the foregrounding of the consciousness of the poet, the writer as a conduit between nature and humanity – resurface in much American poetry of the nineteenth and twentieth centuries. However, Wordsworth also stressed that the artist should think 'long and deeply': spontaneous feeling is the result of constant intellectual analysis.

There is a strain of twentieth-century American poetry that recognises and foregrounds this. While the 'visionary' poet (as discussed in Part Three: 'Visionary Poetry') is a recognisable archetype, a claim might be made for the 'revisionary' poet, who writes the processes of re-seeing and reconsideration into his or her work. Readers are used to treating the poem on the page as a fait accompli; without access to the original manuscripts and notebooks of the writer in question, it is difficult for readers to imagine the processes of correction and cancellation that are an inevitable part of composition. Some poets, however, write these processes into the poetry itself, so that the reader might be privy to the making and remaking of an image. For Allen Ginsberg, sight is actually a kind of sixth sense. To 'see' is to have a vision, with all the metaphysical implications of that word: a vision of the future, a conceptual or artistic belief system, a worldview, as in the opening line of 'Howl', where Ginsberg comments on the state of his generation as he sees them.[6] However, for some poets, to 'see' is to train the eye on the details of the physical world, to continually perfect one's focus, as in the work of the three poets discussed below: Marianne Moore, Elizabeth Bishop and their contemporary James Merrill (1925–95). Moore, Bishop and Merrill were all much less interested in poetry as a fundamental expression of Americanness than the likes of Ginsberg or O'Hara. Merrill spent much of his time in Europe, as his memoir *A Different Person* (1995) testifies; equally, Bishop spent a great deal of her life in Brazil. In some ways it is their marginality, their resistance to the national narrative, that allows their 'revisionary' perspectives to take hold.

Marianne Moore and 'Plain American' Poetry

The poetry critic Grace Schulman sees Marianne Moore's art as one of constant adjustment to the physical properties of her environment; she writes that 'to read a poem by Marianne Moore is to be aware of exactitude. It is to know that the writer has looked at a subject ... from all sides, and has examined the person looking at it as well.'[7] Moore is celebrated for her eye, for possessing sharp and accurate sight. Her 1910s poems bear some resemblance to the work of the imagists,[*] and she was a friend of Ezra Pound and H. D. (Hilda Doolittle), but she diverged from Imagism by frequently using the first person in her work, sometimes casting explicit judgement on the scenes and objects described. Even her earliest poems, which are usually very short, even epigrammatic, combine visual perspicacity with critical pithiness. 'Qui S'Excuse, S'Accuse',[†] for example, is an ideal introduction to this voice (p. 20). Initially, it seems that in this poem Moore claims the artist is unimpeachable, and therefore to some degree exceptional, above the reader and the critic. This is actually not so, for nowhere does Moore make a case for the artist as a being of higher intellect or standing; the artist of the poem could in fact be anyone who has experienced what she terms 'exact perception'. Nor does Moore speak from a privileged position of accumulated wisdom, for she is susceptible to the poetic temptations of metaphor and symbol that sometimes obscure 'perception'. In 'A Red Flower', she keeps the likelihood of interpreting objects with emotion in check by using very short lines and plain words, but acknowledging the possibility of emotional 'overflow' nonetheless. In other poems, such as 'To a Stiff-winged Grasshopper', she understands that her poetic eye is not necessarily unique. She parts the wings of the insect, examining it and thinking she has discovered something new. She does not have time to take pleasure in her discovery, for just as quickly she realises that other poets too have thought they have discovered something, and that she stands with them like a coiled snake swallowing its tail. Here, Moore references the Ouroboros, an ancient mythical symbol. In the case of her experience with the grasshopper, the tail-eating serpent illustrates that there are no real beginnings, and that all is recurrence. There is nothing that has not been seen before; every vision is a revision

---

[*] See Gary Day, *York Notes Companions: Modernist Literature (1890–1950)* (London: Pearson Longman & York Press, 2010), for a detailed explanation of Imagism.

[†] 'Qui s'excuse, s'accuse' is a French phrase, sometimes used proverbially in English, meaning 'he who excuses himself too much, accuses himself of the wrong'.

or refocusing. However, just when it seems that Moore's poem is straying into abstraction, she comments on the extreme symbolism of the ring, reminding the reader both that she would rather not use figurative language in order to be philosophically suggestive and that she is nevertheless susceptible to this type of writing. This predilection for self-correction is a key part of Moore's 'exactitude', for she is 'exacting' in both senses of the word: accurate in her description, and at times, self-punishing in her desire to be so.[*] In some of the early poems, this tendency is almost overstated; pieces with titles such as 'My senses do not deceive me', 'Things are what they seem', 'I tell you no lie' and 'All of it, as recorded' might almost be accused of protesting their empiricism too much.[†] Though at times Moore's razor-sharp perception approaches a theory of poetry, it is more often borne of a desire to be clear and intelligible. As her frequently quoted poem 'England' has it, America is a county with a language so plain that even animals can read it (p. 141).

Though some of her work is almost disarmingly 'plain', almost whimsically so, much is the very opposite: allusive and, on first reading, difficult. Her longest poem, 'Marriage', is also one of the most analysed. Moore threads it with long quotations from other writers, either to illustrate her own ideas on the subject of matrimony, or to move her onto new ones.[8] It initially comes across as an arcane game of free association, but she does not quote in order to prove the extent of her literary knowledge, or the gravity of being weighed down by poetic precedent (see another poem, 'Picking and Choosing', (p. 138). Reassessing 'Marriage' in 1961, she recounted some of the questions critics and readers have asked of it, concluding that 'the thing (I would hardly call it a poem) is no philosophic precipitate'; rather, it is nothing more than 'a little anthology of statements

---

[*] Moore once remarked to the poet Donald Hall, 'Do the poet and scientist not work analogously? … Both are willing to waste effort. To be hard on himself is one of the main strengths of each.' Moore, 'Interview with Donald Hall', *A Marianne Moore Reader* (New York: The Viking Press, 1961), pp. 253–73 (263).

[†] Empiricism is a mode of enquiry that takes personal experience as the basis of fact.

that took my fancy'. When asked why she uses so many quotation marks, she replied, 'When a thing has been said so well that it could not be said better, why paraphrase it? Hence my writing is, if not a cabinet of fossils, a kind of collection of flies in amber.'[9] Moore, characteristically, conjures a highly visual image from the animal world to describe her work. She has clearly considered her oeuvre itself as a collection of objects, an exhibition, and intends to describe it to others as objectively as she can.

However, what also emerges from 'Marriage', and Moore's subsequent explanation of its devices, is a kind of paradox: that even when she is at her most challenging, Moore is striving for simplicity. If readers trust her eye and her judgement, they can forgive her certain whims. There is a point to be made here about the seriousness of poetry. Poetry that thinks of itself as poetry is perhaps more antipoetic than that which does not acknowledge it; self-consciously 'poetic' poetry cannot let its subject speak, or do it any service. This inversion is behind Moore's 'Poetry', discussed earlier. It also leads to her seemingly eccentric reluctance to brand herself as a poet, and her mischievous claim that her work can only be called poetry because it cannot really be categorised in any other way.[10]

The Novelty of the Everyday Object

Moore's 'exactitude', then, comes about through a loosening of poetic discipline, and a refusal to expect miracles of the form. She is as highly meta-poetic as many of her predecessors and contemporaries; that is to say, she is just as likely to write a poem about poetry as any other great poet, from Wordsworth to Whitman, Keats to Eliot. What marks her out is her determination to see poetry as another ordinary or everyday object, much like the snails and steamrollers and bowling balls she examines in the poems themselves. In 'Why That Question', she remarks how tiresome it is to be asked what the difference is between poetry and prose (p. 75). Theories of poetry and poetics do not appeal to her. As a corrective, a Moore poem might begin with a counterintuitive contention, such as in 'Poetry', or a statement of the ordinariness of poetry, as in the opening lines of 'Critics and Connoisseurs' (p. 106). In this poem, Moore goes on to say that Ming vases and imperial decorations are all very well in their way, but a child's simple games can be more poetic. Notably, these are actions rather than perfectly finished artefacts. Where her contemporary and sometime champion T. S. Eliot ventured that humankind's propulsive urge to move and mutate can be countered by art, a 'still point of the turning world' such as might be found in a Chinese vase or the ideal poem,[11] the objects Moore privileges in her own poetry are rarely or barely fixed. To return to her statement about the poem 'Marriage', her works are flies in amber, not fossils; not timeless relics, but living things caught in a moment.

Many of Moore's poems about what in other contexts might be thought of as banal minutiae capture such moments. 'Holes Bored in a Workbag by the Scissors' is one such, where Moore turns the 'fabric' of the workbag into the verb that created it, 'fabricate', so that the bag is involved in its own making and unmaking (p. 114). Meanwhile, in 'An Egyptian Pulled Glass Bottle in the Shape of a Fish' the work of art is compared to a wave (p. 173); despite its solidity, it retains a liquid vitality, as if caught mid-leap or mid-swim. The play between solid and fluid objects is worked out more fully in 'Walking-Sticks and Paper-Weights and Water Marks'. It begins with the image of the 'triskelion', a symbol comprising a three-legged figure common to many ancient cultures, most visibly in the Isle of Man. Though it is a fixed motif on the page, the jointed triskelion is all motion (p. 227); if one limb moves, then so do the other two. Moore proceeds to describe the paperweight of the title in startlingly vivid language, as though it were a living organism (p. 229). The abundant hyphens of this poem are a visual representation of the object's own sense of propulsion, even as it sits still on its shelf. They also suggest concatenation, the linking together of elements in a chain; perhaps the paperweight reminds us that even the most solid of structures have molecules moving in and around them. The poem ends on a musical motto, a rhyme about a juniper tree, which is then repeated endlessly. Everything in the world of the poem is connected to something else, and so none of these objects exist in vacuums. They are understood more completely through an understanding of what has gone into their construction, and what is placed around them in a continually shifting environment. Unlike Eliot's vases, then, Moore's artefacts absorb and reflect the properties of their situation at any given moment. As 'When I Buy Pictures' concludes, after divulging that paintings should provide pleasure in ordinary moments and should not attract intellectual analysis that spoils this pleasure, Moore highlights the essential life and spirituality of paintings, in acknowledging the forces that have made them (p. 144).

Elizabeth Bishop: Vision and the Visual

The poetry of Marianne Moore, then, might be less driven by 'vision' than 'visuality'. Any 'vision', in the sense of a grand or prophetic poetic project, or moment of epiphany, issues from a 'visual' response to the world around her, rather than from the 'mind's eye'; even her praise for the Brooklyn Bridge in 'Granite and Steel', borrowing liberally from Hart Crane, is centred around the fact that architects and engineers had the vision, so that Moore herself might see the fruit of it. She thus revisits or revises the visions of others, albeit in her own distinct voice. Her revision is literally that – a 're-seeing'.

The same might be said of the poems of Elizabeth Bishop, whom Moore befriended and mentored. Bishop, like Moore, is celebrated for her 'eye', and Moore was certainly one of her early tutors in the act of seeing; Bishop called her 'The World's Greatest Living Observer'.[12] She also pays an affectionate tribute to her in 'Invitation to Miss Marianne Moore', beckoning the elder poet to walk with 'pointed toe' over the very Brooklyn Bridge she celebrated in 'Granite and Steel', because she desires to see her 'black capeful of butterfly wings and bon-mots'.[13] The words she associates with Moore in the poem – 'pellucid' and 'unnebulous' – point to what she values in poetry more generally: clarity, precision and a love of the elements. At the beginning of her career in the 1940s, critics warmed to these attributes, while acknowledging that these attributes made her somewhat difficult to place. Even her good friend, the poet Robert Lowell, wrote of her first collection *North and South* (1946) that 'on the surface, her poems are observations – surpassingly accurate, witty and well-arranged, but nothing more'.[14] Accurate, witty and well-arranged poetry was not especially modish in the decades immediately following the Second World War. In the 1950s, the egocentric 'I' of the Beats and the Confessional Poets alike dominated the bookshelves and speaker circuits. Where the 'confessionals' eked poetic inspiration from the darker recesses of their private lives, and the Beats published their personal testimonies in a seemingly uncorrected and uncensored fashion, Bishop remained assiduously private and, by and large, trimmed her poems of excess.

It is the visual, rather than the visionary, that is thus integral to Bishop's work. Like Moore, she frequently writes about animals with diligence and exactitude. More often than not, however, she must confront their sentience as well as describing their features, and this mostly happens in a momentary flash of eye-to-eye contact. In 'The Man-Moth', for instance, Bishop urges the reader to observe mankind, trapped in the city subway like an insect in a jar. 'If you catch him', she writes, 'hold up a flashlight to his eye. It's all dark pupil, / an entire night itself' (p. 12). To see or to watch somebody is invariably to make an object of them, but in Bishop's poetry, to observe the eyes of another being is to use one's own subjectivity to recognise theirs. This occurs to startling effect in 'The Fish', where:

> I looked into his eyes
> which were far larger than mine
> but shallower, and yellowed,
> the irises backed and packed
> with tarnished tinfoil
> seen through the lenses
> of old scratched isinglass. (pp. 33–4)

A line or two later, his eyes move, but 'not to return [her] stare', so that it is 'more like the tipping / of an object toward the light'. However, for the brief moment she first fixes his gaze, she and the fish are both subjects with possible histories and narratives; she visualises his fate, to be wrapped in aluminium for cooking, and her pun on 'isinglass', the fish-derived gelatine used to clarify jellies, associates the commodification of the animal with the decline of his own sight, which the (isin)glass cannot arrest. Similarly, in 'Roosters', the death of the bird's 'wives' is marked by their 'open, bloody eyes / while those metallic feathers oxidize' (p. 29), though the inglorious declines of the fish and the roosters are perhaps atoned for in a later Bishop poem, 'The Moose', in which a coach party of gossipy townspeople is stopped in its tracks by an 'antlerless' mammal, 'high as a church'. Initially, the moose is an 'it', but observation reveals its sex: '"Look! It's a she!"' announces one of the passengers (p. 162). The moose responds to her newly conferred identity in kind, through her own act of seeing: 'Taking her time, / she looks the bus over, / grand, otherworldly'. Bishop appears to be saying that we become ourselves through these acts of looking.

Indeed, Bishop's art is dedicated to this deceptively simple act. Bishop herself was fascinated by the science of the eye; she worked for a brief time in the optical shop of the American navy base in Key West during the Second World War. She urges her readers to use all their visual resources, and they respond in kind; it is highly appropriate that the poet Anne Stevenson called her critical study of Bishop 'Five Looks at Elizabeth Bishop'.[15] Looking, however, is distinct from 'vision'. Like Moore, Bishop considers 'vision', in its most grandiose sense, to be one of the potential excesses of poetry. In 'Poem', from the final collection to be published in her lifetime, *Geography III* (1979), Bishop pays tribute to a painting of a Nova Scotia farm that has become a 'minor family relic'. After some concentration, she realises that she knows the place depicted: the farm, the Presbyterian church, and 'Mrs Gillespie's house' are all discernible. Although she 'never knew' the artist, they 'both knew this place'. 'How strange', she exclaims, before trying to explain the type of connection she feels with the painter:

> Our visions coincided – "visions" is
> too serious a word – our looks, two looks:
> art "copying from life" and life itself,
> life and the memory of it so compressed
> they've turned into each other. Which is which? (p. 166)

'Vision' and 'look' are not synonyms. 'Vision' lends itself too readily to portentousness, and also has undertones of a project completed; it bespeaks a vast synthesis, perhaps, as in *A Vision* by W. B. Yeats (1865–1939), in which the Irish poet attempts to explain the philosophical and symbolic systems behind his work. But here, 'life and the memory of it' are 'compressed', rather than expanded upon. They have taken on each other's physical properties. Visions are metaphysical; Bishop, on the other hand, is more concerned with the textures and energies of the world than the philosophies that might impose themselves upon them. To say 'life' in 'Poem' is not to invoke the conceptual tangles of ontology, but to speak of a situated life, a here and now, in a particular location at a particular time.

Refining and Re-viewing

The substitution of 'look' for 'vision' in 'Poem' exemplifies the 'surpassing accuracy' so esteemed by Robert Lowell. In order to maintain her accuracy, Bishop must show herself in the act of 'surpassing', replacing an original term with a better one. This is a process of clarification; it demands that the poet rewrite in order to write more clearly. It is also a self-correction, a characteristic Bishop device. The poet refines her terms within the poem, writing the process of emendation into the finalised line. In 'Poem', she does it twice, in the aforementioned example, and immediately afterwards, adding extra detail by making 'our looks' into 'two looks'. This is a particularly fine example of an art that makes revision its subject, as Bishop narrates how she re-views the scene depicted in the painting. It was originally seen by the artist so that it might be sketched, and sketched so that it might be seen. 'Our looks' thus become 'two looks'; the textual correction coincides with the shift in perspective.

These moments abound in Bishop's poetry. In 'The Weed', the eponymous plant shakes its dew into Bishop's face, 'so I could see / (or, in that black place, thought I saw) / that each drop contained a light' (p. 16); the poem, which recounts a dream, is full of such parentheses, as if to represent the strange, sometimes dissociative logic of the sleeping mind. In 'Brazil, January 1, 1502', the corrective qualification is used more visually, almost as if mimicking the composition of a picture, the overlaying of different pigments in flowers of purple, yellow, and pink (p. 72). Sometimes the refocusing is a dramatic rejection of what has come before, as in 'Questions of Travel', in which Bishop interrupts her own thought process at the end in order to try to force the poem's central question: 'Continent, city, country, society: / the choice is never wide and never free. / And here, or there... No. Should we have stayed at home, / wherever that may be?' (p. 75). Each of these examples graphically argues for continual shifts of focus. These poems also show that spontaneity, one of Bishop's key poetic conditions, can be written into a verse that nevertheless foregrounds the work of refinement and revision underlying the finished poem.

In some poems, self-correction is shown to be a natural process. For example, 'The Map', the opening poem of her debut collection *North and South*, begins with a statement of apparent fact – 'land lies in water; it is shadowed green' – but is immediately followed by an admission of doubt: 'shadows, or are they shallows, at its edges' (p. 3). The doubt then subsides into out-and-out questioning, as Bishop asks 'does the land lean down to lift the sea from under?' and 'is the land tugging at the sea from under?' These questions do not disrupt the poem, though, for they are presaged in the first line; if the land is shadowed, it follows that a great part of it is unknowable, and so the facts lead soon enough to questions. Bishop knows that the observation of nature requires constant readjustment of the poet's lens, and this is especially true in the case of 'The Map', which itself 'shadows' the erosive transformations that the sea visits upon the land. Revision in this context becomes almost geological, reminding us that the earth is in constant flux and, consequently, so is the representation of it. As she writes in 'North Haven', 'nature repeats herself, or almost does: / Repeat, repeat, repeat: revise, revise, revise' (p. 178): she corrects her initial interpretation of nature's repetitions to an appraisal of its revisions.

Finally, the impulse towards revision is shown to be central to the creation of art itself. 'The Monument' is illustrative here. It is a study in perspectival change, ostensibly presented as a kind of dialogue between two visitors to a gallery, but really an appeal from Bishop for her readers to join her in viewing it. It opens with an invitation, to look at the monument, before trying to ascertain its nature (p. 18). Again, there is a refinement of focus as Bishop gets more of a purchase on the interlocking wooden components. Her museum partner is impatient with it, believing it cannot be representative of anything, being a collection of boxes or crates (p. 19). But for Bishop, its ability to both absorb the gaze of spectators and to elude it is what marks it out as art. She speculates that it may be solid or hollow, and suggests that it must be studied intently to reveal its meaning (pp. 19–20). The vigilance espoused here could be extended to all art. Works of art are subject to their own erosions. The paint in the background scene of the monument here is chipping; the elements chisel it. The complete artefact is only the beginning of the work; hence it must be watched and re-watched. The underlying implication of 'One Art', perhaps Bishop's most widely known and best-loved poem, is similar. It is a villanelle, a poem of six stanzas, three lines apiece, which makes use of recurring lines with small variations. In this case, the recurring line about mastering the art of losing is always rhymed with the word 'disaster', though Bishop's point is that loss is actually no disaster at all (p. 166). In fact, attrition is built into the economy of poetry itself, for form often requires the potential loss of spontaneity or representativeness; there is also the physical 'loss' of the poem on publication as it becomes the possession of the reader. As in 'The Monument', all art contains the germ of its own decomposition, its lack of permanence; thus, there is only 'one art', that must accept this destiny. The last two lines, however, show how art can mitigate against its own losses (p. 167). As Seamus Heaney has pointed out, the parenthesised exhortation to 'write it' expresses Bishop's faith in poetry to 'set the balance *right*'.[16] Her intervention, yet another characteristic self-correction, assures us that loss is not a disaster, it only looks like one. It also reminds us that writing is only ever about resemblance, and this extends to Bishop's oeuvre as a whole. Though she may possess one of the finest eyes in the poetic canon, even her own poetry cannot become the objects it puts into words, and it knows and embraces this with humility. As Marianne Moore wrote of her follower and friend, 'why has no-one ever thought of this, one asks oneself; why not be accurate and modest?'[17]

James Merrill: The Revival of Form

Like Marianne Moore and Elizabeth Bishop, James Merrill is, to a degree, a poet *sui generis** and perhaps for similar reasons. Both Bishop and Merrill were people of private means, born into family money, which allowed them to travel extensively and cultivate a certain detachment from the frequently factional post-war American poetry scene. Both poets were also gay, but at a time of growing candour on such matters, they were reluctant to discuss their sexuality with much openness. While Bishop never really broached her lesbianism in her poems, Merrill's poetry did become progressively more relaxed about his homosexuality, though he nevertheless kept his HIV status

* *Sui generis* is a phrase of Latin origin, meaning 'without category' or 'in a category of its / his / her own'.

secret to all but a few intimates for the best part of a decade. The perceived detachment of Bishop and Merrill did not preclude them from championing and befriending other poets; indeed, with some of his inheritance from his father's investment banking company, Merrill Lynch, James set up the Ingram Merrill Foundation to give financial help to aspiring poets. Nevertheless, an air of cultured reticence surrounded Bishop and Merrill during their lifetimes.

This was not just a consequence of personal behaviour and circumstance. Bishop and Merrill mostly wrote to established formal models; not always strictly, but definitely with a respectful nod towards traditional structures and strictures, which in the age of Charles Olson, Robert Duncan and Robert Creeley seemed almost subversive. Some critics have attempted to reconstruct Merrill as a founding father of the 'New Formalism'. The New Formalists were a group of poets formed in the 1980s who reacted against the dominance of free verse and experimental structures in the poetic establishment; if, in the much-used distinction outlined by Robert Lowell, the 'Language Poets'* were the 'raw', then the New Formalists represented the 'cooked'.† These binary oppositions were common across campuses and in American poetry periodicals. It has long been tempting for critics to sort poets into two major camps – the conservative and the avant-garde – especially since the so-called 'anthology wars'. In 1960, Donald Allen edited *The New American Poetry 1945–1960*, which aimed to trace a new line of 'third generation' modernists continuing the work of Pound and Williams. A diverse

---

* The Language (or L=A=N=G=U=A=G=E) Poets were a loosely connected group who published in the journal of the same name in the 1970s and 1980s. Their work is perhaps the equivalent of what in the other arts might be termed postmodernism, breaking down established structures and questioning assumptions about the relationship between language and truth. Poets identified with the movement include Lyn Hejinian (1941–), Ron Silliman (1946–) and Bob Perelman (1947–).

† Robert Lowell divided poetry into the 'raw' (that which expressed the personality of the poet directly and without formal constraint) and the 'cooked' (poetry which valued impersonality, that was more tied to the academy) in 1960 in this acceptance speech for the National Book Award.

range of poets was included, but they all had their experimentalism in common; among the subsequently significant names to make the roster were John Ashbery, Allen Ginsberg, Denise Levertov and Frank O'Hara. Meanwhile, Donald Hall's anthology, *New Poets of England and America* (1957), centred around a very different cohort of poets, who were often branded as anti-progressive in light of the Allen anthology published three years later; on this list were Robert Bly, Anthony Hecht and Richard Wilbur, all writers of measured, metred verse. James Merrill was also included, and such is the powerful memory of the 1960s and 1970s poetic divides that he is still often considered a somewhat conservative figure, not quite of his time, an 'academic poet'.[18] This belies his fluency in many forms, not to mention his sometimes outré riffs on the tried and tested. What Merrill feels uneasy about is experimental poetry that announces itself thus. In a 1968 interview with Donald Sheehan, he admitted that he has 'always been suspicious of the word "experimentation"' because 'it partakes too much of staircase wit'. It is a misconception that poets outwardly aim to experiment; 'they've simply recognized afterward the newness of what they've done'.[19]

Looking at Words Anew

On initial reading, Merrill's poetry would not seem particularly concerned with 'newness'. As discussed earlier, newness suggests spontaneity. However, as far as it exists, the popular perception of him is of a rarefied, opera-loving aesthete with an almost seventeenth- or eighteenth-century fondness for puns and mannerisms, 'a Renaissance princeling' in the words of John Simon.[20] Some of the tautly rhymed and regulated *First Poems* (1951) do seem like exercises to keep the poet amused. 'Alone, one can but toy with imagery', he writes in 'Hourglass', keeping himself at arm's length by way of the third person;[21] similarly, the dancing in 'Dancing, Joyously Dancing' turns out to be the implied movement in a Breughel painting, rather than a real-life ball. Nevertheless, other poems indicate Merrill's own way of seeing, just as peculiar to him as that of Moore or Bishop; where they train their eye in the observation of objects, Merrill observes words – he treats them as objects to be analysed and seen anew. Even in his childhood, he was aware of the strangeness of words. Remembering how a favourite book related the story of a man 'sampling the port', he argues it could just as easily have meant someone sewing a picture of a harbour (creating a 'sample' of the port) as enjoying a tipple; 'the mother tongue could inspire both fascination and distrust', he writes in 'Acoustical Chambers'.[22]

This love of verbal duplicity stretches the forty or so years between his first and last poems. It is there in 'The Peacock' (1951), which encourages us to 'consider other birds' such as the 'dodo now undone'; the appeal to the reader's sight is akin to Bishop's similar technique, but the visual pun that ensues would be too metaphysical for her. It is also present in the 1995 poem 'b o d y', the spacing of whose title almost calls to mind the work of the 'Language' poets. Merrill beckons his readers to 'look closely at the letters' (p. 646); he shows us how the '*o* plots her course from *b* to *d*', and we realise that the letter 'o' does indeed enter 'stage right' in the body of the letter 'b', leading to a brief appearance in its own right before 'heading off – so soon' into the body of the letter 'd'. Here, Merrill is really musing on mortality and the transience of human existence, where life is the 'o', 'b' stands for birth, and 'd' for death. Meanwhile, '*y*, unanswered, knocks at the stage door'; the 'why' or mystery of existence is left unexplained. The minor miracle of this poem is that despite its morbid premise, Merrill manages to convey the movement of life by forcing the reader to reflect on the motion of reading.

'b o d y' is a study in the minute, and Merrill is often fascinated by the smallest of elements. The later poems, in *The Inner Room* (1988) and *A Scattering of Salts* (1995) especially, draw on the figure of the microscope, as in 'Vol. XLIV, no. 3' and 'The Instilling'. Such images stem from Merrill's amateur interest in the language of science; as he once explained in an interview, the 'vocabulary' of science can be 'unconscionably beautiful, like things a child says ("red shift", "spectral lines")'.[23] Science and poetry have not always been easy partners, but Merrill encourages the reader to find aesthetically pleasing language in what might seem unlikely arenas of discourse. In a historical sense, this too is a 'revision'; after all, 'metaphysical' poets of the Renaissance period such as John Donne saw no division between the natural sciences and literary arts. Merrill's abiding interest in minuscule scientific units might also go some way to explaining his predilection for etymological investigation. Words also have their atoms and molecules, their morphemes and phonemes.* In 'A Room at the Heart of Things', an 'actor and lover' seeks sexual communion (p. 510). He journeys towards his lady's 'chamber', or a 'stanza' as it is referred to earlier in the poem; Merrill is fully aware that this synonym for a 'verse of a poem' comes originally from the Latin for 'room'. Then, 'cell by cell the celebrant attains / a chamber where arcane translucences / Of god-as-mortal bring him to his knees'. Here, as in 'b o d y', Merrill is describing the visual transformation of words on the page. Merrill 'attains' the word 'celebrant', 'cell by cell', where 'cel' is a phoneme of 'celebrant'. If this seems 'arcane', that is to say, obscurely cerebral, then Merrill makes it 'translucent', by revisiting the etymology of 'arcane' itself; its origin lies in the Latin 'arca', meaning 'chest', from whence comes *ark*, a box or coffin. However, the punning goes even further, for the 'chest' leads the reader back to the 'heart' of the title, which we now realise is the 'chamber'; and the heart, being an organ, is made up of 'cells'. In barely two lines, the poem both narrates its character's quest, and its own, into the heart of meaning. 'A Room at the Heart of Things' typifies Merrill's poetic perspective; it requires its readers to see the words on the page, but also see through them, to their origins; it shines a light into language, and allows us the privilege of viewing it, translucent and renewed on the page.

---

* A morpheme is the smallest unit of meaning within a word; a phoneme is the smallest unit of sound.

Extended Commentary: Bishop, 'In the Waiting Room' (1977)

'In the Waiting Room' is the opening poem in Bishop's final collection, *Geography III*, though the volume begins with extracts from a nineteenth-century geography textbook. The very first line of 'In the Waiting Room', then, is in dialogue with the lessons in *Monteith's Geographical Series*. As the topographical questions ('In what direction is the Volcano? The Cape? The Bay? The Lake?') subside, the poem establishes two apparently irrefutable facts: that it is set in a waiting room, as the title makes clear, and that this waiting room is 'In Worcester, Massachusetts' (p. 149). The gap between these assertions and the emotional and psychological 'truths' of the poem's speaker, however, is the real subject of 'In the Waiting Room'; a concern characteristic of much of Bishop's greatest poetry.

The speaker appears to be Bishop herself, recalling a childhood visit to the dentist with her 'Aunt Consuelo'. While her aunt is treated, the young Bishop bides her time in the waiting room, taking in her surroundings and choosing magazines to keep her occupied. The youth of the speaker is underscored by sparse vocabulary: 'I went with Aunt Consuelo / to keep her dentist's appointment / and sat and waited for her / in the dentist's waiting room'. The repetition here ('dentist', 'waiting') also reminds the reader that the voice is that of a grown woman trying to communicate the psychology of a child not yet prone to periphrasis or the use of synonyms. The adult self interjects from time to time, using parentheses to qualify statements: 'I could read', she says in brackets, as if anticipating possible doubts about the legitimacy of her story. Nevertheless, the diction is clear and unaffected overall. In common with many Bishop poems, there is a reluctance to make too much metaphor of the situation or deploy gratuitous adjectives; if anything, it is even more necessary to avoid such literariness in this poem, for to do otherwise would be to impose an adult tone on the consciousness of a child, thus compromising the accuracy of Bishop's account.

The poem's initial resistance to figurative language is also of thematic, as well as tonal necessity. A metaphor transfers the properties of one object onto another; in the original Greek, it is literally an act of 'carrying'. In the first instance, Bishop's poem narrates the feelings of a young girl who desires to be separate from the world around her, and endeavours to maintain this distinctiveness. This is reflected in the terseness of the language, with short sentences that are often clauses in their own right: 'It was winter. It got dark / early', she writes, spurning conjunctions. Her ordered perception of her relation to the world is only threatened once she begins to read the *National Geographic* magazine. Within it, she immediately finds a volcano, 'spilling over / in rivulets of fire', as if the lava were erupting from the page. Attempting to contain it within the magazine, she tries to describe the rest of the contents impassively. There are 'babies with pointed heads / wound round and round with string; / black, naked women with necks / wound round and round with wire'. When she does choose a figurative expression, it is a simile, and a very inhuman, impassive one at that: their necks are 'like the necks of light bulbs', perhaps a subconscious nod to the glare of the surgery lamps. The women appear as anthropological specimens on the page, and she is complicit in their objectification.

When Bishop realises this, it is a jolt. On one level, a simple description of the material features of a periodical follows, 'the yellow margins, the date'; but suddenly, she is aware that she is reading these people, and that this is an act of consumption, even cannibalism, which has been hinted at in her description of one of the magazine images, 'a dead man slung on a pole', captioned 'Long Pig'. Reminding herself that *National Geographic* actually has margins, and that she is reading an outdated issue is a way of attempting to reassert her separateness from what lies inside. However, inside and outside are liable to merge perilously, as the beginning of the next section immediately makes clear with 'an *oh!* of pain' from Aunt Consuelo, wincing 'inside' the dentist's room. For Bishop, it is as if the cry emerges from her own larynx: 'What took me / completely by surprise / was that it was *me*: / my voice, in my mouth' (p. 150). And then:

> I – we – were falling, falling,
> our eyes glued to the cover
> of the *National Geographic*,
> February, 1918.

The push and pull of a split self is represented visually in these lines, the dashes between 'I' and 'we' playing out a tug of war on the page. The repetition of 'falling', however, confirms that the space the dashes create around the pronouns cannot hold. It appears that Bishop is forced into an identification with her aunt, but this 'we' really signals a fracturing of her own self. The shift from the first person singular to the plural is one of Bishop's characteristic corrections of vision, but here it is a double vision, as she visualises herself forking into two. In other words, it is not a vision but a division: a division chiefly between physical and metaphysical ways of knowing the 'self'.

Up to this point in the poem, the implication is that as a six year old, Bishop did not see herself as others might, namely as a white girl, with all the attendant assumptions about such an identity. 'In the Waiting Room' pivots on the realisation that subjectivity is as much constructed by society as self-conferred, and that it is multiple rather than holistic. Consequently, the young Bishop must restate to herself that she will be seven 'in three days' 'to stop / the sensation of falling off / the round, turning world / into cold, blue-black space'. Neutral facts are preferable to dangerous feelings, which threaten the solidity of the physical body on which selfhood and subjectivity are based. Nevertheless, facts too are compromised by this sudden threat, as we see in the lines:

> But I felt: you are an *I*,
> you are an *Elizabeth*,
> you are one of *them*.
> *Why* should you be one, too?

To talk to oneself is to make a 'you' of 'I'. In the theories of the Marxist philosopher Louis Althusser (1918–90), this is an act of 'interpellation', in which the subject is formed only when it is addressed thus; hence, this is the moment that Elizabeth becomes Elizabeth, and recognises that she is implicated in the ideologies of identity that underpin the judgements people make of their peers.[24] She does this by questioning herself, but this makes her aware that she is 'one of them'; that is, she is an addresser as well as an addressee.

It also becomes clear to her that she will grow up to be a woman, for this is a sexual awakening of sorts too. She ponders whether the 'awful hanging breasts' of the tribeswomen in the magazine 'held us together / or made us all just one'. The 'us' here is an acknowledgement of sisterhood, though it also registers doubt over the security and validity of gendered identification. Bishop writes, 'How – I didn't know any / word for it – how "unlikely"... / How had I come to be here, / like them' (p. 151). Although she recounts the elusiveness of *le mot juste*,* it is in fact accentuated within the poetic line, preceded by dashes that point to it visually, and enclosed within inverted commas. The whole poem climaxes in the discovery of this word, which carries two related senses. It is 'unlikely' that she would arrive 'here', in that it is not her destiny to find commonality with her fellow women, nor is it fated that she should find it in the waiting room; and this is because she is 'unlike' them, ultimately an individual, not an archetype.

On realising this, it seems Bishop is about to be overcome by her material surroundings; the waiting room is 'bright / and too hot', and it is 'sliding / beneath a big black wave, / another, and another'. The natural disasters of the *National Geographic* re-enact themselves in the waiting room; what were discrete images threaten to transgress the boundaries of the magazine page. However, the final stanza restores some sense of equilibrium, as a calmer voice intervenes:

* *Le mot juste* is a French term for the precise, correct word.

Then I was back in it.
The War was on. Outside,
in Worcester, Massachusetts,
were night and slush and cold,
and it was still the fifth
of February, 1918.

There is an abrupt shift from Bishop's inner world to the bare facts of what surrounds her, as if to correct the lens from interior to exterior. It seems, perhaps, that she has divulged too much, and must regain her poise; the world must once more spin perfectly on its axis, and not give in to the 'falling' and 'sliding' of the preceding stanzas. She reminds us that outside the waiting room life proceeds as normal, indifferent to the turmoil within. These final lines mark her passage from reader to writer, from the pages of *National Geographic* to a re-established, authoritative narrative voice, and in this sense, the waiting room is a transitional stage between one persona and another. The link between the world's perpetual geomorphologic forming and reforming and the mutations of identity and selfhood remains. Life is full of these waiting rooms, passages between one state and the next; they are the common spaces in which one's place in the world is always under scrutiny. 'In the Waiting Room', then, constitutes the Bishop oeuvre in miniature, a poem driven by constant self-revision, and, at the same time, an awareness that all selfhood is a state of perpetual becoming.

Notes

1   Ezra Pound, 'A Pact', *Personae: Collected Shorter Poems of Ezra Pound* (London: Faber & Faber, 1952), p. 98.
2   Elizabeth Bishop, 'Efforts of Affection: A Memoir of Marianne Moore' (*c.* 1969), *Poems, Prose, and Letters* (New York: Library of America, 2008), pp. 471–99 (489).

3   Marianne Moore, *The Poems of Marianne Moore*, ed. Grace Schulman (London: Faber & Faber, 2003), p. 135.

4   See Charles Olson, 'Projective Verse' (1950), *Selected Writings of Charles Olson*, ed. Robert Creeley (New York: New Directions, 1966), pp. 15–26.

5   William Wordsworth, 'Preface' to *Lyrical Ballads, with Pastoral and Other Poems* (1802) (Oxford: OUP, 2000), pp. 595–615 (598).

6   *Allen Ginsberg, Collected Poems, 1947–1997* (London: Penguin, 2009), pp. 134–41 (134).

7   Schulman, Introduction to *The Poems of Marianne Moore*, pp. xix–xxx (xxvi).

8   A good checklist of all the quoted passages in 'Marriage' can be found in Darlene Williams Erickson, *Illusion is More Precise than Precision: The Poetry of Marianne Moore* (Tuscaloosa: University of Alabama Press, 1992).

9   Marianne Moore, 'Foreword', *A Marianne Moore Reader* (New York: The Viking Press, 1961), pp. xiii–xviii (xv).

10 See Moore, 'An Interview with Donald Hall', *A Marianne Moore Reader*, pp. 253–73.

11 T. S. Eliot, 'Burnt Norton' (1935), *Collected Poems 1909–1962* (London: Faber & Faber, 1974), pp. 189–95 (191).

12 Bishop, 'As We Like It: Miss Moore and the Delight of Imitation', *Poems, Prose, and Letters*, pp. 680–6 (680).

13 Bishop, *Poems, Prose, and Letters*, pp. 63–4.

14 Reprinted in Lloyd Schwartz and Sybil P. Estess, ed., *Elizabeth Bishop and Her Art* (Ann Arbor: University of Michigan Press, 1983), pp. 186–8 (186).

15 Anne Stevenson, *Five Looks at Elizabeth Bishop* (London: Bellew, 1998).

16 Seamus Heaney, 'Counting to a Hundred: On Elizabeth Bishop', *The Redress of Poetry: Oxford Lectures* (London: Faber & Faber, 1995), pp. 164–85 (172).

17 Moore, review of *North and South*, reprinted in Elizabeth Dodd, *The Veiled Mirror and the Woman Poet: H.D., Louise Bogan, Elizabeth Bishop and Louise Glück* (Columbia: University of Missouri Press, 1992), p. 102.

18 This is how he is described by Christopher Beach: see Beach, *The Cambridge Introduction to Twentieth-Century American Poetry* (Cambridge: Cambridge University Press, 2003), p. 144.

19 James Merrill, 'An Interview with Donald Sheehan', *Collected Prose*, ed. J. D. McClatchy and Stephen Yenser (New York: Knopf, 2004), pp. 49–61 (50).

20 John Simon, 'Robed in Images: The Memoirs of James Merrill', *Dreamers of Dreams: Essays on Poets and Poetry* (Chicago: Ivan R. Dee, 2001), pp. 22–31 (24).

21   James Merrill, *Collected Poems*, ed. J. D. McClatchy and Stephen Yenser (New York: Knopf, 2001), p. 16.
22   Merrill, *Collected Prose*, pp. 3–8 (5).
23   Merrill, 'An Interview with Helen Vendler', *Collected Prose*, pp. 85–9 (86).
24   See Louis Althusser, 'Ideology and Ideological State Apparatuses: Notes Toward an Investigation', in *Lenin and Philosophy, and Other Essays*, trans. Ben Brewster (London: New Left Books, 1971), pp. 121–73.

Fiction of the American South: Faulkner, McCullers and O'Connor

It is virtually impossible to understand the literature of the South, and what distinguishes it from the literature of other American regions and cultures, without examining the impact of one event – the American Civil War. The states of the antebellum South were highly agrarian, composed of the properties of landowning 'yeomen' (typically subsistence farmers) and the more prosperous owners of plantations, who produced cash crops such as cotton and tobacco.* The plantations usually employed slaves, but by 1860, the Republican government of Abraham Lincoln moved towards banning the further expansion of slavery. The Civil War that ensued pitted the eleven 'Confederacy' states of the South, who opposed the anti-slavery policies of the government, against the twenty 'Union' states of the North and Midwest. The Union won, while the Confederacy collapsed; this outcome led to the abolition of slavery across the USA, enshrined in the Thirteenth Amendment to the Constitution in 1865.

Following the Civil War, there was a period of 'reconstruction'; by the early twentieth century, the culture and the landscape of the Southern states was beginning to change. As the USA forged ahead with industrial innovations and mass urbanisation, the South, though perceived as resistant and increasingly nostalgic for the pre-industrial,

---

* Antebellum literally means 'before the war' and is a term often used by historians to denote the period prior to the American Civil War.

antebellum era, also had to confront environmental transformation and demographic shifts. Flannery O'Connor wrote in 1957 that literary editors and critics were mistaken in thinking that the 'anguish' of the Southern writer could be explained by their 'isolation' from the rest of the country; rather, 'the anguish that most of us have observed for some time now has been caused not by the fact that the South is alienated from the rest of the country, but by the fact that it is not alienated enough, that every day we are getting more and more like the rest of the country'.[1] The literary critic and historian Richard Gray has noted how such changes were more 'accelerated and traumatic' than in other American regions, provoking artistic and literary responses that were 'without parallel', whose Southern setting was 'at once typical and special'.[2]

There had been notable Southern writers before the 1920s, such as Mark Twain (1835–1910) and Kate Chopin (1850–1904), but the period after the First World War initiated what came to be seen as a 'Southern Renaissance'. Much of the literature of this period tried to make sense of the fallout of the Civil War and the direction that the South had taken since the collapse of the Confederacy. 'Ode to the Confederate Dead' (1928) by the Kentucky poet and essayist Allen Tate (1899–1979) depicts a decimated Southern landscape. Its recurring references to the wind and 'the leaves flying', and the almost biblical register, call to mind T. S. Eliot's landmark 1922 poem, *The Waste Land*; but the 'mummies' that lie in waiting under the ravaged earth and the 'decomposition' of the land are peculiarly Southern, not only because of the direct references to the Civil War but also because they are touched with an aching sense of nostalgia.[3] This nostalgia is one of the characteristics most readily associated with twentieth-century writing of the South. It is recognisable in the 'Belle Reve' ('beautiful dream') of Blanche Dubois' imaginings in Tennessee Williams's *A Streetcar Named Desire* (1947), an illusory land of 'Southern belles', gentlemen callers and romance that never was,* and in the hugely popular novel *Gone with the Wind* (1936) by Margaret Mitchell (1900–49), which

* See Part Three: 'The American Stage' for a detailed discussion of *A Streetcar Named Desire*.

plays on the sentimental attachment of many Southerners to the pre-war plantation way of life – a way of life that, as the title suggests, has long since been swept away, never to be recovered.

The literature of the so-called 'Southern Renaissance' from the 1920s through to the Second World War and beyond often has loss at its core. However, many writers were keen to stress that the South of the popular imagination was mythical. They suggested that far from being organised around a culture of orderly hierarchies, manners and social codes, the Southern way of life, both before and after the Civil War, had always carried an undercurrent of violence, ugliness, and even psychosis. Through the twentieth century, the 'Southern Gothic' has become the most one of the most recognisable subgenres of American literature; its elements can be found in the works of many great Southern writers, including William Faulkner, Flannery O'Connor, Katherine Anne Porter and Eudora Welty. Southern Gothic literature is often profoundly concerned with the nature of good and evil, and other universal moral dilemmas, but these issues are mapped onto a highly distinctive physical and cultural geography. In this way, Southern Gothic literature might also be considered 'at once typical and special', as Richard Gray contends. The three writers examined in this chapter are all fascinated by the dualities of the real and imagined South. They write of the allure of the agrarian myth by using tropes of lost innocence, often depicting the South as a kind of fallen Eden, but they also suggest that the region is and has always been characterised by the equally biblical potential for theatrical drama and hellfire.

Inventing the South: William Faulkner

At the end of one of William Faulkner's (1897–1962) most complex and difficult novels, *Absalom, Absalom!* (1936), Shreve suspects his Harvard roommate Quentin Compson of despising the land from which he came – the American South. Compson's dramatic rejoinder closes the novel: '*I don't. I don't! I don't hate it! I don't hate it!*'[4] The attentive reader might think that Quentin protests too much; his attitude towards the land of his youth is ambivalent and highly conflicted. Much the same could be said of his creator, the majority of whose novels are set in the Southern state of Mississippi. Faulkner was born, brought-up and educated in the state, and seldom left the South; if he strayed from it, he was never long in returning. His fiction is perhaps the benchmark by which all other Southern novels are judged. Nevertheless, his works do not occupy a realistic space. Faulkner's depictions of the South are not interested in verisimilitude or documentary; rather, they often use highly experimental narrative techniques to suggest that the very category of the 'South' might be nebulous or even imaginary. In Faulkner's greatest novels and short stories, the South is nothing more or less than the stories people tell about it. It is constructed through narrative, and self-consciously so, as characters constantly try to be heard over others amid a clamour of voices vying for attention and supremacy. The fictiveness of Faulkner's South is also inherent in his invention of Yoknapatawpha County, the backdrop to his most famous novels. Yoknapatawpha is representative, but also imaginary; in time, it comes to represent the very imaginariness of the South itself.

Absalom, Absalom! might be considered the culmination of Faulkner's experimental output; with the exception of *Go Down, Moses* (1942), few of his post-1936 novels challenge formal norms in quite the same way as *Absalom* and its predecessors, *The Sound and the Fury* (1929) and *As I Lay Dying* (1930, discussed in the Extended Commentary below). *The Sound and the Fury* is often considered a modernist novel; its avant-garde approach to the narrative voice, in which all four sections are devoted to the interior monologue of a particular character, often sparsely punctuated and heavy with idiolect, are reminiscent of other great 1920s novels such as James Joyce's *Ulysses* or Marcel Proust's *Remembrance of Things Past*. However, modernism in the United States was disparate and localised, particularly as so many American writers of the time relocated to Europe in the 1920s and 1930s.[*] Faulkner claimed to be generally impervious to these cultural developments, going as far as to suggest rather insouciantly that he had never read *Ulysses*, though he certainly owned a copy; nevertheless, there is a case to be made for him at the height of his powers as an American novelist

---

[*] See Part Two: 'A Cultural Overview' for further details of this migration.

sui generis.[*] It was with the publication of *The Sound and the Fury* in 1929, so markedly different from its predecessors, the relatively realist novels *Soldiers' Pay* (1926) and *Flags in the Dust* (1927), that this case was almost made for him overnight.

The Sound and the Fury not only sets itself the stylistic challenge of the stream-of-consciousness, but does so three times over. It is divided into four sections, three of which chart the inner psychologies of the Compson brothers, Benjy, Quentin and Jason; the voice of the fourth is unspecified, though it tracks the movements of the family's black domestic servant, Dilsey. In their sections, the Compson brothers all attempt to work through their relationships with their sister, Caddy; indeed, Faulkner himself confessed that the novel grew from a single image of her 'muddy drawers' as she climbs the tree in the Compsons' garden, an episode recounted impressionistically by Benjy, whose repeated claim that Caddy smells 'like trees' furnishes the novel with one of its most memorable leitmotifs. Benjy's section of the novel is perhaps the most notorious, a disorientating study of the mind of a thirty-three-year-old man-child whose development has been arrested. He is the 'idiot' implied in the title, which alludes to Macbeth's Act Five soliloquy on the futility of life;[†] and despite Faulkner's use of italics to distinguish Benjy's memories from the action of the present, the section is mostly marked by fluid reportage of the dialogues that go on around him, with no clear descriptive demarcation of time or place. Nevertheless, in contrast to European 'modernist' novels, Faulkner's writing here is minimalist, rather than maximalist. Benjy's vocabulary is limited by his brain condition; the novel therefore begins tentatively, and on reduced resources. The opening of the novel also depends on the mistaking of one word for another – between the 'caddie' called for

---

[*] Allen Tate goes as far as to say that this is a Faulkner 'legend', that 'he did appear, like the sons of Cadmus, full grown, out of the unlettered soil of his native state, Mississippi'. See Tate, 'A Southern Mode of the Imagination', *Essays of Four Decades* (London: Oxford University Press, 1970), pp. 577–92 (577).

[†] 'Life's but a walking shadow, a poor player / That struts and frets his hour upon the stage, / And then is heard no more. It is a tale / Told by an idiot, full of sound and fury, / Signifying nothing'. William Shakespeare, *Macbeth*, V.v.23–7, *The Complete Works*, ed. Stanley Wells and Gary Taylor (Oxford: Oxford University Press, 1999), pp. 975–99 (998).

by the golfers who play their game round the commercially exploited Compson estate, and 'Caddy' Compson herself, invoked by the characters in the novel but denied by Faulkner any opportunity for her own unmediated voice to be heard.

These aspects of the novel convey the slipperiness of language, but also return the reader to its primal roots, in noises and overheard sounds. The characters come into their voices gradually through Benjy's perception, as if to mimic how consciousness itself begins; sound, after all, is the first sense to develop in the womb. The novel never entirely gives up this nebulous quality, even in the more matter-of-fact section that charts the most materialistic and conniving Compson, Jason. If anything, Benjy sets the tone. The second section, in the voice of the university-educated and apparently eloquent Quentin, seems to be constantly on the brink of disintegration, until eventually it descends into an unpunctuated confusion of barely processed thoughts. The passage seems to suggest that inarticulacy need not be restricted to those with diagnosable mental pathologies. Indeed, as the title of the novel indicates, chaos and noise ultimately win out. The novel closes on a sequence in which the black servant Luster rides on horseback with a querulous Benjy back to the Compson house. As they pass a monument to a Confederate soldier, Luster hits the horse, Queenie, to make her go faster. Faulkner describes Benjy's subsequent bellowing thus: 'it was horror, shock; agony eyeless, tongueless; just sound'.[5] Equilibrium is barely restored in a cryptic and most probably ironic final paragraph:

> Ben's voice roared and roared. Queenie moved again, her feet began to clop-clop steadily again, and at once Ben hushed. Luster looked quickly back over his shoulder, then he drove on. The broken flower drooped over Ben's fist and his eyes were empty and blue and serene again as cornice and facade flowed smoothly once more from left to right; post and tree, window and doorway, each in its ordered place. (p. 278)

Benjy is comforted by the apparent 'order', but the usually solid cornices and facades are still 'flow[ing]'; this seems very much like a temporary settlement. Faulkner's Mississippi barely labours under the illusion of having been 'reconstructed'; even an incognisant man-child wails on passing the statue of a fallen Confederate hero.

Haunted by History

While *The Sound and the Fury* makes a virtue of its discordance, *Absalom, Absalom!* sees Faulkner attempting to organise a historical narrative ranging over many decades into orderly sequence. The novel begins with an almost precise statement of the time, 'a little after two o'clock' (p. 5); however, it quickly becomes apparent to the reader that just as in *The Sound and the Fury*, when Quentin is given a pocket-watch by his father to remind him 'not that [he] may remember time, but that [he] might forget it now and then' (p. 65), so does time move tortuously and illogically in *Absalom, Absalom!*. The end of the novel is even followed by Faulkner's own chronology, laying out the main events in its back-story. It helps the reader, though it also necessarily presumes they re-read. This is entirely apt for a novel comprising retellings of the same tale, a novel about how stories which exist in multiple versions quickly pass into myth, thereby facilitating a further chain of omissions, paraphrases and elaborations.

The tale in question is that of Thomas Sutpen, a plantation owner with grandiose plans for his land; these plans are described as 'Sutpen's Design' by the various narrators of the novel, who include Quentin Compson and his father, and Rosa Coldfield, the younger sister of Sutpen's wife, who was once promised to Sutpen himself. Sutpen's story is emblematic of the history of the South, and it is told without idealism or romance. As recounted, he acquires his acreage through the force of his personality, bullies his way through family crises, and implements his 'design' for the sole purpose of gaining material wealth and inflated standing within his corner of Mississippi. He is called into military action during the Civil War, and on returning finds his estate torn up by Northerners, fallen into ruin; he nevertheless insists on regaining what has been lost, by replanting and re-employing. These circumstances would be easy to romanticise, but Faulkner's narrators are both fascinated and repelled by Sutpen, who appears to embody the extremities of Southern plantation culture.

These extremities only increase his mythical qualities, to the extent that Quentin's friend Shreve, a bookish Northerner, insists on calling Sutpen a 'demon' with almost comical ferocity. This is the kind of response that constructs a 'Southern Gothic' archetype out of Sutpen. The frequently melodramatic plotlines of revenge, barely averted incest and disownment also contribute to the novel's 'Gothic' quality, and even one of the narrators, Rosa, is a Miss Havisham-like figure draped in black, passing the 'forty-three summers' since breaking her engagement with Sutpen in 'a dim hot airless room with the blinds all closed' (p. 5).* For the non-Southerner, Shreve, it is almost impossible to take seriously: 'Jesus, the South is fine, isn't it', he says, 'It's better than the theatre, isn't it. It's better than Ben Hur, isn't it' (p. 179). This in itself is a parody of the incredulous Northerner, whose views on Southern literature were summarised by Flannery O'Connor thus:

> When we look at a good deal of serious modern fiction, and particularly Southern fiction, we find this quality about it that is generally described, in a pejorative sense, as grotesque. Of course, I have found that anything that comes out of the South is going to be called grotesque by the Northern reader, unless it is grotesque, in which case it is going to be called realistic.[6]

Nevertheless, the extremity of some of Faulkner's narrative is also a comment on the self-mythologising tendency of many Southerners, of which Sutpen's case is metonymic. The breathless quality of some of the writing itself, layered as it is with coinages and compounds, 'distilled and hyperdistilled' (p. 5), marks a new idiom that endeavours to convey not only the sometimes melodramatic history of the South but also the collapse of its apparently binary oppositions. Words merge into each other or pile up in strange formations; as Rosa says at one point, 'I became all polymath love's androgynous advocate' (p. 121),

---

* Morbid elderly women are a common feature of Faulkner's South. As Rosa says, 'I waited not for light but for that doom which we call female victory which is: endure and then endure, without rhyme or reason or hope of reward' (p. 119). See also the short story, 'A Rose for Emily', *The Penguin Collected Stories of William Faulkner* (Harmondsworth: Penguin, 1985), pp. 119–30.

indicating the possibility of multiple types of knowledge coexisting in minds unhindered by the usual gendered divisions. Antonyms go unheeded or ignored in *Absalom, Absalom!*, nowhere more than in race relations. Miscegenation abounds: it emerges that Sutpen has an illegitimate child, Charles Bon, from an affair with a mixed-race Caribbean woman, and Bon himself is described in androgynous terms. These examples would appear to deconstruct the oppositions between black and white, and male and female, on which the antebellum, and indeed the post-war South depended; yet in many ways, Faulkner is arguing that this is the typical history of the region, convoluted and riddled with contradiction. The most friable of all these either/or distinctions is that between past and present. In a South so fascinated by its own history, there is no clear boundary between now and then. Any linearity in Faulkner's writing, would thus in some senses compromise its Southernness; instead, the past is always happening, destined to be repeated, to spark 'repercussions', a word which in Faulkner's frequent use comes to act out the very process it describes. The effect is to make all the characters half-haunted; Quentin's body is

> an empty hall echoing with sonorous defeated names; he was not a being, an entity, he was a commonwealth. He was a barracks filled with stubborn back-looking ghosts still recovering, even forty-three years afterwards, from the fever which had cured the disease. (p. 9)

The Shadow of Race: Faulkner and McCullers

Such ghostliness, prevalent in much twentieth-century Southern literature, denotes a kind of fall; the Southern man is unwhole, forever tracked by loss. This is not just confined to the Southern imagination. It speaks of America more generally too, the fall from the innocence of the New World. After the Civil War, the blank slate had been written on with blood. Though he does not mention the slaughter of Native Americans directly, Faulkner nevertheless suggests that America's original innocence was bought with similar belligerence.

Sutpen originally hails from Virginia, but has always been corrupted by hubris; the virgin earth contained the seeds of its own destruction from the very beginning. Similar views of the fate of the land can be found beyond the literature of the South, in the work of Faulkner's contemporaries, in particular John Steinbeck.

However, any consideration of the divisions within the Southern man, or his fall from innocence, must take full account of the complex racial issues that ensued from antebellum slavery, and the climate of white paranoia that followed the Civil War, when black men and women were technically freed only to find themselves trapped into segregation and the constant threat of the lynch-mob. Much of Faulkner's work makes familiar archetypes of the black man in particular; for example, the fugitive, animalistic slave Tomey's Turl in *Go Down, Moses* (1942), and the patient, submissive Loosh in *The Unvanquished*. Nevertheless, Faulkner acknowledges in 'The Bear', one of the constituent stories in *Go Down, Moses*, that the fates of black and white alike are inextricable, for 'the whole land, the whole South, is cursed, and all of us who derive from it, whom it ever suckled, white and black both, lie under the curse'.[7] Undoing this curse depends on mutual understanding, and a turn away from the essentialism that underlies many of the South's racist assumptions. Faulkner's work concludes that 'the best way to take all people, black or white, is to take them for what they think they are, then leave them alone'; his view is that 'a nigger is not a person so much as a form of behaviour' (p. 74). In *The Unvanquished* (1938), the young white child Bayard grows up with the young black child Ringo; before long, Bayard decides that his friend is no longer a 'nigger' because their closeness makes the term redundant.[8] Meanwhile, the novel *Light in August* (1932) is mostly given over to the problems caused by mixed-race identity in small-town Yoknapatawpha. The troubled protagonist, Joe Christmas, is neither black nor white; he appears white, but he also has African blood. He fits into no easily definable geographical or cultural category, and is destined to be marginalised. It would seem the South of his time can only deal with clear binaries.

The work of Carson McCullers (1917–67) also explores the divided identities of Southerners who wish to achieve wholeness. Out of all her works, her last novel, *Clock Without Hands* (1961), deals with race issues most explicitly and profoundly. One of the main relationships at the heart of the novel is between the respected county judge and former congressman, Clane, and his grandson Jester; Jester, whose father, Clane's son, committed suicide, and whose mother died in childbirth, has grown up with the judge. In the novel, Jester is a young adult developing his own perspective on the world. As he explains to Judge Clane at lunch one afternoon, the painting on the wall gives him a rather different impression than at first glance. Where Clane sees 'an orchard and clouds and a Nigra shack', Jester picks out a 'pink mule'.[9] It is a 'symbol', according to Jester, for 'all my life I've seen things like you and the family wanted me to see them. And now this summer I don't see things as I used to' (p. 31). Jester begins to feel an antipathy towards his grandfather, who firmly believes in racial segregation. Clane is dismayed by the prospect of a black boy sitting in the same classroom as a white girl, and entertains fantasies of turning back the clock to the pre-war period. He has a grand plan if he is re-elected to congress; namely, to pass a bill to redeem all Confederate monies that were in circulation from the time of the Civil War. He claims it will be a huge cash injection, 'a New Deal for the economy of the South' to rival Franklin D. Roosevelt's 1930s programme of Depression relief. McCullers satirises this nostalgia masquerading as optimism; Clane soon enough references the *ne plus ultra* of Southern melodramas:

> What happened after the War Between the States? Not only did the Federal Government of the United States free the slaves which were the sine qua non of our cotton economy, so that the very resources of the nation were gone with the wind. A truer story was never written than *Gone With the Wind*. Remember how we cried at that picture show? (p. 36)

He also confesses that he wishes he had written the book. Jester, on the other hand, is keen to cross the colour line, and befriends Sherman, a young black man with whom he discusses politics and race, as well as the more typical topics of juvenile discussion – alcohol and sex. Sherman has an ambivalent attitude to his own racial inheritance. He hates spirituals, because they are a type of 'nigger music' (p. 74); he also regularly engages in bouts of cultural one-upmanship with Jester, trumping his facts and declaring a wish to play Othello on stage or sing Tristan at the Metropolitan Opera House. The relationship between Sherman and Jester is thus mutually necessary; it allows both parties to escape the roles defined for them by previous generations.

However, Sherman is subsequently employed by Clane as a personal assistant, and must confront still-ingrained prejudices. Acting as amanuensis for Clane's drafted currency plans, Sherman comes to realise that his employer still believes in slavery. For Sherman, this is truly shocking, though in the mid-twentieth century, many black people in the South had rights in name only. Sherman knows that 'The Fifteenth Amendment of the American Constitution had guaranteed the right to vote to the Negro race, yet no Negro Sherman had known or heard tell of had ever voted' (p. 143). Furthermore, he has seen the lynching of black men for little more than whistling at white girls, the type of incident readers might be familiar with from *To Kill a Mockingbird* (1960), a novel by the Alabaman writer Harper Lee (1926–), published the year before *Clock Without Hands*. Sherman refuses to write from Clane's dictation, announcing, 'I won't be a party to turning the clock back almost a century' (p. 150). He leaves and heads back to his beautifully furnished rooms, only to be killed in a racially motivated bombing. Jester warns him of the danger prior to his death, asking why he doesn't 'go North where people don't mind so much' (p. 197); in the early 1950s and 1960s, America is just as divided as it was during the Civil War, only in the arguably worse position of systematically ignoring and wilfully contravening its own constitution in the desire to turn back the 'clock without hands'.

An American Malady

Despite spending most of her years in New York, all of Carson McCullers's major works are set in the South; unlike Faulkner, who seldom left Mississippi, she was a novelist in exile, and, perhaps understandably, more overtly nostalgic and romantic in her recollections. *Clock Without Hands* is her most overtly political novel; her others deal primarily with personal grief and melancholy, rather than collective community trauma (though even *Clock Without Hands* features the private deterioration of J. T. Malone into leukaemia as its other major plotline). In McCullers's works, the South is not generally a place for communality or conviviality. The town in her novella, *The Ballad of the Sad Café* (1951), is much more typical: 'lonesome, sad, and like a place that is far off and estranged from all other places in the world'.[10] This present-day scene is offset by the recounted history of Miss Amelia. Although she is now a 'sexless and white' face with a 'secret gaze of grief' staring out of an upstairs room, she was once the proprietor of a popular cafe that spread warmth and fostered a sense of well-being in the town; 'there, for a few hours at least, the deep bitter knowing that you are not worth much in this world could be laid low' (p. 66), and the cafe made those on the margins of respectability – 'bachelors, unfortunate people, and consumptives' – feel included and as central to the life of the town as any of its other inhabitants. The cafe was also the backdrop for her love affair with a hunchbacked cousin, Lymon; but the return of her ex-husband Marvin Macy, referred to as the 'loom-fixer I was married to', caused trouble between them, and eventually they both fought her in the cafe in front of an audience of gossipy customers, before wreaking cosmetic damage to the premises and absconding into the night together. Most of the novella is taken up with this tale, which in its brevity and wistful mood becomes a kind of parable, a warning against fleeting love. Once more, at the end, 'the soul rots with boredom' (p. 84). There is a sense that the episode in the cafe is the town's only folklore, an incident whose very exceptionality sums up the tedium and loneliness of this unnamed, and thus emblematic, Southern outpost.

'Loneliness' is undoubtedly McCullers's watchword. In an article for *This Week* in 1949, she called it the 'American malady', an inevitable consequence of the tendency 'to seek out things as individuals, alone'.[11] That it is a 'malady' rather than a 'sickness' or 'illness' is telling; the more poetic word indicates to the reader that, for McCullers, this suffering is not necessarily aesthetically or artistically negative. Indeed, even the most cursory reading of any of her three other novels, *The*

Heart is a Lonely Hunter (1940), *Reflections in a Golden Eye* (1941) and *The Member of the Wedding* (1946), reveals that she is uniquely fascinated by it. *The Heart is a Lonely Hunter*, perhaps McCullers's most popular novel, tells of John Singer, a deaf mute, who despite the potential to be an outcast, becomes a focal point for the loneliness and disillusionment of the others around him in a small Georgian town. Jake Blount, a troubled drunkard, finds solace in Singer, whose 'eyes made a person think that he heard things nobody else had ever heard, that he knew things no one had ever guessed before'.[12] Mick Kelly, a young girl whose parents run the boarding house in which Singer lodges, also looks to him for advice, and some means of escape from the cacophony of noise in the house. She thinks that there is something about him, like the 'Motsart [sic.]' that she hopes to play on the piano; she wishes there were 'some place to hum it out loud' (p. 51). This underlines the irony of Singer's name; though he cannot emit a sound himself, his silence allows others to find their voice.

A third character, Dr Copeland, is a black physician struggling determinedly to continue his professional life with dignity in a culture that defaults to suspicion or outward racism. Later in the novel, Copeland's family get into trouble. His son is convicted of manslaughter on a dubious charge, and his feet are cut off after turning gangrenous in prison; but the mysterious serenity of Singer establishes a counterpoint to the bigotry, as Copeland recalls the white man lighting his cigarette for him, their black and white faces respectively lit up for a moment in the flame. These individual points of connection are often the most that can be hoped for in the South of McCullers's fiction, for just as in *The Ballad of the Sad Cafe*, the nascent sense of community is all too brief. Singer shoots himself after discovering that his friend Antonapoulos, another deaf-mute, is dead. Though Singer has gathered new acquaintances, there is no insurance against the ultimate loneliness, for losing Antonapoulos is like losing a central part of his own self; in a sense, Antonapoulos is to Singer what Singer is to Mick, Jake and Dr Copeland. Singer's demise leads to other departures. Jake decides to restart his life somewhere else, while Dr Copeland, now too sick to manage in his own home, is sent to Grandpapa's farm. Copeland's rueful tone towards the end of the novel, when he considers the failure of his mission to empower his fellow black citizens, connects the loss of Singer more sweepingly to the incompleteness of the South, destined never to achieve equality or enlightenment. His idealism, based around an understanding of the ethical philosopher Baruch Spinoza and the political theorist Karl Marx, leads him to think this may not be 'the end', that 'the calling voices of all those who had fought', the 'grief-bound voices of his people' and of the 'mute Singer, who was a righteous white man of understanding', might be heard (pp. 287–8). However, he realises that opportunities for connection and wholeness were momentary and anomalous. Equally, Biff, the cafe owner whose premises provides the setting for many of Singer's encounters, figures this lost chance as symptomatic of the Southern problem in general. On the final page of the novel, he has an epiphany, followed immediately by a sense of foreboding:

> Then suddenly he felt a quickening in him. His heart turned and he leaned his back against the counter for support. For in a swift radiance of illumination he saw a glimpse of human struggle and of valour. Of the endless fluid passage of humanity through endless time. And of those who labour and of those who – one word – love. His soul expanded. But for a moment only. For in him he felt a warning, a shaft of terror. Between the two worlds he was suspended. He saw that he was looking at his own face in the counter glass before him ... affrighted into a future of blackness, error and ruin. And he was suspended between radiance and darkness. Between bitter irony and faith. (p. 312)

When all has passed, there are no mutual understandings in the flicker of a cigarette flame; the mirror only reveals the reflection of a divided self. As in *The Ballad of the Sad Cafe*, the town has had its chance, but once that chance has lapsed, it takes on an unreal quality. Binary oppositions form once more. The townspeople will be permanently 'suspended' between 'radiance and darkness' and 'irony and faith'; a united South, and indeed a union of its lonely souls, is beyond possibility.

Irony and Faith: Flannery O'Connor

'Irony and faith' could well be a pairing that sums up the oeuvre of Flannery O'Connor (1925–64). Her take on the Southern novel was markedly different to that of either of the writers already examined in this chapter; she claimed to have not read Faulkner and to detest McCullers.[13] Much of her studied antipathy can be explained by her refusal to be categorised. As mentioned earlier, she was profoundly sceptical of the 'Southern Gothic' genre, complaining that it was used by non-Southern critics to make generalisations about 'freakish' goings-on; and in her 1960 essay 'Some Aspects of the Grotesque in Southern Fiction', she registers irritation at the so-called 'School of Southern Degeneracy', writing that 'there was a time when the average reader read a novel simply for the moral he could get out of it', whereas 'today, novels are considered to be entirely concerned with … social or economic or psychological forces'.[14] She is therefore quick to dismiss writing that conforms to outsiders' ideas of 'Southernness'; yet at the same time, she is equally interested in the singularity of much Southern literature. Its relative isolation from the artistic and publishing centres of the coasts place its fictions in a unique sphere, because they still chronicle a people. As O'Connor writes,

> The best American fiction has always been regional. The ascendancy passed roughly from New England to the Midwest to the South; it has passed and stayed longest wherever there has been a shared past, a sense of alikeness, and the possibility of reading a small history in a universal light. In these things the South still has a degree of advantage.[15]

As in Faulkner's work, this 'shared past' is the history of the antebellum plantation, the Confederacy, the Civil War and the Reconstruction. This is where the two writers' concerns overlap. O'Connor knows that the South is other to the rest of the USA because 'we have had our Fall', which has led to 'a sense of mystery which could not have developed in our first state of innocence – as it has not sufficiently developed in the rest of our country'.[16] Where Faulkner and O'Connor differ is in their religious emphasis. For Faulkner, this 'fall' is arguably a philosophical and narrative concern, whereas for O'Connor, it is examined through a Christian lens. Her Catholicism placed her at an angle to her mostly Protestant counterparts. Keeping this in mind while reading her work is not an instance of biographical fallacy, but a key strategy of interpretation, not least because she was explicit about it herself, partly in defence of those aspects of her art that seemed most typically 'Gothic'. In her essay 'The Fiction Writer and His Country', she argues that 'the writer who emphasizes spiritual values is very likely to take the darkest view of all of what he sees in this country today', for 'the sharper the light of faith, the more glaring are apt to be the distortions the writer sees in the life around him'.[17] Writing of the problem of a less-than-devout readership, O'Connor defends the extremities of some of her work by arguing that the Christian novelist's task is to communicate what he sees as 'repugnant' distortions. Many readers are likely to consider them 'natural' and thus the writer 'may well be forced to take ever more violent means to get his vision across to this hostile audience'; 'you have to make your vision apparent by shock – to the hard of hearing you shout, and for the almost-blind you draw large and startling figures' (p. 33).

O'Connor's first novel, *Wise Blood* (1952), is populated with such 'large and startling figures', and uses macabre irony in its enquiry into Tennessean religious mores. Hazel Motes, a demobilised wanderer, has always believed that 'the way to avoid Jesus was to avoid sin'.[18] Since leaving the South for his army career, any longing he has for Christianity is explained by a nostalgia for his lost sense of place; he keeps his Bible with him 'because it had come from home' (p. 15). He nevertheless has a pious quality; when mistaken for a preacher by a taxi driver, he is at great pains to correct him, announcing that he doesn't believe in anything, but the driver says 'that's the trouble with you preachers ... You've all got too good to believe in anything' (p. 20). This is the irony of Southern Christianity, a situation in which the culture of churches and ministries has become quite separated from matters of personal belief.

In a street scene of comical consumerism, in which a vendor tries to sell potato peelers to a crowd, Hazel is approached by a blind preacher who can 'smell the sin' on his breath and wants to save him. This is another irony – that the Christian uses the very tactics of persuasion that he reprehends and seeks to redress in the salesperson. A fracas between Hazel and the preacher ensues, during which the latter says, rather cryptically, 'I can see more than you ... You got eyes and see not, ears and hear not, but you'll have to see some time' (p. 36). This sequence culminates in Hazel founding his own anti-denomination. 'I don't say [Jesus] wasn't crucified, but it wasn't for you', he announces to the gathering crowd; 'Don't I have eyes in my head? Am I a blind man? Listen here ... I'm going to preach a new church – the church of truth without Jesus Christ Crucified' (p. 37). During the course of the novel, it is revealed that the blind preacher is not in fact blind – it is a gimmick and a trick. Instead, it is Hazel who becomes blind by the end of the novel, having deliberately destroyed his own sight with quicklime. After his death in a police car, his landlady, Mrs Flood, observes that 'the outline of a skull was plain under his skin and the deep burned eye sockets seemed to lead into the dark tunnel where he had disappeared' (p. 160). In this novel, sight and vision are, appropriately enough, never what they appear to be; the apparently unspiritual Hazel has turned out to be, in O'Connor's words, a 'Christian malgré lui' (a Christian 'despite himself'), martyred by a community of the venal and the self-interested.*

The Next Generation

Writing as she was in the 1950s and 1960s, much of O'Connor's work is concerned with the shifting values during the transitional period between nominal but segregated freedom and the Civil Rights Movement. Her short stories, as well as her second and final novel, *The Violent Bear It Away* (1960), often focus on differences of opinion between the generations, moments when the 'old' South, still inclined to racism and nostalgic for a time prior to African-American empowerment,

---

* 'Christian malgré lui' is how O'Connor described Hazel in her prefatory note to the second edition of *Wise Blood*.

comes face to face with the conscience of the young. 'Everything That Rises Must Converge' (1961), from the collection of the same name, is exemplary here. It opens with Julian preparing his mother for her slimming class. They must take the bus, and on the way their exchange is fractious. Julian's mother laments the diminished value of 'graciousness' in a modern world that does not reward the Southern values it once held dear. Julian's rejoinder is typical of his generation's desire for equality and resistance to social and racial hierarchies: 'knowing who you are is good for one generation only', regardless of whether, as his mother reminds him, 'your great-grandfather had a plantation and two hundred slaves'.[19] For Julian, 'culture is in the mind', but for his mother it is 'in the heart ... because of who you *are*' (p. 410); an antipathy is clearly set up here between intellect and superstition. To demonstrate his independence of the family name and his resistance to the values of the old South, Julian sits next to a young black businessman on the bus, much to his mother's chagrin. Later, a 'coloured' lady and her child position themselves beside him. His mother's prejudice does not extend to infants, and she plays peek-a-boo with the child; the child's mother is angered by this hypocrisy. The story ends with Julian's mother offering a penny to the child. The child's mother refuses violently, and Julian says 'don't think that was just an uppity Negro woman ... That was the whole coloured race which will no longer take your condescending pennies'. However, his defiance turns to anguish as his mother dies of shock; the black woman's dismissal of her sends her reeling onto the pavement, presumably exacerbating the hypertension that required the slimming classes.

This story pitches the personal against the political, the irony being that Julian's principles are seen to lead, if indirectly and somewhat grotesquely, to family grief. The accursed South has the last laugh, perhaps. This can be seen in other O'Connor short stories too. For example, 'The Enduring Chill' (1958) also revolves around the antagonism between a mother and her son. Mrs Fox is a dairy farmer, while her son Asbury is almost a caricature of the pneumonic, effete 'artist', who must return to Timberboro from New York to recover his health. Asbury's values bewilder his mother. He claims to be writing a play 'about Negroes'. Mrs Fox cannot understand his motivation, for 'why anybody would want to write a play about Negroes was beyond her'.[20] Nevertheless, she does think that his literary talents could be put to a specific Southern use, presumably without addressing 'Negroes' as free citizens: 'When you get well', she says, 'I think it would be nice if you wrote a book about down here. We need another good book like *Gone With the Wind*' (p. 370). O'Connor uses this textual example ironically on more than one occasion; in the short story 'A Good Man is Hard to Find' (1953), John Wesley asks his grandmother what happened to the old plantation, to which she replies, 'Gone With the Wind ... Ha. Ha'.[21] It is a shorthand metonym for everything that 'Southern' literature is expected to be, both by Southerners and by Northern outsiders, the 'grotesque' art of which O'Connor was so sceptical. Yet O'Connor is also laughing at the pretensions of Southern writers who disavow their heritage. Talking to Father Finn from his sickbed, Asbury asks the priest what he thinks of Joyce. The priest asks 'Joyce who?' 'James Joyce', comes Asbury's clarification, to which the priest responds, 'I haven't met him' (p. 375). This manages to parody both the stereotype of Southern insularity and the young expat Tennessean determined to show off his knowledge and cultivation. But again, the changeless South wins. Asbury turns out not to be dying, only to have an 'undulant fever' that will return sporadically throughout his life. To him this is far worse than the romantic, artistic death whose suicide note he has already drafted. By the end of the story, 'he saw that for the rest of his days, frail, racked, but enduring, he would live in the face of a putrifying terror' (p. 382). It would seem that the grip of the South seldom relents, and the younger generations are powerless to change it from within. This might be noted in the aforementioned short story, 'A Good Man is Hard to Find', one of O'Connor's most anthologised, all the children, and their grandmother, travelling from state to state, are killed at gunpoint by the Misfit. It is not the politically empowered and egalitarian next generation that will be legatees of the Southern inheritance, but the lonely, criminal or psychotic. This is the South that has extended so far into the popular imagination that even the Australian-born, British-by-adoption rock musician Nick Cave (1957–) has written of it in his novel *And the Ass Saw the Angel* (1989). The South in literature is frequently as divided and troubled as it was in the work of Faulkner, McCullers and O'Connor; they have in their different ways set the template.

Extended Commentary: Faulkner, *As I Lay Dying* (1930)

Irving Howe once described *As I Lay Dying* (1930) as 'the warmest, the kindliest, and the most affectionate' of all Faulkner's novels.[22] It is a commonly held view, though of course the novel's warmth or kindliness must be measured against works of great turmoil and trauma such as those already discussed throughout this chapter. It does contain moments of clear comedy, made possible by its central narrative device. Each of the major characters is given his or her own voice, and the novel is divided into short sections headed up with the name of the character whose first-person testimony follows. This allows for multiple dramatic ironies; and the fact that the novel tells of a pilgrimage to bury the Bundren family matriarch, Addie, with characters speaking their thoughts along the way, nods towards much earlier comical texts such as Chaucer's *Canterbury Tales*.* The novel also makes use of slapstick and bathos. The coffin is constantly imperilled by the less-than-steady hands of its carriers, even overturning at one point, and Anse, the late Addie's husband and head of the family, appears to have a more selfish investment in the journey to Jefferson than the burial of his wife – namely, that he will soon be able to get 'them teeth'; the banalities of life do after all continue beyond the loss of a loved one.

Despite such surface light-heartedness, *As I Lay Dying* shares many of the concerns of *The Sound and the Fury*, *Absalom, Absalom!* and others of Faulkner's great novels, containing key elements of his canon in miniature. As one of his more recognisably 'modernist' texts, it is profoundly concerned with communicating the life of the mind, and the frequent inarticulacy that attends any attempt to represent it. The most apparently eloquent of all the novel's voices is that of Darl,

---

* This connection was made more explicit by the British novelist Graham Swift (1949–), whose *Last Orders* (1996) is a self-confessed homage to Faulkner's 1930 novel. In *Last Orders*, a group of men travel from London to Margate to scatter the ashes of a mutual friend. Chaucer's pilgrims journeyed from London to Canterbury, which is about sixteen miles from Margate.

one of the grieving sons of Addie and the first character to 'speak' to the reader. His language is poetic and alive to the music of the world around him. In his words,

> I enter the hall, hearing the voices before I reach the door
> ... A feather dropped near the front door will rise and brush
> along the ceiling, slanting backward, until it reaches the down-
> turning current at the back door: so with voices. As you enter
> the hall, they sound as though they were speaking out of the
> air about your head.[23]

Darl is almost the authorial consciousness of the novel; this passage borders on the metatextual, as if he were commenting on the narrative mechanics of *As I Lay Dying* itself. It also points towards later Faulkner works, its spectral acoustics prefiguring the 'empty hall echoing with sonorous defeated names' experienced by Quentin in *Absalom, Absalom!*.

Darl's sometimes abstract voice contrasts sharply with that of his brother Cash, who constructs Addie's coffin, the coffin that the family must carry all the way to Jefferson to bury her as she wished. Cash's language is precise and logical. One of his sections begins with the statement, 'I made it on the bevel', before explaining this decision in thirteen numbered points (p. 66). These points are not all statements; number six is merely the word 'except', a graphic illustration of how Cash the carpenter deconstructs language into its constituent building blocks, as if prepositions were screws or nails. Faulkner represents Cash and his achievements with such visual puns throughout. In the real-time narrative of the pilgrimage, he falls prey to a fit of vomiting; one of his sections is a mere two lines, 'It wasn't on a balance. I told them that if they wanted it to tote and ride on a balance, they would have to –' (p. 131). The dash at the end of the line represents Cash's inability to finish his sentence because of physical convulsion, and it is almost an image of projectile vomit in itself. The next time the reader encounters him, in one of Darl's sections, 'he tried to say something. Dewey Dell wiped his mouth again' (p. 143). Elsewhere, the coffin itself is given its own physicality on the page. In one section Vernon Tull, a close friend of the family, testifies that Cash made the coffin 'clock-shaped like this', inserting a line-drawn depiction. It literally interrupts the text, which continues to be arranged around it; again, the joins and seams of grammar are exposed, as Tull unknowingly reveals the inherent absences behind deixis, and beyond that, the gaps within written communication for which the reader usually compensates automatically.*

Faulkner places Addie herself at the centre of this exploration of the written word's inadequacies. Addie is dead in the novel, but she does have her own section, unlike the similarly named Caddy Compson, the absent woman at the heart of *The Sound and the Fury*. This voice from beyond the grave might fulfil the 'Southern Gothic' expectations of some readers, but her testimony actually proves to be the philosophical heart of the novel. It is she who most fully explores the territories beyond language, saying that 'words are no good ... words don't ever fit even what they are trying to say at' (p. 136). Experience is greater knowledge than language; Addie 'knew that fear was invented by someone that had never had the fear; pride, who never had the pride'. Most of all, the word 'love' is 'just a shape to fill a lack'. Language points only to the absences that underlie it. There is no real or fundamental relationship between word and thing, merely a mutually agreed, nominal one; this projects the novel's philosophies almost beyond modernism, into a kind of proto-postmodern understanding of language's arbitrariness and contingency.

Addie's mistrust of words reaches its climax in a blank space, which is placed almost dead centre in her section, arranged as follows:

> The shape of my body where I used to be a virgin is in the shape of a   and I couldn't think *Anse*, couldn't remember *Anse*. (p. 137)

Virginity is a common motif in Faulkner's work. Quentin obsesses over Caddy's virginity in *The Sound and the Fury*; his father explains to him that it is a concept invented by men to dominate women, and that 'purity is a negative state', virginity being 'just words'. There are

---

* Deixis is an instance in which an utterance requires contextual information to be understood; a common example within writing would be a statement beginning 'this proves' or 'here we see...'.

similar observations in *Absalom, Absalom!* and *The Wild Palms* (1939). In Faulkner's novels, virginity is often the subject of some scepticism; it is a kind of paradox, a state only apprehensible through its loss. To obsess over virginity is to be preoccupied with such loss; moreover, it makes a fetish of innocence, which is itself a troubled concept in Faulkner's work. In *As I Lay Dying*, Addie does not directly reference the question of the 'fallen' South and the specific losses that have constituted that fall, but the blank space at the heart of her confession appears to suggest it. There is a desire, perhaps, to regain an Edenic, pre-linguistic state. Her section also concludes with a recognisably 'Southern' piece of religious superstition. Addie recalls that Cora, the novel's Christian conscience, prayed for her once because she claimed that she was 'blind to sin'. Cora's claim is that 'people to whom sin is just a matter of words, to them salvation is just words too' (p. 140). It is, perhaps, a pious warning, that redemption is impossible for those who see religion as a mere linguistic signifier without any real spiritual powers. That Addie should end her monologue with this suggests she is not so worried about her prospects of absolution; to conclude that most of life's great ideas are mere words is not to denounce those ideas, but to move beyond attempts to reconcile a feeling with its mode of expression.

For Darl, the character with the most obvious linguistic facility, language also breaks down eventually. His final section is another example of words severing themselves from the people and things they describe. By the last few pages of the novel, he no longer uses first person; instead, he speaks of 'Darl' in the third person, a Darl who appears to be laughing manically, foaming at the mouth and gibbering 'yes yes yes yes yes yes yes' (p. 202). Like Quentin in *The Sound and the Fury*, he collapses under the burden of his own apparent eloquence. But, unlike the latter stages of Quentin's section of the earlier novel, this passage of *As I Lay Dying* is grammatically straightforward; it is almost as if Darl has broken out of the format of the novel itself, to view himself as a character, an authorial construction. His example might serve as an analogy for Faulkner's art in general; at once both recognisably 'Gothic' yet formally subversive, liberated from the constraints of previous 'Southern' narratives, yet doomed to laugh morbidly into the darkness.

Notes

1   Flannery O'Connor, 'The Fiction Writer and His Country', in Sally and Robert Fitzgerald (eds), *Mystery and Manners: Occasional Prose* (London: Faber & Faber, 1984), pp. 25–35 (29).

2   Richard Gray, *The Literature of Memory: Modern Writers of the American South* (London: Edward Arnold, 1977), p. 38. See also especially the 1930 anthology of Southern writers' views on the period of industrial 'progress' in the South, *I'll Take My Stand* (Baton Rouge: Louisiana State University Press, 1989).

3   Allen Tate, 'Ode to the Confederate Dead', *Collected Poems 1919–1976* (New York: Farrar Straus Giroux, 1977), pp. 20–3.

4   William Faulkner, *Absalom, Absalom!* (1936. Harmondsworth: Penguin, 1982), p. 311.

5   William Faulkner, *The Sound and the Fury* (1929. London: Picador, 1993), p. 277.

6   O'Connor, 'Some Aspects of the Grotesque in Southern Fiction', *Mystery and Manners*, pp. 36–50 (40).

7   William Faulkner, 'The Bear', *Go Down, Moses* (Harmondsworth: Penguin, 1967), p. 212.

8   William Faulkner, *The Unvanquished* (Harmondsworth: Penguin, 1970), p. 9.

9   Carson McCullers, *Clock Without Hands* (London: Penguin, 2008), p. 31.

10 Carson McCullers, *The Ballad of the Sad Cafe* (London: Penguin, 2008), p. 7.

11 Carson McCullers, 'Loneliness...An American Malady', *The Mortgaged Heart*, ed. Margarita G. Smith (London: Barrie & Jenkins, 1972), pp. 259–61 (260).

12 Carson McCullers, *The Heart is a Lonely Hunter* (London: Penguin, 2008), p. 26.

13 See Hermione Lee, 'Introduction' to O'Connor, *Everything That Rises Must Converge* (London: Faber & Faber, 1980), pp. vii–xiv.

14 O'Connor, 'Some Aspects of the Grotesque in Southern Fiction', p. 38.

15 O'Connor, 'The Regional Writer' (1963), *Mystery and Manners*, pp. 51–9 (58).

16 O'Connor, 'The Regional Writer', pp. 58–9.

17 O'Connor, 'The Fiction Writer and His Country', p. 26.

18 Flannery O'Connor, *Wise Blood* (London: Faber & Faber, 2000), p. 13.

19 Flannery O'Connor, 'Everything That Rises Must Converge', *The Complete Stories* (London: Faber & Faber, 1990), pp. 405–20 (407–8).

20 O'Connor, 'The Enduring Chill', *The Complete Stories*, pp. 357–82 (361).

21 O'Connor, 'A Good Man Is Hard to Find', *The Complete Stories*, pp. 117–33 (120).

22 Irving Howe, *William Faulkner: A Critical Study* (New York: Vintage, 1962), p. 141.

23 William Faulkner, *As I Lay Dying* (Harmondsworth: Penguin, 1965), pp. 18–19.

The Society Novel: Wharton, Fitzgerald and John O'Hara

At the turn of the twentieth century, the study of American society was becoming anthropological. Thorstein Veblen, a rather divisive Ivy League academic, published *The Theory of the Leisure Class* in 1899, an influential treatise on the 'pecuniary' codes behind the value allotted to leisure within American culture. It posits that the prestige of the visibly leisured is the result of hierarchies that extend back millennia, to the first civilisations and societies. Leisure is the privilege of those who do not need to work, and Veblen claimed that many of the indicators of higher 'classes', particularly aesthetic preferences, were a consequence of this assumption. For example, his explanation of the impracticality of much feminine *haute couture* is that its very awkwardness is a measure of the prestige of the wearer; it is impossible to do difficult manual work in mink stoles or high heels.

Veblen's theories critiqued what came to be known as 'conspicuous consumption', the need for personal wealth to be on constant display so as to maintain a position of social prestige. As the world's leading exponent of market capitalism, the USA has also led in a particular kind of novel of manners, in which such consumption, and the leisure it signifies, plays a key part. The USA's expansion in the nineteenth century created many new millionaires who came to define the ideal of the self-made man; it is an archetype that endures, integral to how many Americans view their place in the national narrative. Where the Old

World had its prominent families, with heritages of wealth extending back centuries into feudalist aristocracy, the New World had its 'new money'. Nevertheless, at the turn of the twentieth century, America had 'old money' too, and a discernible snobbery and scepticism towards the self-made classes attended it. The very language used by long-prominent families to denote what they saw as upstarts – nouveau riche, parvenu and arriviste – sought to create a distance between the Europhilic establishment, with its tendency to look to France and England for guidance in taste, and the all-American chutzpah of the industrialists, financiers and advertisers whose wealth apparently blossomed from the humblest of beginnings.

For American men and women of letters, this distinction made for a 'novel of manners' quite different from that of other countries and cultures. Many readers would associate the 'novel of manners' with early nineteenth-century Britain, and in particular, the works of Jane Austen (1775–1817), whose nuanced observations on the landed upper middle class did not generally have to contend with 'new money' (though Captain Wentworth in *Persuasion* is a notable exception). In the USA at the turn of the twentieth century, however, 'old' families were not much 'older' than the recently moneyed; those with 'old money' were the descendants of the European upper-middle and upper classes, after all. The emphasis on self-reliance and equality of opportunity within much American rhetoric was at odds with the concept of an aristocracy or pseudo-aristocracy. Even those from well-regarded families advocated a combination of inherited standards and a semi-puritan accent on working to maintain them; a peculiarly American ethic. As the novelist Edith Wharton (1862–1937) writes in her memoir, *A Backward Glance* (1934), it might seem odd to a reader that her family and their peers, 'a group of *bourgeois* colonials and their republican descendants', should become 'a sort of social aristocracy'.[1] Nevertheless, it is true that the majority of New York's upper middle class, for example, were of 'bourgeois' descent; that is to say, of the merchants and businessmen of industrial trade and entrepreneurialism. As such, their standing in society was ultimately determined by the fact that they had acquired a great deal of wealth.

By way of comparison, this could not always be said of the English aristocracy, to whom breeding could trump affluence. Good standards in uptown Manhattan depended on being of private means, whilst at the same time not drawing unbecoming attention to it. This is the 'Old New York' that Wharton chronicles in the 1924 short story collection of the same name and in many of her novels. Nevertheless, her greatest novels plot the points at which the nouveau riche intersects with genteel Upper East Side society; where the 'standards' she cherishes nostalgically in *A Backward Glance* come up against the shifting socioeconomics of early twentieth-century New York, in all its Veblen-like conspicuousness.

Edith Wharton and the *'Roman de Moeurs'*

After reading Wharton's 1905 novel *The House of Mirth*, the American-born novelist Henry James (1843–1916) wrote to her, suggesting that the best way he could offer constructive criticism was 'by coming back to the U.S. to deliver a lecture on "the question of the *roman de moeurs* in America – it's deadly difficult"'.[2] By 1905, James had lived in Great Britain for nearly thirty years, having decided that the gentlemen and ladies of European society offered the novelist more scope for observing the minutiae of gentility than their counterparts across the Atlantic. His earliest novels, such as *The American* (1877) and *The Europeans* (1878) explored the cultural differences between the Old and New Worlds, a theme that continued to occupy him into the early twentieth century, though by then the novels were almost exclusively set in England or elsewhere in Europe. His use of the French term *'roman de moeurs'* is telling. The phrase implies his belief that the American novel of manners is almost a contradiction of terms, to the extent that there is not even a language for it; the short history of the nation has allowed for little of the social stratification upon which English masters of the form such as Samuel Richardson and Jane Austen could draw, and this is what makes any attempt at an American equivalent 'deadly difficult'. It also bespeaks the tendency among cultured New Yorkers to look to Europe for acceptable aesthetic sensibilities, a tendency Wharton knew well; she frequently conceded her preference for the customs of the English, and spent much of her life in France.

Most aptly of all, however, the word '*moeurs*' is a useful conflation; it means both 'manners' and 'morals'. This equivalence was essential to the values of the 'Old New York' of Edith Wharton's childhood memory. In *A Backward Glance*, she notes how 'the qualities justifying the existence of our old society were social amenity and financial incorruptibility'; 'a strict standard of uprightness in affairs' was an essential indicator of both manners and morals, effectively making them synonymous. For Wharton and James, manners should be in service to morals and vice versa, but in the United States, this simple equation is complicated by a cultural imperative to acquire and maintain wealth, and that wealth is necessary to maintain the illusion of manners and morals. Wharton makes this her subject many times over. The early short story 'A Cup of Cold Water', for example, tells of the well-bred but impecunious Woburn, who fritters his limited savings on keeping up with a richer social set, in order that he might court and marry Miss Talcott. Miss Talcott's own view of his endeavours is typical of her class and position:

> To the girls in Miss Talcott's set, the attentions of a clever man who had to work for his living had the zest of a forbidden pleasure; but to marry such a man would be as unpardonable as to have one's carriage seen at the door of a cheap dress-maker. Poverty might make a man fascinating; but a settled income was the best evidence of stability of character. If there were anything in heredity, how could a nice girl trust a man whose parents had been careless enough to leave him unprovided for?[3]

'Stability of character' here is largely dependent on 'a settled income'; wealth outweighs birth because only those of dubious standards would make bad investments or squander their assets.

The gap between appearances and means, and the possible personal tragedies such a gap might provoke, are scrutinised thoroughly in *The House of Mirth*. However, it does not focus on 'old' New York, but on the venal and corrupt behaviour of an ostensibly respectable social set. The novel follows the misfortunes of Lily Bart, a society woman of good breeding who is nevertheless in a precarious financial position. At twenty-nine, little of her paltry inheritance is left. She is also unmarried, which only exacerbates her material disadvantage, for she must spend a large proportion of her remaining funds on the best dresses and accessories in the hope that she can find a suitable husband. She also has a weakness for beautiful things, and at the beginning of the novel the reader finds her attempting to ward off 'dinginess' at all costs. It is a characteristic Thorstein Veblen would recognise; Lily Bart's 'whole being dilated in an atmosphere of luxury; it was the background she required, the only climate she could breathe in'.[4] Nevertheless, her attitude to the fashionable circles in which she moves is dichotomous; for example, she both 'ridicule[s]' and 'envie[s]' Gus and Judy Trenor's set (p. 44). Furthermore, like Wharton herself, whose artistic impulses were at odds with the intellectual staleness of Old New York, Lily has a 'broad-minded recognition of literature' that 'would have had its distinction in an older society' (p. 57). Miss Bart's Europhilic romanticism is antithetical to the harsh social and economic necessities of her milieu, but paradoxically, it is this very milieu which would allow such romanticism to flourish.

Lily's conflicting impulses are what ultimately prevent her from marrying and so accelerate her decline into social ostracism. Wishing to marry for love not fortune, she rejects the possibility of a financially advantageous union with the socially awkward Percy Gryce, and instead asks the husband of her friend Judy, Gus Trenor, to invest her money in stocks and shares. She knows that others might construe this as risky behaviour, but it turns out to be a catastrophe. The 'returns' Lily receives from Trenor are nothing of the sort; instead, he is trying to buy her affections. Keeping him onside necessitates meeting him, and gossip spreads about their liaisons. After he threatens her, Lily 'realis[es] for the first time a woman's dignity may cost more to keep than her carriage', and 'that the maintenance of a moral attribute should be dependent on dollars and cents made the world appear a more sordid place than she had conceived it' (p. 149). Trenor's is not the only corruption she must confront. Lily's fall is further precipitated when she becomes an unwitting decoy to the adultery of Bertha Dorset, a supposed friend who is later revealed to be a schemer. Bertha conducts an extramarital dalliance with a young poet, but frames Lily as her husband's own mistress; Lily's rapidly deteriorating social status offers inadequate protection against these claims, and so the rumours spread, eventually causing her aunt, Mrs Peniston, to disinherit her. The later part of the novel sees Lily forced to take on work, the ultimate loss of prestige; furthermore, she performs her tasks badly, eventually being dismissed from a milliner's for producing substandard hats. The observations of Lawrence Selden, Lily's chief admirer, that 'a society like ours wastes such good material in producing its little patch of purple' (p. 62) turns out to be grimly prophetic; Lily dies ignobly from an overdose of sleeping draught, penniless, unmarried and, through various misunderstandings and missed opportunities, she is denied Selden, the one person whose respect and love for her have never wavered.

Innocence and Experience

In *The House of Mirth*, Lily's situation grows ever more desperate, to the point where it seems inexorable, even inevitable. Her tragedy is partly one of being born into the right class at the wrong time, as 'new money' eclipses the values attending the 'old'. Wharton was clearly sceptical about the nouveau riche class, their motivations, tastes and opinions. Banker and businessman Simon Rosedale in *The House of Mirth*, for example, is almost a grotesque. The old guard clearly view him as an impostor, an arrogant Jewish upstart. He is the focus of much anti-Semitism throughout, described as having small, suspicious eyes and held in contempt by the Dorsets and Trenors for living in a house of disharmonious design, a visible expression of his perceived lack of aesthetic standards and the ostentation of his newfound wealth. He is nevertheless acute in his vision, taking note of those around him as if they were 'bric-a-brac' (p. 13); in many ways he is the most objective of all the novel's characters, being at an angle to the society in which he moves.

In other works, Wharton places the parvenu* at the very centre of the narrative. Undine Spragg in *The Custom of the Country* (1913) is transferred from the Midwest of America to uptown Manhattan; she is a young woman on the make, determined to maintain her social status at all costs. Undine is the target of some ruthless satire and not a little snobbery on Wharton's part. Her non-New York roots mark out her lack of respectable heritage, while her name, with shades of Dickens or Trollope, pairs fanciful pretension with unbecoming vulgarity. As Lorna Sage notes, it cannot be accidental that her initials spell out US; her shallowness and materialism are the very condition of the America that Wharton herself decried.[5] Undine is the antithesis of Lily Bart. She is a serial divorcee, living proof that in the America of the early twentieth century it is always possible to erase the past and start again. Although this possibility can be personally empowering, Wharton recognises all that is sacrificed in pursuing it to its utmost. In the less critically lauded, though commercially successful, novel *The Glimpses of the Moon* (1922), a rootless couple, Nick and Susy Branch, extend their honeymoon indefinitely. They request cheques rather than wedding presents, and with the accumulated money travel through Europe, taking advantage of the hospitality of as many rich acquaintances as possible. This would never have done in 'old' New York society, but in the 1920s, frivolous gaiety is the order of the day; friends of the Branches 'were interested in seeing how long [the cheques] could be made to last. It was going to be the thing, that year, to help prolong the honey-moon by pressing houses on the adventurous couple'.[6]

Wharton's attitude to the faddish hedonism of the 1920s was sceptical. She was keen to stress that she did not write 'jazz-books' – that is, the type of novel popularised by F. Scott Fitzgerald or his lesser followers.[7] Her most celebrated works of the 1920s, in particular the stories of *Old New York* (1924) and the novel *The Age of Innocence* (1920), were marked by a nostalgia for a fast-disappearing Manhattan, a Manhattan which had often provoked mixed feelings within Wharton, but nevertheless provided an antidote to the new turn of

---

* A parvenu is a person from humble origins who has rapidly risen to a position of social prominence or affluence.

fashion towards cocktail party witticisms. The title of Wharton's 1920 novel is touched with irony. The 1870s would appear to be 'innocent' of anything outside narrow 'uptown' society that might challenge social codes and expectations. Yet this 'innocence' is often extremely knowing; some of those in society are certainly cognisant of that which they must repress in order to maintain their status. The male protagonist, Newland Archer, is the most apparent example of this self-knowledge; the novel relates his swift transition from conformity to questioning. The woman he marries, May, is conventional to a fault, a perfect society lady. The woman he falls in love with, Ellen, is at a remove for several reasons; although she is May's cousin, she has led quite a different life, having married an abusive Polish count and lived in Europe only to come back to the USA to escape her ill-fated union. Her European tastes and standards are quite different from those of the New Yorkers around her, making for a potentially Jamesian contrast between the sophisticated mores of the Old World and the apparent green naiveté of the New. Archer himself soon realises how 'elementary' his principles have hitherto been, conjecturing that in the 'complicated old European communities ... love-problems might be less simple and less easily classified'.[8] Nevertheless, at the end of the novel long after May has died, their son Dallas reveals that his mother always knew about Archer's love for Ellen, but that ultimately she trusted him not to act on it because his sense of duty was too strong. This New York society is aware of what it represses in order to maintain a respectable facade. It is not so much innocent as engaged in maintaining an illusion of innocence; it depends upon a continuum of decorum. Thus it is that the end of the novel sees Archer turn away from the possibility of an encounter with Ellen Olenska. The memory of 'innocence' overpowers any need to advance or progress beyond it.

Flappers and Philosophers: F. Scott Fitzgerald

The ending of *The Age of Innocence* is not so dissimilar from that of a novel that appeared five years later, *The Great Gatsby* by F. Scott Fitzgerald. Edith Wharton met Fitzgerald only once, at the height of his fame in 1925. Their rendezvous was not a success; a drunken Fitzgerald told a rather risqué story, and Wharton later wrote in her diary that the incident was 'awful'.[9] This anecdote neatly demonstrates the strained connections between the 'old' and 'new' literary scenes in 1920s America. The writers of the 'jazz age' were sexually candid where their predecessors were erotically inhibited, and they paid little heed to the established methods of measuring social status. Wharton was seen increasingly as a literary aristocrat, aloof from the American artistic scene: as Frederick J. Hoffman puts it in his summary of the jazz decade, *The Twenties*, 'in a genuine sense the opportunity for a formalized comedy of social manners had passed'.[10]

'Formalized' is the key word here. The almost anthropological scrutiny to which Wharton subjected the minute social divisions of the affluent classes depended to a great degree on discrepancies between expected or prescribed behaviour and the human instincts that might contradict it. In the novels of the emerging generation of 1920s writers, however, characters write their own codes of conduct: newness is valued over tradition. They reflect the tone set by a burgeoning magazine culture; the 1913 arrival of *Vanity Fair* was particularly significant, publishing some of the most famous writers of its generation, including Dorothy Parker, Aldous Huxley and D. H. Lawrence. Much 1920s literature also reflects the new demographics of the age. New York continued to grow in size and confidence through the 1920s; by 1925, it had overtaken London as the most populous city on the planet. To F. Scott Fitzgerald, New York in 1919 had 'all the iridescence of the beginning of the world'.[11]

This fetish for the new and contemporary spawned its own micro-trends, but the turnover of fashion was often so rapid that elegant distaste and disaffection were equally voguish among the young 'flappers and philosophers' of Fitzgerald's writing. A delight in the latest prestigious goods was matched by a simmering disquiet at the potential for vulgarity in the promotion of the consumer product. Not unlike Wharton, Fitzgerald looked to Europe as a possible antidote to Manhattan's brash materialism. Like other writers of the so-called

'Lost Generation', he felt drawn to France especially.* In his memoir *A Moveable Feast*, Ernest Hemingway recalls that Fitzgerald insisted his 'congestion of the lungs' was an exclusively European condition, and not, as his fellow writer suspected, a euphemism for pneumonia; even disease was liable to become a function of Fitzgerald's ambivalence towards America and his sometime self-construction as a kind of effete old-world aesthete.[12] This uneasy push and pull between the modish and the nostalgic marks a good deal of Fitzgerald's writing. It is central to his most widely read novel, *The Great Gatsby* (1925), whose famous last line reads, 'so we beat on, boats against the current, borne back ceaselessly into the past'.[13] The 'current' here is both the wave crested by the metaphorical boat, and more generally a synonym for the contemporary, the today; progress is, invariably, illusory, a case of going forwards to go backwards.

The central figure of Fitzgerald's first novel, *This Side of Paradise* (1920), Amory Blaine, is a preppy young rake with literary pretensions. He cultivates a snobbish attachment to continental art and custom, while nevertheless becoming almost emblematic of a particular type of Ivy League-educated American youth. His family provenance, in any case, comes by way of a kind of peripatetic Europeanism; Fitzgerald lets the reader know that 'the Blaines were attached to no city. They were the Blaines of Lake Geneva.'[14] His mother broadly dislikes American women – 'they have accents, my dear', she says to Amory rather dismissively – but she is nevertheless sceptical of too much anti-Americanism; she considers 'regret' at one's nationality a 'vulgar' preoccupation, even if she would rather have been born into 'an older, mellower civilization' (pp. 20–1). There is thus a sense of both delight and dismay at being born American, which Amory himself shares. Being both involved in the world of the beautiful young people and somewhat sceptical of it allows Amory to satirise those around him, much like Fitzgerald himself. While at Princeton, he thinks up ironic commentaries on the various types represented in his circle, such as the 'slicker', who 'derive[s] his name from the fact that his hair was inevitably worn short, soaked in water or tonic, parted in the

---

* For a discussion of the 'Lost Generation', see Part Two: 'A Cultural Overview'.

middle, and slicked back as the current of fashion dictated' (p. 32). However, his mentor, Monsignor Darcy, reminds him that there is a distinction between 'personalities', who are shallow and transient, and 'personages', who grow in eminence over time.

Blaine seemingly desires to be a 'personage', to distinguish himself from all the 'personalities' around him. He searches for inspiration in his contemporaries, looking for someone in his class at Princeton who might found 'The Great American Poetic Tradition', but his hopes are thwarted: as he goes on to suggest, 'we *want* to believe' in great artists and politicians, but it is impossible (p. 197). The superficiality of the age is marked by a desire to be *seen* to be reading and thinking whatever is in vogue, without appreciating the potential for deeper significance. Many of Fitzgerald's short stories from the time also deal with this. However, they often hint that the surfaces in which they revel are cracked. In 'The Cut-Glass Bowl', for example, Fitzgerald writes that 'there was a rough stone age and a smooth stone age and a bronze age, and many years afterward a cut-glass age', but though this age is 'especially busy reflecting the dazzling light of fashion from the Back Bay to the fastnesses of the Middle West', it is easily fractured nevertheless.[15]

Materialism and Romanticism

Sometimes, Fitzgerald's exposure of the hollow venality of high society is merciless; his shorter works often have the qualities of moral allegory. 'The Diamond as Big as the Ritz', perhaps the most popular of his stories, tells of a young man, John T. Unger, who goes to visit his friend Percy's family in the deep recesses of Montana. Percy's parents are direct descendants of America's first family, the Washingtons, and thus already have a certain mythic quality before the plot unfolds. Percy's father's house sits on the biggest reserve of diamonds in the world, which would make Braddock Washington the richest man to walk the earth. However, he cannot speak of his treasures to anyone, because of a paradox; to divulge the abundance of diamonds would be to drive down their market value. He must therefore employ slaves to work the diamond mine, slaves whom he has subjected through the false claim that the South won the Civil War.* He trades just enough diamonds to keep him wealthy, but not so many that suspicion can be aroused. This illusion requires him to maintain a morbid routine, whereby any visitors to the house are prevented from leaving; they are either incarcerated or killed. It is an extreme fable, akin to a Grimm fairytale. Fitzgerald's descriptions of the house and its environs are larded with hyperbole; there are rooms that 'dazzled the eyes with a whiteness that could be compared only with itself, beyond human wish or dream',[16] and landscaped gardens in which John would not be surprised to see 'a goat-foot piping his way among the trees or to catch a glimpse of pink nymph-skin' (p. 928). It is an unreal territory, uncharted too, 'the only five square miles of land in the country that's never been surveyed' (p. 918). It appears to exist outside of America; yet it is indeed a nightmare mythical America, so concerned with the measuring the value of its own uniqueness that it has almost made a Mephistophelean pact with itself. Braddock makes an offering to God, holding his arms out into the night air, but God is nowhere to be found; he has long since departed from the United States.

The Washington family in 'The Diamond as Big as the Ritz' are completely isolated from society, but some of the themes of the story re-emerge in later, more socially conscious work, particularly in *The Great Gatsby* (1925), whose subject is the gap between a romanticised America of unlimited natural and material potential and the realities of its fascination with money and acquisition. The initial depiction of Gatsby himself is even reminiscent of Braddock Washington in the short story; the narrator, Gatsby's neighbour Nick Carraway, encounters him standing in his garden, holding his arms out over the bay towards the other side of Long Island as if 'determin[ing] what share was his of our local heavens' (p. 27). However, his back-story, if similarly allegorical, is much more typically 'American'. Formerly James Gatz, Gatsby is a self-made man, an opportunist whose

---

* If the South won the Civil War, slavery would have continued in Montana.

somewhat ostentatious displays of wealth – a cavalier disregard for electricity bills as he illuminates his house like the 'World's Fair',* a collection of beautiful shirts purely for aesthetic rather than sartorial use – conceal his somewhat tawdry means of acquiring it, namely bootlegging alcohol during the Prohibition period. Nevertheless, Gatsby is far from a textbook example of Thorstein Veblen's theories of conspicuous consumption. His flamboyant displays are all geared towards the reclamation of an ideal rather than the maintenance of social cachet. This ideal is romantic in both senses of the word. Gatsby is perhaps an American version of the typical 'Romantic' associated with the late eighteenth and early nineteenth century, an ultimately solitary figure who rejects reason in pursuit of sensation; in the novel, Nick describes Gatsby's romanticism as an awareness of 'a secret place above the trees' in which his hero can 'suck on the pap of life, gulp down the incomparable milk of wonder' (p. 118). His *raison d'être* is also romantic in the more recognisable sense of being tied to his relationship with a woman. His claim that it is possible to turn back the clock comes from his unwavering belief that he can win back his old flame Daisy, who in the timeframe of the novel is now married to the rather brutish Tom Buchanan. It is for this reason that he invents his extravagant persona, to woo her back.

The novel is on one level a chronicle of individual tragedy. Gatsby's naive faith in Daisy collides with the harsher exigencies of the New York social order, a collision that ultimately leads to his own death at the hands of the grieving husband of Tom's mistress. The way in which Nick describes Gatsby's demise makes clear that the 'milk of wonder' has curdled; his body floats in his swimming pool, a trail of leaves on the surface suggesting that Gatsby's 'secret place above the trees' has been demolished. But *The Great Gatsby* also charts the corruption of the 'fresh, green breast of the new world' that Dutch settlers encountered in the seventeenth century. That early optimism,

---

* This is Nick's impression of Gatsby's house (p. 88). It seems that Nick is not referring to a specific World's Fair, but the general idea of one; world's fairs are international exhibitions designed to reflect the cultural eminence of a particular city or country.

on some level embodied by the Gatsby who suckles the 'milk of wonder' from that 'fresh, green breast', is now shown to be little more than a gaudy illusion; it is no accident that the title of the novel depicts its hero almost as a circus conjuror, and that his 'greatness' is on many levels ironic, even empty. In this at least, Fitzgerald and Edith Wharton have one thing in common – a tendency to hold the ideals of the past, however hypocritical or ill-founded they might be, above the society doings of the present. Gatsby, like Lily Bart, is shown to be almost tragically at odds with his own time, ill-equipped to deal with the ruthless machinations of his peers and neighbours.

The Society Novel after Fitzgerald: John O'Hara

Post-Fitzgerald, American 'society novels' became increasingly acerbic and self-critical. *Parties: A Novel of Contemporary New York Life* by Carl Van Vechten (1880–1964) perhaps foreshadows the future of the *roman de moeurs*, its self-explanatory title indicating blatant pastiche. Like *The Great Gatsby*, it too features a bootlegger, by the satirical name of Donald Bliss; but in this New York, not even the parties are particularly fabulous; for example, Rosalie Keith 'was celebrated for giving the worst parties in New York, but despite this undesirable reputation she never ceased giving them and people continued to go to them'.[17] Wharton and Fitzgerald both relied to some extent on a traditional cornerstone of novel-writing; the assumption that the reader must have at least some sympathy for the main character(s). This requires a 'society' writer to offset the superficial displays of Thorstein Veblen's mass-consumption theories with the struggles of characters to reach beyond and outside of them. However, the work of the novelist and short-story writer John O'Hara (1905–70) frequently allows little possibility of such redemption. The essayist and cultural commentator Fran Lebowitz (1950–), herself infamous for working on a yet-to-be-completed society novel called *Exterior Signs of Wealth*, maintains that O'Hara is 'the real Fitzgerald';[18] he is what Fitzgerald could have been, had he put aside some of his more romantic, nostalgic and Eurocentric inclinations. Even during his initial period of fame, John O'Hara was touted as both a logical successor and an antidote to Fitzgerald. In 1935, *Time* magazine declared him 'the voice of the hangover generation that awakened in the grey dawn of 1930'; these were the society novels that exposed the ugliness of the affluent in the era of the Great Depression, whose personal 'hangovers' mirrored a country that found itself adrift and depleted after the frivolities and speculative economics of the 1920s.

Many of O'Hara's short stories, which were regularly featured in the *New Yorker*, chart this 'hangover generation', well aware of the stagnancy of their own leisure. In 'The Moccasins', for example, 'the people were just sitting around, lying around, waiting for something, but nothing in particular, to happen'.[19] But it is in *Appointment in Samarra* (1934), O'Hara's best-known and most critically feted novel, that he explores this stagnancy most fully. Its principal character, the wealthy car dealer Julian English, does indeed suffer from a significant hangover, during which he ruefully remembers throwing a highball cocktail in the face of Harry Reilly. At its core, English's behaviour seems inexplicable, even to himself: 'why, he wondered, did he hate Harry Reilly? Why couldn't he stand him?'[20] The apparently motiveless incident occurs because 'it was fun to think about it'. English is of a milieu in which any behavioural oddities are immediately the material of golf-club gossip, but it is nevertheless a social environment in which little has real consequence other than the opprobrium of this smart set; in many ways, their self-regard goes beyond even that of Fitzgerald's Princeton roués and jazz girls. The highball incident thus quickly takes on a legendary status made possible only by the hermetic nature of Gibbsville society life. Julian's return to the club after his outburst illustrates this level of self-absorption to great effect. He encounters Bobby, who is sparring for an argument. He quips to his friend Whit, 'depression or no depression, I think the membership committee ought to draw the line somewhere' (p. 61); the wider political context of the era is heeded only insofar as it is relevant to the life of the club. When Bobby says that they should have had 'the God damn marines' in the previous night to deal with Julian's misbehaviour, English retorts, 'there you go, talking about the war again ... You never got over that God damn war', but Bobby goes one better, ironically making the highball incident a historical event on the level of war; he talks of the 'Veterans of 1930', the year of 'The Battle of the Lantenengo Country Club Smoking Room', where the incident took place. His apparently flip sarcasm is telling. Lantenengo Street is full of people for whom Gibbsville society and its history is more important than any national narrative. As O'Hara makes plain in Chapter Three,

> There were a great many people in Gibbsville who had money in 1930. The very rich, who always had money, still had a lot of money. And the merchants and bankers, doctors and lawyers and dentists, who had money to play the market, continued to spend their principal.* (p. 43)

In O'Hara's Pennsylvania, there is a wanton disregard for any greater good beyond the maintenance of wealth and/or social kudos. The eventual fate of Julian English is suicide; he gasses himself in his car, the ultimate symbol of both his wealth and his superficiality. His widow, Caroline, muses that 'he was like someone who had died in the war' but really it is the image of his 'gesture with a cigarette' as he 'swung a golf club back and forth' that stays with her (p. 187). Even in death, his place in Gibbsville society runs no deeper than a frozen memory of affluent leisure. It is a sterile milieu; far from embodying the ideals of social mobility and empowerment we might associate with American opportunity, English's scene is one in which 'by the time a man reached junior year in college he knew how he was situated in the country-club social life' (p. 66). Rather melodramatically, suicide becomes the only way of truly subverting this programmed social order.

---

* The 'principal' is the initial amount of an investment before interest is ever added. O'Hara thus depicts a world in which people are reluctant to give up their affluent lifestyles despite dwindling funds.

Cataloguing Social Ills

This unnerving contrast between Gibbsville's rather prosaic etiquettes and the potential psychological strains underlying them is characteristically expressed by O'Hara through lists, calculations and enumerative descriptions. In the judgement of the prominent literary critic Lionel Trilling, 'the work of no other American writer tells us so precisely, and with such a sense of the importance of the communication, how people look and how they want to look, where they buy their clothes and where they wish they could buy their clothes, how they speak and how they think they ought to speak'.[21] *Appointment in Samarra* is a case in point; for example, Julian English's father's various affiliations, memberships and directorships are fully catalogued for the sake of accuracy and verisimilitude. The paragraph in question is more akin to the pages of the British biographical encyclopaedia *Who's Who* than any American equivalent, perhaps suggesting that while Dr English's connections and achievements may be tied to Gibbsville, the methods by which their prestige are measured once more recall those of the hierarchical societies of Europe, as shown in the works of Wharton and Fitzgerald. However, O'Hara seldom romanticises these details. They are listed almost journalistically, as they might be in a society newspaper or magazine; this is literalised in the short story, 'Other Women's Households', which begins with an account of Phyllis Richardson going through the weekly paper every Friday night 'for mentions of herself'.[22]

The novel *Ten North Frederick* (1955) adopts this technique for rich narrative advantage. It begins with the funeral of a prominent politician, Joe Chapin, listing all the major mourners in turn. Honorary pallbearers are itemised and scrutinised; this is a dramatic device for introducing the reader to an entire community of Gibbsville luminaries, just as the 'busybody' attached to Chapin's widow's house records everything and everyone that passes in the street below.* The novel subsequently pieces together these various lives, and gradually reveals how they coincided,

---

* A 'busybody' was a feature of some nineteenth-century American houses, a mirror attached to a building that reflected views of the street below.

connected and conflicted with that of the protagonist while he was alive. O'Hara makes sure to include what the fictional *Gibbsville Standard* has to say about the ceremony in its feature, 'Notables Attend Chapin Funeral', both to underline the realism of his prose and to justify his own central literary device; the newspaper is chiefly interested in the death of Chapin because it triggers a society gathering, just as O'Hara himself uses that death as a way of anatomising the social structure of a whole town. In this way, he is perhaps more ruthlessly anthropological in his studies of class and social esteem than Edith Wharton ever dared to be. Lionel Trilling suggests that this is not always a positive aspect of O'Hara's writing, arguing that sometimes 'his passion for accuracy is out of control'.[23] Much too has been made, particularly by O'Hara's biographer Geoffrey Wolff, of his unpopularity among many of the social and artistic coteries of his era; he was by all accounts quick to vent his prejudices and his behaviour was often deemed to be arrogant, even guileful.[24] However, according to Fran Lebowitz, his reputation as a 'social climber' was to blame for this; snobbery dictated that his blatant self-promotion be met with disdain. His position on the outside looking in allowed him a greater degree of unsentimental vision into the repetitive, self-perpetuating cycles of social approval and opprobrium that mark a very specific class of people – the Lantenengo and Frederick Street crowds and their associates.

It could also be argued that O'Hara laid the ground for other 'society' novelists to follow, through and beyond the Second World War. In the 1980s, for example, a new nouveau riche emerged in the wake of Ronald Reagan's economic boom. These strutting stockbrokers and drugged-up partygoers were a perfect subject for the timely refashioning of the 'society novel', as exemplified by Jay McInerney in *Bright Lights, Big City* (1984) or Tom Wolfe (1931–) in *The Bonfire of the Vanities* (1987), works which owe more to O'Hara's unsentimental eye than to his more romantic predecessors. It seems as long as there are elites in American society, there will be novelists who excel in cataloguing the minutiae that determine their values.

Extended Commentary: Fitzgerald, *Tender is the Night* (1934)

If *The Great Gatsby* is a narrative of doomed delusions that nevertheless places faith in nostalgia and romanticism, then *Tender is the Night* (1934) depicts a fashionable society without any such crutches. Keats's 'Ode to a Nightingale' is recalled in the title of the novel, but the reference might as soon suggest 'the weariness, the fever and the fret' as the 'immortal' song of the bird.[25] The title was a last-minute alteration, swapping the more prosaic *Doctor Diver's Holiday* for a line from Fitzgerald's favourite poet; a poet attended by a mythology of consumptive youth and otherworldly sensitivity equal to Fitzgerald's own reputation for flights of fancy on what Ernest Hemingway called 'damaged wings'.[26]

Tender is the Night begins with such damaged beauty, in a recent past redolent of faded glamour that was already a little decadent in the time in which the novel is set. 'Now, many bungalows cluster' near to the French Riviera beach of the opening scene, 'but when this story begins only the cupolas of a dozen old villas rotted like water lilies among the massed pines' (p. 11). The young actress, Rosemary Hoyt, holidaying with her mother on this strip of beach, notes the strange coexistence of the gaudy and the morbid. A man tells her after her swim that there are sharks further out to sea, and she is stalked by a 'stale' feeling when travelling by train through Provence. Accustomed to the 'grotesqueries of a continent heavily underlined as comedy or tragedy', Rosemary is unsettled by an ineffable tension in the air. It is partly a consequence of the old world meeting the new, the collision of America and France so often chronicled by writers of the 'Lost Generation', seen through the eyes of a displaced Hollywood starlet. But the Riviera is characterised by other social demarcations and hierarchies too. The beach segregates the tanned, who occupy the sands, from the white-skinned, who are nudged onto expanses of pebble and shingle; American society figures transplanted from their uptown addresses to the Cote d'Azur import their own obsession with social codes, drawing an equivalence between their 'plot' of beach land and the wider 'plot', the narrative of who is 'in' and who is 'out'. From the off, Rosemary is an interloper. She decides to spread her peignoir on the sand 'between the dark people and the light' (p. 14); hers is a threshold presence, not least as she is at a crossroads in her own life, 'hover[ing] delicately on the last edge of childhood' (p. 12). Such youthfulness, redoubled by her growing reputation as a movie beauty, allows a level of access to the heart of the social scene that is denied to most.

In particular, it attracts the attention of Doctor Dick Diver, a respected American psychologist, and his troubled wife, Nicole. Dick and Nicole are the most prominent expat couple on this stretch of the Riviera. They are known for their parties, though Doctor Diver is no Gatsby. He lacks the romanticism of Fitzgerald's other great socialite, instead striking Rosemary as full of 'self-control and of self-discipline' (p. 28). Though his gatherings are as brilliant, Dick is held back by an acute self-awareness. The 'excitement that swept everyone up into it' is 'inevitably followed by his own form of melancholy' so that after attending his guests with 'extraordinary virtuosity', he ends up 'look[ing] back with awe at the carnivals of affection he had given as a general might gaze upon a massacre he had ordered to satisfy an impersonal blood lust' (pp. 36–7). There is something theatrical about these performances, not in the gaudy, delusional manner of Gatsby, but in a calculated way. Dick and Nicole are cognisant of their own artifice. Nicole readjusts the fake camellia on her shoulder and takes delight in her 'lovely grassless garden' (p. 34), while Dick's attitude to the entertainments he organises at their house is knowing almost to the point of irony; at the end of the first Riviera section of the novel, he announces 'this part of the summer is over ... Maybe we'll have more fun this summer but this particular fun is over. I want it to die violently instead of fading out sentimentally – that's why I gave this party' (p. 47).

This self-consciousness is a legacy of the America that Thorstein Veblen anatomises in *The Theory of the Leisure Class*. Dick and Nicole epitomise 'conspicuous consumption'; they wish to be seen as having a high regard for prestige goods, almost for their own sake. Fitzgerald's description of this locates them within a long history of decadence: he writes that 'the Divers' day was spaced like the day of the older civilizations to yield the utmost from the materials at hand, to give all the transitions their full value' (p. 30). 'Value' here is aesthetic, but also, unmistakeably, economic. According to Veblen, the development of impeccable taste in fine goods is really an example of 'honorific' value; it is a classic conflation of beauty and expense.* The Divers' affluence is also matched by a need to prove it, exemplifying another key Veblen principle. Dick is unsettled by this; he notes the 'discrepancy between the growing luxury in which the Divers lived, and the need for display which apparently went along with it' (p. 182). Nicole, on the other hand, could almost be a Veblen case study in this regard. He proposes that 'conspicuous consumption' requires the leisured to be overgenerous: as their wealth 'accumulates', their own 'unaided effort will not avail to sufficiently put [their] opulence in evidence by this method', and 'the aid of friends and competitors is therefore brought in by resorting to the giving of valuable presents and expensive feasts and entertainments'.[27] Nicole conforms to this type; Fitzgerald writes that 'everything she liked that she couldn't possibly use herself, she bought as a present for a friend' (p. 65), then lists some of her miscellaneous gifts, including folding beach cushions and doll's house miniatures.

Nicole's obsession with possessions, however, is perhaps an expression of her lack of self-possession. As the flashback in the second section of the novel recounts, Nicole's sporadic schizophrenia (and behind that, a history of abuse by her father) is what leads her to Dick Diver in the first place, in his professional capacity. The qualities Rosemary associates with Dick – self-discipline, solidity – have been maintained out of necessity, to stabilise his marriage. Rosemary's arrival jeopardises this immediately. Nicole observes the sexual chemistry between her husband and the young actress early in the novel; she 'saw her choose him, heard the little sigh at the fact that he was already possessed' (p. 28). Nicole 'already possesse[s]' Dick, but this sigh could

---

* According to Veblen, 'The superior gratification derived from the use and contemplation of costly and supposedly beautiful products is, commonly, in great measure a gratification of our sense of costliness masquerading under the name of beauty. Our higher appreciation of the superior article is an appreciation of its superior honorific character, much more frequently than it is an unsophisticated appreciation of its beauty' (p. 86).

also suggest that the possession of Dick has already passed from his wife to his future lover, in their very first encounter.

Dick's haphazard extramarital affair with Rosemary sees her come between husband and wife; as in her passage from youth to womanhood, and her decision to place herself in between the dark and light on the beach, she crosses a threshold. However, it is not Rosemary, nor even Nicole, who is undone most by this transgression; rather, it is Dick who falls from grace, into unsteady temper and alcohol dependency. Though it has frequently seemed to him that Nicole's intent is to 'own him', to override his natural inclination to live 'ascetically' with her own tendency towards 'slackness', by 'constantly inundat[ing]' him with 'a trickling of goods and money' (p. 187), the push and pull of extravagance and frugality has helped him define himself. Nicole's ownership of Dick, however, tips the balance of their marriage. For years, Nicole feels that she has been 'planet to Dick's sun' (p. 310), but where once Dick was her psychiatrist and protector, he is now her possession. His amours with Rosemary come to seem a consequence of this conjugal imbalance, rather than a cause. Dick hits his lowest point in Rome, where he is arrested for brawling; Nicole, meanwhile, has embarked on a romance with Tommy Barban, one of the more volatile members of the Diver circle. Fitzgerald pictures her in the ascendant towards the end of the novel, writing that 'Nicole had been designed for change, for flight, with money as fins and wings'. The nightingale of Keats's ode that lies behind the title of Fitzgerald's novel is invoked obliquely here; but it is buoyed by dollar bills. Just as Daisy Buchanan's voice in *The Great Gatsby* is 'full of money', acting almost as a kind of insurance, so too does Nicole's wealth seem innate or destined; it is therefore ultimately triumphant, a default that no physical or mental strain can compromise. The penultimate chapter ends with her viewing Dick from afar; as he walks away from her, he is an ever-decreasing 'dot' in the crowd. By the end of the novel, the reader is not even sure what has happened to him. We are left with Nicole's speculation on where he might be practising, wondering whether he has managed to re-establish his career.

Though the novel sees some potential for social change in the figure of Rosemary, the 'television girl' of the future as Dick sees her, and pays some attention to Doctor Diver's intellectual brilliance, it winds up reinforcing the dominance of the leisured, affluent class. Conspicuous wealth still seems the surest way to guarantee personal success; it is Nicole, after all, who regains herself at the end of *Tender is the Night*; and it is to Nicole's perspective that Fitzgerald turns to close the novel. Just like Wharton before him, and O'Hara after him, Fitzgerald registers ambivalence at the pervasive allure of private means; the rich may be venal, delusional and destructive, but they invariably reserve their right to the last laugh.

Notes

1   Edith Wharton, *A Backward Glance*, ed. Candace Waid (1934. London: J. M. Dent, 1993), p. 5.
2   Henry James, Letter to Edith Wharton, in Edith Wharton, *The Letters of Edith Wharton*, ed. R. W. B. Lewis and Nancy Lewis (London: Simon and Schuster, 1988), p. 374.
3   Edith Wharton, 'A Cup of Cold Water', *The New York Stories of Edith Wharton* (New York: NYRB, 2007), pp. 60–87 (61).
4   Edith Wharton, *The House of Mirth* (London: Wordsworth, 2002), p. 23.
5   See Lorna Sage, Introduction to Wharton, *The Custom of the Country* (London: Alfred A. Knopf), pp. xi–xxiii (xi).
6   Edith Wharton, *The Glimpses of the Moon* (1922. London: Virago, 1995), p. 67.
7   See Hermione Lee, *Edith Wharton* (London: Vintage, 2008), p. 601.
8   Edith Wharton, *The Age of Innocence* (1920. Ware: Wordsworth, 1994), p. 62.
9   See R. W. B. Lewis and Nancy Lewis, eds, *The Letters of Edith Wharton* (London: Simon & Schuster, 1988), p. 482.
10 Frederick J. Hoffman, *The Twenties: American Writing in the Postwar Decade* (1949. New York: Macmillan, 1962), p. 437.
11 F. Scott Fitzgerald, 'My Lost City', *The Crack-Up*, ed. Edmund Wilson (New York: New Directions, 1945), pp. 23–33 (25).
12 Ernest Hemingway, *A Moveable Feast* (1964. London: Jonathan Cape, 2010), p. 138.

13 F. Scott Fitzgerald, *The Great Gatsby* (1925. London: Penguin, 1994), p. 188.

14 F. Scott Fitzgerald, *This Side of Paradise* (1920. London: Penguin, 2000), p. 5.

15 F. Scott Fitzgerald, 'The Cut-Glass Bowl', *Novels and Stories 1920–1922* (New York: Library of America, 2000), pp. 335–55 (335).

16 Fitzgerald, 'The Diamond as Big as the Ritz', *Novels and Stories 1920–1922*, pp. 913–53 (921).

17 Carl Van Vechten, *Parties: A Novel of Contemporary New York Life* (New York: Knopf, 1930).

18 Fran Lebowitz, 'A Humorist at Work: Interview', interview with George Plimpton and James Linville, *Paris Review* 127, pp. 160–88 (185).

19 John O'Hara, *Selected Short Stories of John O'Hara* (New York: Random House, 1956), pp. 19–27 (19).

20 John O'Hara, *Appointment in Samarra* (Harmondsworth: Penguin, 1945), p. 11.

21 Lionel Trilling, Introduction to O'Hara, *Selected Short Stories of John O'Hara*, pp. vii–xiii (vii).

22 O'Hara, *Selected Short Stories of John O'Hara*, pp. 272–82 (272).

23 Trilling, Introduction, p. x.

24 See Geoffrey Wolff, *The Art of Burning Bridges: A Life of John O'Hara* (New York: Alfred A. Knopf, 2003).

25 John Keats, 'Ode to a Nightingale' (1819), *The Major Works*, ed. Elizabeth Cook (Oxford: OUP, 2008), pp. 285–8 (287). Dick Diver, the novel's flawed protagonist, would also appear to be an occasional fan of Keats; Fitzgerald writes that while in Rome 'his spirit soared before the flower stalls and the house where Keats had died'. F. Scott Fitzgerald, *Tender is the Night* (1934. London: Penguin, 1998), p. 240.

26 Hemingway, *A Moveable Feast*, p. 125.

27 Thorstein Veblen, *The Theory of the Leisure Class* (Oxford: Oxford University Press, 2009), p. 53.

The American Short Story: Cheever, Paley and Carver

It has become a kind of received wisdom that American writers have made the short story their own. Other countries and cultures have produced masters of the form: Russia has Anton Chekhov (1860–1904), France, Guy de Maupassant (1850–93), Ireland claims Frank O'Connor (1903–66) and Argentina boasts Jorge Luis Borges (1899–1986). All these writers have influenced and inspired generations of American short-story writers, but the fund of native talent in the field is so vast as to be virtually self-sustaining: as the Russian-American writer Vladimir Nabokov (1899–1977) put it in 1973, 'the greatest Short Stories have been produced not in England, not in Russia, and certainly not in France, but in [the United States]'.[1] While the nineteenth century in European literature marked the highpoint of the realist novel, it could be argued that, with the exception of the great works of Melville, Hawthorne, Twain and James, the greatest American fiction was to be found in miniature. Early trailblazers of the form such as Washington Irving (1783–1859) and Edgar Allan Poe (1809–49) became international ambassadors for American literature in general, and the dominance of their compatriots in the field was remarkable enough for Brander Matthews to declare the short story an American invention: he wrote in 1901 that 'Almost as soon as America began to have any literature at all it had good Short-stories.'[2]

The American short story only grew in esteem through the twentieth century. Just as the great nineteenth-century novelists, such as

Hawthorne and James, excelled in the form, so did the iconic men and women of twentieth-century American letters: Edith Wharton, F. Scott Fitzgerald, William Faulkner and Ernest Hemingway all complemented their longer works with successful examples of shorter fiction.* There emerged subcategories of short story that have since become emblematic of an entire genre; the 'Southern Gothic', for instance, is as much dominated by the short stories of Flannery O'Connor, Eudora Welty and Tennessee Williams as the novels of Faulkner, McCullers or Erskine Caldwell. By the end of the twentieth century, short stories had never sold so well, or been so central to establishing the names of writers.

This is partly explained by the rise in college creative writing programmes. Raymond Carver, for example, attended workshops at the University of Iowa in the 1960s, and he went on to teach on the same programme with John Cheever for a brief period in the early 1970s. Through the 1980s and into the 1990s, critics heralded a new golden age of the short story. Andrew Levy suggests that there was a 'renaissance' of the form,[3] triggered by the liberal arts colleges and their respective publications; new voices emerged, such as Ann Beattie (1947–), Richard Ford (1944–) and Joy Williams (1947–). However, 'renaissance' implies that the previous decades marked a gap. As the short-story writer and novelist Tobias Wolff (1945–) contends, the new generation wrote in a modish, minimalist style appropriate to their age, but they were nevertheless the latest in an illustrious line, for 'the truth is that the short story form has reliably inspired brilliant performances by our best writers, in a line unbroken since the time of Poe'.[4] One of the greatest influences on that long 'line' was not the academy, but a magazine: the *New Yorker*, founded in 1925, which has published some of the most discussed short stories of all time, among them 'The Lottery' (1948) by Shirley Jackson (1916–65), numerous pieces by John Updike and John Cheever, and more recently, work by highly regarded masters of the form such as Lorrie Moore (1957–) and Annie Proulx (1935–), whose 1997 *New Yorker* story, 'Brokeback Mountain'

---

* See especially Wharton, *Tales of Men and Ghosts* (1910); Fitzgerald, *Tales of the Jazz Age* (1922); Hemingway, *Men Without Women* (1927); Faulkner, *Go Down, Moses* (1942).

has arguably become her chief claim to fame since Ang Lee's 2005 film adaptation. Though the novelist James Purdy might sniff that the *New Yorker* is the 'worst influence' on short-story writers, requiring them to conform to its remits, the importance of the magazine is unquestionable.[5]

Other reasons for the ongoing American regard for the form are more difficult to define. The seemingly constant search for 'the great American novel' could be diagnosed as a symptom of a federal country's desire to read itself as an organic whole.* The short story, on the other hand, is often an expression of the particular or the local. Some have thus read it as a key element in the national narrative of individualism. According to William Peden, it offers an antidote to the American predilection for grandeur and scale, and represents 'individuality, freedom and variety'. He also claims that it can form a more immediate response than other literary forms to shifting trends and values. Peden was writing in the 1960s, at a time of almost unprecedented soul-searching within the American populace and body politic. He believed that the short story was the appropriate vehicle for depicting 'the fragmented nature of individual and national life', and that in the Cold War era, it was not possible to grapple with the 'fundamental verities' taken for granted by nineteenth-century realism writers, such as Tolstoy and Dickens.[6] Yet the short story is often valued precisely because it can seem timeless, almost mythical. It might be noted that some of the foundational texts of world literature are, in a sense, groups of short stories, even if rendered in verse; the *Arabian Nights* and Ovid's *Metamorphoses*, for example, or in the medieval period, Boccaccio's *Decameron* and Chaucer's *Canterbury Tales*. American literature has its short-story cycles too. *Winesburg, Ohio* (1919) by Sherwood Anderson (1876–1941) is a useful example. Though it is often considered a novel, it is really a sequence of short stories about the inhabitants of a Midwestern community, 'grotesques' as Anderson refers to them in the prologue.[7] Just as the community is the sum of its individuals, so is the 'novel' composed of its constituent

---

* The USA is a federal country; that is to say, it is a nation comprising semi-autonomous units (states) with their own laws and customs.

stories; both the town of Winesburg and the book that recreates it are federal entities that in some ways mirror the constitution of the United States itself.

Since Anderson, many writers have traced loose communities in short-story sequences. The short form gives an author the opportunity to study characters in isolation. Whether they are emblematic of their neighbourhood and background, or anomalous, they become all the more representative of the American 'everyman' or 'everywoman' in the short story, in which a writer must by necessity give an impression of a whole life within a few pages. Despite frequently adopting symbolism or deploying an allegorical framework, the American short story is predominantly a metonymic rather than metaphorical form.* It is a part of the larger national narratives that becomes representative of them. The three writers discussed in this chapter – John Cheever, Grace Paley and Raymond Carver – may be highly distinct stylistically; they also write from different geographical and cultural positions. Nevertheless, they are all masters of compression, gesturing towards much grander narratives than the particulars of plot or incident in their short stories might suggest.

John Cheever and the City of Broken Dreams

The previously modest critical reputation of John Cheever (1912–82) grew steeply with the publication of *The Stories of John Cheever* (1978), which won the Pulitzer Prize and drew huge admiration from fellow writers. John Irving, whose novel *The World According to Garp* lost the prize that year to the *Stories*, said that he could not imagine 'resenting' Cheever, as he was 'one of the few writers who made me realize that the kind of writing I loved could still be done'.[8] Until 1978, that 'kind of writing' had for many readers and critics been the very epitome of urbane *New Yorker* prose, usually detailing the lives of a certain type of anxious middle-class household in either Manhattan

---

* Metonymy is a type of figurative device by which a concept is referred to or substituted by a related property.

or the far suburban fringes of New York. What was most revelatory to new converts after the collected *Stories* was the range and versatility of Cheever's achievement in this relatively narrow field.

Cheever's Manhattan stories often concentrate on isolated individuals or family units. The form is ideally suited to chronicling flashes of disconnection. Tales of urban alienation are as old as tales of urban life itself, but Cheever is adept at taking the potential cliché and reshaping it in surprising ways. In 'The Season of Divorce', the narrator observes that 'chance meetings' are 'part of the life of any large city', and that 'the city is full of accidental revelation', suggesting that there is a narrative of potential interconnectivity underlying the daily movements and rituals of apparently unrelated New Yorkers.[9] This is borne out when Dr and Mrs Trencher enter the lives of the unnamed narrator and his wife, Ethel. Dr Trencher quickly becomes besotted with Ethel and beckons her to run away with him. The narrator sees this is an unwelcome kind of connection, and takes out his feelings of bitterness on the city itself, reading the word 'disaster' in the smokestacks along the East River and remarking how the light 'convince[s]' him that it is 'the season of divorce' (p. 190). Consequently, even if the tone at the end of the story is a lot less sure of itself than the self-confessedly 'middle class' voice that opens it, the narrator has nevertheless convinced himself that insulation from New York is preferable to immersion in it.

This trajectory from surety to doubt is nowhere more apparent than in 'The Enormous Radio'. The Westcotts's extraordinary ordinariness is established from the very first paragraph of the story. In a characteristically compressed style, Cheever opens with a comprehensive run-through of the norms to which they conform:

> Jim and Irene Westcott were the kind of people who seem
> to strike that satisfactory average of income, endeavour, and
> respectability that is reached by the statistical reports in college
> alumni bulletins. They were the parents of two young children,
> they had been married nine years, they lived on the twelfth
> floor of an apartment house near Sutton Place, they went to
> the theatre on an average of 10.3 times a year, and they hoped
> some day to live in Westchester. (p. 49)

Several sentences convey information both explicitly and implicitly. For example, the 'respectability' reached by 'statistical reports in college alumni bulletins' informs us both that they are college graduates and that they might feel a sense of belonging in the social networks that follow a university education; equally, despite its apparently neutral tone, the voice suggests that the couple's encounters with the theatre are more a token of their class and status than an indicator of artistic interest. This is a couple, after all, whose sole ambition is to move to a more salubrious locale.

Cheever's introduction is a gentle critical poke at the commonplace routines of a particular type of white-collar New Yorker, but it is also a forewarning. When Jim buys Irene a new radio, it soon imperils the entire balance of the house; moreover, it compromises the couple's sanity. For Irene, the radio is an 'aggressive intruder' among her more delicate possessions, giving off a 'malevolent' green light. Initially it offers chamber music, but gradually the Westcotts begin to overhear other lives from other houses in their neighbourhood through the speakers. Irene is shocked to find the Sweeneys's British nurse reading Edward Lear nonsense rhymes, and with each passing day the pitch of other people's lives becomes almost unbearable for her: 'Life is too terrible, too sordid and awful', she cries after a day of listening to her neighbours' cancer diagnoses and domestic disputes (p. 57). The radio, initially a token of smart consumerism, becomes a point of connection with other people's feelings of disconnection. Given the power to eavesdrop on others, Irene feels more, not less isolated. There is a strong suggestion that it is dangerous to become involved in the lives of fellow city-dwellers. 'The Enormous Radio', then, can be read as an allegory of urban dislocation, or even as a parable of Cold War America itself, obsessed by technological advances, paranoid and prone to snooping. But over and above this, it is also a caution against narrative overload, a warning to the author who attempts to write too many stories at once, all competing for the airwaves; with great subtlety, 'The Enormous Radio' justifies its own style and form, arguing for the short story that concentrates instead on one small incident or the travails of one ordinary man or woman, drawing out a single voice from the metropolitan cacophony and making it exemplary.

Other stories turn the desire to make connections in a city of hermetically housed individuals on its head. In 'Christmas is a Sad Season for the Poor', Charlie the elevator operator confesses his loneliness to anyone who will listen. Every one of his passengers hears of his sadness at being alone on Christmas Day. The more he relates it, however, the more he begins to embroider the truth; for example, he invents children he has not fathered. On Christmas Day itself, he receives presents from the inhabitants of the apartment building in which he works, including seasonal puddings, glasses of champagne, and toys for the imaginary children. Buoyed by a strange euphoria, he lets go of the elevator controls while a passenger is travelling. He subsequently loses his job and is filled with remorse. To atone, he decides to give the toys and trinkets to his miserable landlady and her three children; he offloads his guilt in a typical act of Christmas generosity. A reader unused to Cheever's resistance to easy moralising might imagine this to be the natural endpoint of the story. However, the landlady in turn sees that her children have too much, and also resolves to donate the items to someone more deserving; and so a chain of 'licentious benevolence' is initiated (p. 180). Throughout the story, Cheever knowingly plays with the reader's expectations of allegory, only to subvert them: 'Christmas is a Sad Season' resists the usual, potentially trite seasonal messages of goodwill and compassion for the poor, preferring to suggest that the connectivity we seek is often a way of offsetting or allaying guilt. The title is thus ironic; the truly poor are offstage in Cheever's story.

The Suburban Short Story

Cheever also takes his exploration of the guilty, isolated middle classes into suburbia, specifically that enclave so desired by the couple in 'The Enormous Radio': Westchester County. Westchester is a wealthy area bordering New York City. It also has a significant place in the history of the American short story, being the location of Tarrytown, in which Washington Irving's 'The Legend of Sleepy Hollow' is set. In Cheever's world, it might be Shady Hill or Bullet Park, but it is an archetype whose most easily identifiable features, from the wide lawn to the picket fence, are immediately familiar from a thousand teen movies, horror films, post-war novels and primetime drama series.

Such familiarity makes 'suburb' a loaded word. In 'The Housebreaker at Shady Hill', even to say it seems a bad omen; the narrator, Johnny Hake, sidesteps it carefully, instead referring to the eponymous neighbourhood as a *'banlieue'*, a French word he misguidedly believes to be equivalent.* This introduces a note of whimsy, as does the fact that Johnny initially works for a 'parablendeum' manufacturer. Parablendeum appears to be a kind of plastic wrapping, a Cheever coinage spoken of as if it were as ordinary as polystyrene or linoleum. The invention takes the story out of purely referential territory and more into allegory; indeed, the imaginary plastic suggests nothing so much as 'parable'. It is even symbolic to Johnny himself, who confides to the reader that he dreams of 'wrapping bread in coloured parablendeum Filmex' (p. 333). However suburban living might be geared towards the maintenance of social order and the continuation of the American nuclear family, it is really as driven by capitalist gusto as the city to which its inhabitants commute; its subconscious is commercialised.

Hake rebels against his surroundings by breaking into neighbours' houses in the middle of the night and stealing their wallets. That he should resort to petty crime for no apparent gain is appropriate not only to the spirit of Cheever's satire but also to the short story form more generally; it is a small event that gestures towards a much more all-encompassing anxiety about the emptiness of much material acquisition. Simultaneously, it is a crime completely commensurate with the time it takes to narrate. In a novel, its impulsiveness might be lost in a flood of psychological speculation, or else attract disproportionate consequences. The short story liberates Cheever from such consequences. His achievement is to make the crime seem flippant, and it is the apparent slightness of the form that enables it to be so.

The short story form is also a metaphor itself for the often hermetic claustrophobia of suburbia, as in 'The Wrysons' and 'The Worm in the

* Though the French word *banlieue* roughly translates as 'suburb', its connotations are quite different. Suburbia in the USA and the UK tends to describe middle-class, white-collar commuter territory, but the *banlieues* are nearer to what would be called the 'projects' in America: cheap or social housing.

Apple'. The Wrysons, also occupants of Shady Hill, are continually stalked by fear of the outside. They 'dread' any 'irregularity', continually fear 'a stranger at the gates', and their desire to 'preserve the character of the community' is not quite 'natural'. Like Johnny Hake, Irene Wryson dreams, but her subconscious is stalked by the nuclear threat. Her recurring nightmare is of waking up to find that a hydrogen bomb has been detonated in Shady Hill. As in 'The Enormous Radio', the Cold War looms constantly, but in 'The Wrysons', this bomb also dramatises the potentially implosive tensions that underlie suburbia's meticulous domestic maintenance. The story ends with Irene discovering her husband burning a cake in the kitchen. She mistakes the smell of cinder for bomb ash. Clearly, the trials of the suburban household are as traumatic as any grand international standoff; as a result, the story implodes on itself, ending not in progress but stasis as its characters are 'more mystified by life than ever, and more interested than ever in a good appearance' (p. 419).

'The Worm in the Apple', meanwhile, is a précis of the lives of another suburban couple so typical that they become grotesque. The narrative voice registers a deeply ironic incredulity at itself. The story appears to be narrated by a near neighbour who cannot quite believe that the Crutchmans exist: they 'were so very, very happy and so temperate in all their habits and so pleased with everything that came their way that one was bound to suspect a worm in their rosy apple' (p. 370). They are blatantly offered up as a case study, as the narrator by turns plays observer, critic and psychoanalyst. Helen has the 'pallor' of a nymphomaniac; Larry's tendency to garden bare-chested betrays 'a tendency to infantile exhibitionism'. The tone then changes to that of the sleuth: 'Why did they only have two children? Why not three or four? Was there perhaps some breakdown in their relationship after the birth of Tom?' (p. 371). The effect on the reader is disconcerting, as there is no room left for interpretation beyond the exegetic cross-questioning of the prose itself; all the while, the pronoun 'we' is used to include the reader, but the tone set by the narrator is almost that of a delivered demonstration or lecture. Racing through the upbringing of the Crutchmans' children, their education, relocation and marriages, the narrator writes that in their prime of life the couple 'might be expected to suffer the celebrated spiritual destitution of their age and their kind – the worm in the apple would at last be laid bare', but this does not surface; instead, as the last sentence tells us, through the 'prudence and shrewdness' of Helen's broker, 'they got richer and richer and richer and lived happily, happily, happily, happily' (p. 374). 'The Worm in the Apple' is the opposite of 'The Housebreaker of Shady Hill'. Where the latter concentrates the emptiness of suburbia into one major incident, the former charts it over an entire life: 'The Worm' is diachronic, while 'Housebreaker' is synchronic.* The contrast between the two stories exemplifies the range of Cheever's short fiction, forever working within the limitations of its form to assert itself as the only form for its subject.

The Loudest Voice: Grace Paley

Grace Paley (1922–2007) and John Cheever would apparently have little in common, either biographically or stylistically, yet Paley understands equally well as Cheever that compression is a major precondition of the effective short story. They also share a belief that the cacophonous multiplicity of New York can best be examined through the eyes and voices of its individuals. In Paley's case, it is the voices especially that motivate her short stories. When asked in a 1985 interview whether these voices follow from strains of people's speech in Paley's head, she replied, 'You've got it!', going on to say that 'I heard enough voices so that I could make my own out of them'.[10] They are often, like Paley's, female and Jewish; but their range over the three major collections she published, *The Little Disturbances of Man* (1959), *Enormous Changes at the Last Minute* (1974) and *Later the Same Day* (1985), is an impressive act of compression in itself.

'The Loudest Voice', from *The Little Disturbances of Man*, follows one character's journey from a bit-part in the polyphony of everyday

---

* The terms diachronic and synchronic are most commonly used in linguistics to denote different methods of studying a language. Diachronic study is that which takes a view over a long period of time, while synchronic study is that which takes its view from one particular time or place.

life to the discovery of her own individuality, her own 'voice'. Shirley Abramowitz knows she has a loud voice, but at first it competes with the chaotic noise around it, where 'dumbwaiters boom, doors slam, dishes crash' and 'every window is a mother's mouth bidding the street shut up'.[11] In this symphony of daily routines, it is difficult to distinguish individual sounds, something Paley describes with great economy, imagining the windows not to convey the sounds of mothers' mouths but to actually be them. The metonymic substitution here also suggests that noise even emanates from inanimate objects; it is in the very architecture of the neighbourhood.

Shirley is always being admonished for her noisiness, reading the flavours on the sides of Campbell's soup tins in the grocery store, or answering questions too boldly in the classroom. She must discover there is a time and a place for her booming and bawling, and it comes with the school's Christmas production. Having been tipped off by another teacher about Shirley's reading of a psalm in assembly, Mr Hilton asks her to narrate a part requiring 'stamina'. Her mother disapproves; she is disappointed that her child, and other Jewish pupils of the school, must celebrate a Christian festival, though her husband reminds her that this is America, and that Christmas is far less objectionable than subjection to the state-sponsored anti-Semitism they might find in other countries. After the production is over, Shirley concludes, 'My voice was certainly the loudest' (p. 41), a defiant reconfirmation of her physical vocal prowess that is also a figurative expression of a kind of Jewish empowerment within a predominantly Christian context. Nevertheless, its social value is ambiguous; the loudest voice is a mark of audibility, but whether this translates into political visibility is uncertain. Though its socio-cultural position differs from those in Cheever's work, Paley's metonymic facility is comparable; an ordinary and rather comical social mismatch ends up making a valuable point about community and assimilation.

The relationship between these literal and political 'voices' underpins many of Paley's stories. Everybody is 'noisy' in 'A Woman, Young and Old', also from *The Little Disturbances of Man*. The cacophony of the family acts out more general societal discord – 'wars, deception, broken homes, all the irremediableness of modern life' – on a domestic level (p. 14). 'Politics', from Paley's second collection, *Enormous Changes at the Last Minute*, makes more explicit connections between the personal and the political, inferring that in New York, the two are frequently one. The 'mothers from our neighbourhood' go down to the Board of Estimate to agitate for improved municipal playgrounds, and sing songs to tunes learnt in their mothers' kitchens. It is an act by which the domestic literally becomes the public, though any potential activist earnestness is kept in check by Paley's sense of mischief; the singer pleads for a perimeter fence because 'the Commies just walk in the gate / and put shit in the sand' (p. 226). The fence is erected, but soon violated when a policeman constructs a hole in it so that he might get to the baseball bats in the locker room. A female journalist happens to be nearby, and follows him in. She asks him what he is doing, and he replies that the New York police service, 'stripped of its power' by 'vengeful politicians', should arm itself by whatever means it can. The story ends with the policeman 'inject[ing] her with two sons, one Irish and one Italian, who sang to her in dialect all her life' (p. 227). Over and above the irony of the newly protected playground becoming a site of illicit sex, the ending of the story invests even this somewhat sordid encounter with a wider socio-political significance. Just like the women, the policeman is protesting, and this protest courses through him as he fathers the next generation. It is an apparently random act; the politics of people's so-called private lives surfaces without having to stage the threshold between private and public, as the women do. Most crucially, it then runs in the blood of future generations, whose voices or 'dialect[s]' continue the spirit of 'our moldy pot New York'.

The smallest and most spontaneous acts, be they 'little disturbances' or otherwise, therefore support the weight of past and future narratives. In 'Faith in the Afternoon', also from *Enormous Changes*, the narrator addresses an ambiguous 'you' in the opening paragraph. This links the subsequent introduction of young Faith (presented under her pillow at midnight trying to keep overactive thoughts of her 'antecedents' at bay) with the need to make history in the present so that future generations can learn from their forebears.

The narrator calls on the addressee as a fellow independent thinker of the Western Bloc to speak out now, for '[in] twenty years, give or take a spring, your grandchildren will be lying in sandboxes all over the world, their ears to the ground, listening for signals from long ago. In fact, kneeling now on the great plains in a snootful of gray dust, what do you hear? Pigs oinking, potatoes peeling, Indians running, winter coming?' (p. 150). This passage epitomises Paley's style, dancing between the breathless and the concise, between colloquial and florid registers, and placing the mundane and the grand narrative on an equal footing. It is immediately political; she reverses the Cold War rhetoric of the 'Eastern Bloc' and makes the West into a mirror image of the Soviet empire. It is also immediately on a grand geographical scale, invoking the Great Plains of America's Midwest. However, the sweep of the USA's historical narrative, suggested by the 'Indians running', goes side by side with the intimate and the ordinary, the sound of pigs in the barnyard and peelers in the kitchen. It is the short story itself, with its ability to mine the profounder implications of one single moment, which is being described here too. If attuned to the 'ground' correctly, the 'ears' of which Paley writes will be able to receive 'signals from long ago'; the smallest of gestures reveal the longest and grandest of histories.

Stories About Stories

The above passage from 'Faith in the Afternoon' also exemplifies another of Paley's traits: her short stories are often about the act of storytelling itself. The very first story in her published oeuvre, 'Goodbye and Good Luck', which opens *The Little Disturbances of Man*, is formed from Lillie's narration of her Aunt Rosa's account of her past life, working in the ticket office of a Broadway theatre. She meets and eventually marries an actor, Volodya Vlashkin, and after the twists and turns of this plot, encourages Lillie to 'tell this story to your mama from your young mouth', to 'tell her after all I'll have a husband, which, as everybody knows, a woman should have at least one before the end of the story' (p. 13). This knowing signoff really refers to readers' expectations of novels; it could be a paraphrase of the first line of Jane Austen's *Pride and Prejudice*, the 'truth universally acknowledged' that a man in possession of a fortune is in want of a good wife, the truth that the reader knows from the beginning will be reached by the novel's conclusion. It is amusing in this context precisely because a short story does *not* require such a teleology.[*]

'A Conversation with My Father', from *Enormous Changes*, expands on the self-conscious narrativity of 'Goodbye and Good Luck'. It features a writer figure whose aged father urges her to 'write a simple story just once more', a work of 'the kind Maupassant wrote, or Chekhov ... Just recognizable people and then write down what happened to them next.' She would like to try to do so, to write the kind of story that begins 'There was a woman...' followed by the plot, what she describes as 'the absolute line between two points which I've always despised. Not for literary reasons, but because it takes all hope away. Everyone, real or invented, deserves the open destiny of life' (p. 237). She tells her father a 'story' about a junkie who lives on her street, but he is dissatisfied. He complains that she has 'left everything out', a mistake that Turgenev or Chekhov would never make. He orders her to try again. She obliges, but with much elaboration; the boy no longer simply turns to heroin as a teenager, but rather falls 'into the fist of adolescence'. His mother falls prey to the same addiction, which causes her to cry 'terrible, face-scarring, time-consuming tears' (p. 241). These passages are deliberately overwritten, but her father relates to them, particularly after she closes her second attempt with 'The End'. She is being ironic, but her father recognises in this stark, if clichéd closure 'a tragedy. The end of a person'. The writer argues that it doesn't have to be the end; the character could overcome her dependency and become a social worker. Her father is not impressed, exclaiming 'Jokes ... As a writer that's your main trouble.' He then has the last word: 'Tragedy! You too. When will you look it in the face?' We realise that this is almost an anxious note-to-self on Paley's part – that

---

[*] To read 'teleologically' is to read always in the knowledge or desire of the final end of a work.

'A Conversation with My Father' actually gives us the prospect of Paley herself telling a story twice in order to put off staring down the tragedy of which the father speaks. Storytelling is a form of deferment, after all, a way of filling time, and Paley is acutely conscious of this fundamental human need.

Later stories, particularly those in *Later the Same Day*, are less meta-textual, though their titles ('The Story Hearer', 'This is a Story about My Friend George, The Toy Inventor', 'Zagrowsky Tells') still place the act of storytelling at the top of the agenda. The very last story in *Later the Same Day*, indeed in *The Collected Stories*, is called 'Listening'. It appears to be a conclusion to some of the other stories featuring the recurring 'Faith' character who becomes a writer herself across Paley's collections, but it ends with Faith's friend Cassie's incredulity that she has been left out of her stories. 'Why have you left me out of everybody's life?' she asks (p. 398). Faith realises her error, and asks forgiveness. Cassie's response brings the story to a close: 'From now on, I'll watch you like a hawk. I do not forgive you.' It would seem that Paley registers doubt at the short story's inclusive capabilities in 'Listening', but really this conclusion is a mission statement too. It is a reminder to the writer to keep 'listening', to keep her ear close to the ground as Paley has Faith do in her first featured story. Out of all the voices that populate Paley's work, the reader's emerges as strongly as any; they too are part of the ongoing story of New York.

Seeing the Smallest Things: Raymond Carver

In the earlier work of Raymond Carver (1938–88), it seems both the reader and the writer are largely absent. Objects and people simply exist; the prose that represents them, then, is stripped of all possible excess. This style came to be known in the 1980s as 'dirty realism', and along with writers such as Frederick Barthelme (1943–) and Tobias Wolff (1945–), Carver was seen as one of its chief exponents. His essay, 'On Writing' makes a strong case for the minimalist approach. He affirms that 'it's possible, in a poem or a short story, to write about commonplace things and objects using commonplace but precise language, and to endow those things – a chair, a window curtain, a fork, a stone, a woman's earring – with immense, even startling power'.[12] This suggests a highly symbolic imagination, but in many of the early stories especially, the opposite is true; they actively resist metaphor. 'The Father', which is barely two pages long, satirises the human tendency to read meanings into objects that are merely projections of desire. Phyllis, Carol and Alice have a new baby brother. They coo over him, and insist on asking 'Who does he look like?' The grandmother maintains he has 'his grandfather's lips', but the mother disagrees. Phyllis then suggests that 'he doesn't look like anybody', only for Carol to burst out that 'he looks like *Daddy*!'[13] This would appear to be the answer, but it only leads to the next stage in a chain of enquiry: 'But who does Daddy *look* like?' Phyllis believes he '*has*' to look like somebody, but the story ends, 'He had turned around in his chair and his face was white and without expression' (p. 34). Carver's story suggests that relentlessly searching for likeness, connection or meaning is most likely to be met with absence or blankness; or even, in this case, with something slightly sinister or ghoulish.

Other stories from Carver's first collection, *Will You Please Be Quiet, Please?* (1976), see the potential for philosophical enquiry submerged under the banal absurdity of everyday life. 'Collectors' features a door-to-door salesman and his customer. In a comical scenario, Aubrey Bell, the salesman, attempts to demonstrate a vacuum cleaner to a nonplussed narrator. Bell is desperate to talk, particularly to relay facts about writers and artists. He spies the narrator staring at the indoor slippers he dons as he steps out of the rain and into the house, and remarks that 'W. H. Auden wore slippers all through China on his first visit there. Never took them off. Corns' (p. 79). Later, the narrator recounts Bell's patter: 'Rilke lived in one castle after another, all of his adult life. Benefactors, he said loudly over the hum of the vacuum' (p. 81). His attitude to vacuuming also appears to be rather metaphysical. Over the hum of his appliance, he declaims,

Every day, every night of our lives, we're leaving little bits of ourselves, flakes of this and that, behind. Where do they go, these bits and pieces of ourselves? Right through the sheets and into the mattress, *that's* where! (p. 80)

What would appear to be an acute moment of existential perception is actually a medium of selling consumer goods; the sublime and the ridiculous meet in one almost tragicomic moment. The vacuum cleaner is what it is, nothing more; it is almost a literal object of 'dirty realism', sucking up dust and resisting Bell's attempts to philosophise it.

In 'I Could See the Smallest Things', from Carver's second collection, *What We Talk About When We Talk About Love* (1981), Nancy suffers from insomnia. Her husband, Cliff, prevents her from sleeping: his 'breathing [is] awful to listen to' and he takes up most of the bed (p. 240). She goes out into the moonlight, and encounters her next-door neighbour, Sam, in his garden with a flashlight, trying to exterminate slugs. They are minute, commonplace things; one of life's niggling little problems. Nancy thinks nothing of it, until she gets back to bed. She gives Cliff 'a little shake' and he clears his throat, whereupon 'something caught and dribbled in his chest' (p. 243). She notes that 'it made me think of those things that Sam Lawton was dumping powder on'; she is about to connect her husband's phlegm to the writhing of lowlife invertebrates. This is the first point in the story in which metaphor seems possible. As Nancy puts it, 'I thought for a minute of the world outside my house'; she is about to understand the minutiae of her life on a more universal or allegorical level. But then immediately, she concludes that 'then I didn't have any more thoughts except the thought that I had to hurry up and sleep'. The slugs have been significant in the moment, but not epiphanic. Carver's approach here follows the maxim of the British short-story writer V. S. Pritchett, whom he quotes with admiration in the 'Author's Note to *Where I'm Calling From*' (1988): 'V. S. Pritchett's definition of a short story is "something glimpsed from the corner of the eye, in passing". First the glimpse. Then the glimpse given life, turned into something that will illuminate the moment and just maybe lock it indelibly into the reader's consciousness. Make it a part of the reader's own experience, as Hemingway so nicely put it' (p. 748).

Under the Surface

The slugs also play out Carver's fascination with the currents of darkness under the suburban veneer. A fascination not unlike that of Cheever. As he explains in 'On Writing', 'I like it when there is some feeling of threat or sense of menace in short stories ... the things that are left out, that are implied, the landscape just under the smooth (but sometimes broken and unsettled) surface of things' (p. 732). Some of his most famous stories engage with this threat directly and playfully; a good example is the conclusion of 'Tell the Women We're Going', which sees two female cyclists murdered by the protagonist after a suburban barbecue. Many of his stories also deal with the sexual peccadilloes of suburban families. Transvestite husbands ('Neighbors'), compulsively masturbating teenagers ('Nobody Said Anything'), and couples discussing violent sexual undercurrents with candour ('What We Talk About When We Talk About Love') seem familiar from the work of other bards of suburbia, such as John Updike and Rick Moody. However, the economy with which Carver describes them does not suggest dysfunction, but ordinariness; he turns the subversion of suburban mores back in on itself.

One of the devices he returns to intermittently is to have his characters indulge in acts of voyeurism, which has the effect of making the character who is the viewer as unsettling as the viewed, if not more so. In 'The Idea', Carver sets up a whole community of peeping Toms. The story focuses on a couple, Vern and his unnamed wife, who crouch below their windowsill in order to spy on their neighbour; the neighbour in turn walks out onto his back porch at a certain time every night so that he might catch a particular woman undressing at her window. 'Someday I'm going to tell that trash what I think of her', Vern's wife avows (p. 15). This projection into the future, of course, does not happen in the story; the reader is only subjected to the resolution to do something about the apparently exhibitionistic woman, for whom Vern's wife 'use[s] even worse language, things I can't repeat' (p. 17). The story exemplifies the 'glimpse' of which Carver writes in his 'Author's Note', and it reminds us that there is perhaps something voyeuristic about all his short stories.

This is dramatised self-reflexively in 'Viewfinder', which begins with a typical juxtaposition of the ordinary and the eccentric: 'A man without hands came to the door to sell me a photograph of my house. Except for the chrome hooks, he was an ordinary-looking man of fifty or so' (p. 228). This man takes Polaroid snaps in the street, then tries to sell the customer images of his or her own house.* The narrator watches him taking the photographs, in an act of mutual spying, then the Polaroid man offers the image to the narrator, who is startled to discover his own head, '*my head*, in there inside the kitchen window'. There is no privacy in this world of cold callers and commercialists. The narrator decides to make this work for him, and asks the photographer to 'sympathize' with him fully by capturing him in a staged moment of abandonment. They set up a scene in which the narrator climbs onto his own roof, whereupon he discovers some rocks that have been lobbed by juveniles. He begins to throw the rocks in a kind of primal ritual. The photographer protests that he doesn't do 'motion shots', but the narrator is oblivious; being the subject of voyeurism has turned him into an exhibitionist.

The power of the momentary 'glimpse', then, can unleash the primal forces that the orderliness of suburbia tries to sublimate. However, not all of Carver's stories depend on these devices. One of his most affecting, 'Cathedral', from the collection of the same name (1983), asks how we might perceive everyday objects without the power of sight. The narrator is initially jealous of his wife's friendship with a blind man, Robert, who comes to stay one evening on his way to a family gathering. His remarks are petty and prejudiced:

---

* The Polaroid Corporation produced instamatic cameras from 1947 to 2008. The film self-developed and the camera printed the photograph within minutes.

> I wasn't enthusiastic about his visit. He was no one I knew. And his being blind bothered me. My idea of blindness came from the movies. In the movies, the blind moved slowly and never laughed. Sometimes they were led by seeing-eye dogs. A blind man in my house was not something I looked forward to. (p. 514)

However, once they have eaten, and smoked a little cannabis, and his wife has fallen asleep on the sofa, the narrator begins to warm to Robert. They watch a programme about cathedrals on television. Robert then asks the narrator to describe the cathedrals to him, but his version seems inadequate; thus, in a literal act of the 'blind leading the blind', Robert clutches the narrator's hand as he draws a cathedral on paper, so that he can follow its lines and features. This act of re-seeing the world is complete when the narrator closes his eyes on finishing the drawing. He finds it liberating, as he explains to the reader: 'My eyes were still closed. I was in my house. I knew that. But I didn't feel like I was inside anything' (p. 529). Paradoxically, simulating blindness is an eye-opener for him; it releases him from the confines of his walled and bordered suburban space, and from the sometimes suspicious relationship between the watcher and the watched, a relationship with which much of Carver's fiction concerns itself. He has done little more than draw a church on a scrap of A4; but that small act changes the entire atmosphere of the house. It is a tiny creative step that opens up a world, much as the smallest gestures and most concise descriptions of them in the work of Cheever, Paley and Carver signify grander narratives without writing them.

Extended Commentary: Cheever, 'The Swimmer' (1964)

Like many of Cheever's short stories, 'The Swimmer' was first published in *The New Yorker*. It then reappeared in the 1964 collection, *The Brigadier and the Golf Widow*. Many believe it to be the very epitome of Cheever's art, and consequently it is often regarded as one of the most important of all American short stories. In the words of the *New York Times* critic A. O. Scott, 'no sprawling, anguished epic of marital unhappiness or suburban malaise can match [its] insight and elegance'.[14] At barely twelve pages long, it is not so much a vignette as a novel in miniature, as trenchant and complex a diagnosis of suburban malaise as anything by Updike or Franzen. Compressing a whole life into one ongoing incident on a particular day, 'The Swimmer' initially seems fairly realistic, but as it unravels, it becomes more and more allegorical. By the end, it seems almost fully mythical; a poignant example of the elusiveness and illusiveness of contentment in suburban America, and ample evidence, if any were needed, that the short story can cover diverse generic ground without compromising its concision.

Cheever's story is immediately both universal and particular, a key duality in much of his work. The opening paragraph is a perfect example: 'It was one of those midsummer Sundays when everyone sits around saying, "I *drank* too much last night"', writes Cheever, before fleshing out his 'everyone' with a roll-call of individuals: Donald Westerhazy, Lucinda Merrill, Helen Westerhazy. He imagines that his readers have experienced these circumstances; 'one of those midsummer Sundays' implies that such weekend mornings are instantly recognisable, to the degree that he can speak of them in an almost clichéd narrative voice. 'The Swimmer', then, is both about poolside suburbanites and for them; the Westerhazys and Lucinda Merrill are avatars of the reader, and indeed they will turn out to be a bit-part audience to the behavioural quirks of Neddy Merrill, the protagonist.

The reader knows very little of Neddy Merrill except that he lives in Bullet Park (the scene of Cheever's novel of the same name), is married to Lucinda and has four daughters. From the outset he appears to be an exuberant optimist, pictured sliding down banisters and taking delight in even the most basic of human activities; he breathes 'as if he could gulp into his lungs the components of that moment, the heat of the sun, the intenseness of his pleasure' (pp. 776–7). He decides to find his way home by swimming a length in each of his neighbours' pools, to a distance of a few miles, and the novelty of the adventure whets his senses. Responding to his immediate environment with such pin-sharp perspicacity that his perception is almost visionary, he applies the eye of the pioneer to suburbia:

> He seemed to see, with a cartographer's eye, that string of swimming pools, that quasi-subterranean stream that curved across the county. He had made a discovery, a contribution to modern geography; he would name the stream Lucinda after his wife. (p. 777)

Like many of Cheever's characters, Neddy attempts to regain a kind of innocence in an overdeveloped human landscape that has been corrupted by materialist desire. The domestic swimming pool epitomises suburban artifice; it is a replica of nature regulated to strict measurements. Neddy wants to be free of such regularity. He yearns for a space still unmapped, on which he can imprint himself through the act of calling the 'stream' Lucinda; it is a classic American desire for the prelapsarian, pre-colonial New World, with Neddy as a 1960s Adam naming the features and creatures of his Eden.[*]

When Neddy announces at the Westerhazys' pool party that he is about to swim 'home', he is referring not only to his own house, but also to a point of geographical and temporal origination. 'Home' also denotes a kind of sporting victory, as in the 'home run' of a baseball match, and Neddy not only visualises himself as 'a pilgrim, an explorer, a man with a destiny' but also an athlete whose 'friends would line the banks of the Lucinda River' (p. 778). This is a good example of how a short story can work on both an immediate, real-time level (the sense almost of a race against the clock) and allegorically, gesturing towards grander narratives of national self-realisation. 'Home', as ever in American literature, is heavily invested with often contradictory meanings. It is a set of fashionable furnishings, but also a set of values; it is a clearly demarcated, walled and bordered space, as measured by the hedges Neddy must traverse in order to travel from one family residence to another, and yet it is also a word for America itself, expanding to absorb multiple interpretations of the nation.

---

[*] In *Genesis* 2: 19–20, Adam is called upon by God to name the animals around him.

At first, Neddy's swims are invigorating, and the people he meets on them are receptive and generous. However, the story darkens as it progresses. After taking shelter during a thunderstorm in the Levys' gazebo, Neddy resumes his watercourse, but he begins to encounter emptiness and absence. He is surprised to find the Lindleys' riding ring overgrown, its jumps dismantled. At this point, his previously acute senses lose their power and accuracy. He remembers hearing something about the Lindleys' horses, but the 'memory was unclear' (p. 781). The Welchers' house, meanwhile, shows every sign of them having left for good; garden furniture is stacked, and visitors are greeted by a 'for sale' sign. Neddy can barely believe this evidence; he thinks he only got a party invitation from them a week or so ago. The character's memory is playing tricks on him.

His journey into innocence takes a wrong turn from here too. He is left, rather humiliatingly, in a near-naked state at a Route 424 junction, whereupon passengers hurl verbal abuse and beer cans from their cars. He is not so much man before the Fall as a man before his own fall. Cheever momentarily separates the character of Neddy from the metaphor of him; he even recalls the reader directly, musing that 'had you gone for a Sunday afternoon ride that day you might have seen him' (p. 781). Then, the free indirect discourse becomes a meta-commentary on the trajectory of 'The Swimmer' itself: 'At what point had this prank, this joke, this piece of horseplay become serious?' (p. 782) appears to be one of several questions Neddy asks himself, but Cheever might be asking it of his own writing process. The sureties of suburban life become all the more warped as Neddy enters the public pool, here depicted as a kind of pseudo-fascistic nightmare in which prohibitions are printed in capital letters, lungs are overwhelmed by chlorine, and 'a pair of lifeguards in a pair of towers' blow police whistles and 'abused the swimmers through a public address system' (p. 782). He is routed out of the pool for failing to display an identification disk; at the height of the Cold War, Middle America could almost be a Soviet outpost. As he inches closer to the 'home' he plans to reach, he is taken ever further away from the ideals and values that created America in the first place.

By the time he reaches the Biswangers, all the talk is of money; even when he finds himself at the house of his sometime mistress, Shirley, she presumes he has come to extort cash from her.

Ultimately, it is the hollowness at the heart of materialist, capitalist America towards which Neddy has been swimming. He reaches his own house, knowing that 'he had swum the county, but he was so stupefied with exhaustion that his triumph seemed vague' (p. 788). He emerges as the downtrodden Everyman, recognisable from countless American novels, plays and films, who has sacrificed his sanity and health for the sake of keeping face among his fellow suburbanites. His eccentric wish to swim through the neighbourhood may be a resistant expression of individuality, but any race against personal targets is subsumed by the rat race. He arrives at his front door to find that nobody is home; more agonisingly, he is locked out. The America that was meant to offer opportunity to all has delivered a decisive interdiction; it is boarded up, out of bounds. 'The Swimmer' is masterly in compressing this verdict into the space of a single afternoon, but its claim to be exemplary of the best of Cheever's art, and of the short story as a genre, goes even further. Neddy's home, locked and broken, resembles the type of haunted house that might feature in one of Edgar Allan Poe's *Tales of Mystery and Imagination* – the House of Usher, perhaps. Poe's stories are among the first great American examples of the form; Cheever takes the reader full circle, suggesting that there was never an innocent time before, only an America of corruption and barely concealed horror. It would seem that in the universe of the short story, it was ever thus.

Notes

1   Vladimir Nabokov, 'Inspiration', *Saturday Review of the Arts* 1 (January 1973), p. 32.
2   Brander Matthews, *The Philosophy of the Short-story* (New York: Longmans, Green, and Co., 1901), p. 49.
3   See Andrew Levy, *The Culture and Commerce of the American Short Story* (Cambridge: Cambridge University Press, 1993), p. 1.

4   Tobias Wolff, Introduction, *The Picador Book of Contemporary American Stories*, ed. Wolff (London: Picador, 1993), p. viii.
5   Quoted from private correspondence by William Peden in Peden, *The American Short Story: Front Line in the National Defense of Literature* (Boston: Houghton Mifflin, 1964), p. 21.
6   Peden, *The American Short Story*, pp. 5–8.
7   Sherwood Anderson, *Winesburg, Ohio* (Oxford: Oxford University Press, 1999), pp. 7–10.
8   Quoted in Scott Donaldson, *John Cheever: A Biography* (New York: Random House, 1988), p. 323.
9   John Cheever, *The Stories of John Cheever* (London: Vintage, 1990), pp. 181–92 (185).
10   Peter Marchant et al., 'A Conversation with Grace Paley', *The Massachusetts Review* 26:4 (Winter 1985), pp. 606–14 (607).
11   Grace Paley, *The Collected Stories* (London: Virago, 1998), pp. 35–41 (35).
12   Raymond Carver, 'On Writing', *Collected Stories*, ed. William L. Stull and Maureen P. Carroll (New York: Library of America, 2009), pp. 728–33 (730).
13   Carver, *Collected Stories*, p. 34.
14   A. O. Scott, 'Brevity's Pull: In Praise of the American Short Story', *New York Times*, 4 April, 2009.

The American Stage: O'Neill, Williams and Miller

In December 1936, Eugene O'Neill was awarded the Nobel Prize for literature. He saw his international accolade as a watershed in the history of American letters: in his words, 'this highest of distinctions is all the more grateful to me because I feel so deeply that it is not only my work which is being honored, but the work of all my colleagues in America – that this Nobel Prize is a symbol of the recognition by Europe of the coming-of-age of the American theatre.'[1] O'Neill's statement sums up the position of American drama in the first third of the twentieth century. By the 1930s, a poetic tradition was well-established, and there were already scores of internationally regarded American novels, but few plays had made any lasting impact. Dramatic activity was looked upon with some suspicion in the nineteenth century, one of the many legacies of Puritanism.* The most popular forms of drama – vaudeville and melodrama, for example – generally adhered to stylised formulae, and more literary plays performed in American theatres were usually adaptations or productions of European classics. While many writers emphasised the importance of poetry and prose in the construction of a national literary heritage, few saw a thriving theatrical culture as a vital element of that heritage. Those who did lamented the lack, seeing the paucity of good theatre as symptomatic of an incomplete civilisation. In 1833, William Dunlap,

---

* For an overview of these legacies, see Part Two: 'A Cultural Overview'.

one of the few pre-twentieth-century American playwrights to find acclaim, proposed that 'the rise, progress and cultivation of the drama mark the progress of refinement and the state of manners at any given time and in any country.'[2] It would take another hundred years, and O'Neill's Nobel address, for American theatre to voice confidence in its own direction and significance.

Eugene O'Neill in Context

It is possible to read O'Neill's progress as metonymic of the emergence of American theatre as an international force. His father, James, was an Irish-American actor who found fame playing the eponymous character in a stage adaptation of Alexandre Dumas's *The Count of Monte Cristo*. He performed the role thousands of times, but his son disapproved of what he saw as artistic integrity compromised for financial gain. The emergence of O'Neill's own talent thus marked a rebellion against American populism, and a decisive statement of serious artistic intent. To this end, he had much in common with other newly emerging American dramatists of the 1910s and 1920s, such as Susan Glaspell (1876–1948) and Paul Green (1894–1981). Glaspell in particular played a crucial role in O'Neill's own career. She was a founder member of the Provincetown Players, a group of writers and performers who first assembled in July 1915. Though the Players only held two seasons in Provincetown (1915–16) before transferring to New York, their name carried echoes of the vanguard and the pioneer; Provincetown, at the very tip of Cape Cod, was the first port reached by the Pilgrim Fathers in 1620, and though they did not settle there permanently, they did stay long enough to sign the Mayflower Compact, their first governing document. The parallels are acute: the Provincetown Players were the Pilgrim Fathers of the American stage, and they gave Eugene O'Neill the vital platform to make the case for both himself and American drama as a whole.

O'Neill went on to write some fifty plays, establishing himself as the de facto father of modern American drama. His reputation abroad was, and arguably still is, almost greater than in the USA. He is especially popular in Scandinavia, a reflection, perhaps, of the often overt influence of dramatists such as Henrik Ibsen (1828–1906) and August Strindberg (1849–1912). One of his most significant achievements is the way in which he infuses these older European models with a new American voice. To date he remains the only American playwright to win the Nobel Prize. However, critical assessment of O'Neill's work has been shifting and complex, not least because of the scope of its ambition to establish a new American dramatic tradition. Its self-conscious literariness has sometimes been perceived as both a strength and a weakness, and to an extent this duality continued through the course of American drama in the twentieth century.

Page and Stage

Most of O'Neill's earliest plays were one-act pieces. By the time he joined the Provincetown Players, he had already self-financed the publication of five in a 1914 omnibus edition, *Thirst, and Other One-Act Plays*. Many of these works were set at sea, on passenger steamers, or were concerned with the lives of marine captains and their families, drawing on O'Neill's own post-Princeton experience as a vagabond seaman.[*]

The first O'Neill play to be performed by the Provincetown Players was *Bound East for Cardiff* (1915), set on the British ship, *SS Glencairn*. Even at this early stage, many of what would emerge as O'Neill's most recognisable traits and techniques can be identified in the play. For example, Yank's morbid concern with his own death reverberates through most of O'Neill's best-known works. *Bound East* also introduces some characteristic dramatic devices. The seamen speak in various vernaculars, establishing the play's claims to social realism: Driscoll the Irishman is given Celtic vowels, while Scotty

---

[*] O'Neill enrolled at Princeton in 1906, but was expelled after a year. For several years, he embarked on various sea voyages as a jobbing sailor, living a somewhat disorderly and drunken life in various ports across the world, before attempting suicide in 1912. It was only on contracting tuberculosis and being admitted to a sanatorium later in 1912 that he began to read and write plays.

pronounces Cardiff 'Carrdiff'. The action is also preceded by detailed stage directions, outlining every object on stage and even calling for '*clammy perspiration*' on Yank's forehead (p. 187). Both of these techniques are designed to make the play more immediate, more vital than the formulaic conventions of nineteenth-century American drama would have allowed, but they also create their own questions and problems. Readers of Hardy or Dickens novels might well be used to the inclusion of dialect words and the phonetic representation of accents, but in fiction such devices are a useful component of the realist mode. In theatre, however, the text must go through extra processes of interpretation before it reaches the audience. Directors and actors must re-imagine and reconstruct the script; the necessity of an extra 'r' in Cardiff is perhaps questionable. Similarly, O'Neill's copious stage directions and character descriptions unsettle the play's relationship to the theatre and its audiences. In a work of fiction, clammy beads of sweat might be a necessary indication of a character's anxiety, but on stage they can only be visible to a tiny proportion of the audience, even if performed to O'Neill's exact specification.

These are examples of the gap between the two 'texts' that make up any dramatic work, as outlined by the Polish philosopher of aesthetics Roman Ingarden (1893–1970). In his 1931 book, *The Literary Work of Art*, Ingarden makes a distinction between the *haupttext*, that which the audience experiences during a live theatre performance, and the *nebentext*, comprising the published parts of the play that are not meant to be spoken, such as lists of dramatis personae and stage directions.[3] In Shakespeare, for example, there is virtually no *nebentext*; except for indications of character entrances and exits, an uncut production of *King Lear* is almost identical to the play as printed. By contrast, the *nebentext* and *haupttext* in many of O'Neill's works are radically different, creating a considerable discrepancy between page and stage. Some critics have read this as a 'novelistic' tendency, arguing that O'Neill's plays test the generic limits of dramatic literature.[4] Others have even branded them 'antitheatrical',[5] a term O'Neill himself would not necessarily have shunned, not being an avid theatregoer himself.

Notwithstanding the question of whether 'novelistic' tendencies imperil the dramatic form or extend its possibilities, the gaps between the written text and performed text in O'Neill's plays express one of his central thematic concerns, the interface between the public and the private, inside and outside. O'Neill's work is often preoccupied with these issues on both a local and a national level, and in his best work, he uses the structure of his plays analogically and allegorically, suggesting that the contradictions and limits of dramatic form might comment upon the inherent dichotomies and boundaries of American experience.

Staging the Psyche

As O'Neill said in a 1946 interview, 'instead of being the most successful country in the world, [America] is the biggest failure', because 'its main idea is that everlasting game of trying to possess your own soul by the possession of something outside of it, thereby losing your own soul and the thing outside of it, too'.[6] The crisis of American experience, then, would appear to be a fatal trade-off between the possibility of self-possession and the pursuit of material gain so associated with Western capitalism. It is a fatal malfunction in the relationship between inner and outer, between the domestic sphere and the big, modern, acquisitive society that lies beyond it. This is a familiar motif across all genres of American literature, but O'Neill shows that drama can be more effective than poetry or prose in communicating it, because it can actually stage the threshold between the public and the private. In one of his earliest successes, *The Emperor Jones* (1920), O'Neill charts the decline of an African-American fugitive, Brutus Jones, who settles on a Caribbean island and proclaims himself its emperor. Rebels stalk him through the play's eight scenes, waiting to kill him with a silver bullet. While the two outermost scenes concern the observations of a Cockney trader, Smithers, the central six are Jones's monologues. They present the audience with the doomed emperor talking to himself as he escapes into the dark of the forest, which symbolically represents his retreat into the recesses of his own consciousness. This is a mark of the play's expressionism; that is, its distortion of the physical conditions of the outer world in order to portray the conflicts of the inner soul or consciousness. The drum tattoos of the rebellious natives further dramatise the difficulty of separating the inner soul from outside threat. They gain volume and pace as the play goes on, coming to represent Jones's own increasing heart-rate as anxiety impedes his progress; when the internal beat coalesces with the external, the game is up.

Strange Interlude (1928) carries the tensions between the inner soul and public persona even further, perhaps to their extreme. It met with controversy on hitting Broadway, partly for its portrayal of adultery and abortion, but in the main because of its length: nine acts and over four hours of performance time, not counting intervals. Its length is a consequence of O'Neill's application of the recent modernist techniques more widely found in fiction of the 1910s and 1920s, in particular the experiments of James Joyce's *Ulysses* (1922), a novel the playwright greatly admired. The modernist fiction of Joyce (1882–1941), Marcel Proust (1871–1922) and Virginia Woolf (1882–1941), among others, often uses interior monologue or the 'stream of consciousness' to convey the innermost thoughts and feelings of characters, and in *Strange Interlude*, O'Neill experiments with these techniques on stage. In the very first scene, we encounter the novelist Charles Marsden in the library of Professor Leeds, ruminating aloud:

> He hasn't added one book in years ... how old was I when I first came here? ... six ... with my father ... father ... how dim his face has grown! ... he wanted to speak to me before he died ... the hospital ... smell of iodoform in the cool halls.[7]

O'Neill collapses the *nebentext* into the *haupttext* here. Thought processes that would usually go unexplored or else be included in detailed stage directions find themselves staged and voiced, as characters speak their lines to each other then comment upon their own actions in lengthy asides. Public and private personae are thus both represented in the public space of the playhouse, but at the risk of a paradox: the more O'Neill writes his characters' unconscious into their script, the less representative of it his play becomes. To paraphrase his own thoughts on the American soul, he reaches for both the consciousness itself and that which might express it, thereby losing both. *Strange Interlude*'s main protagonist, Nina, has an early epiphany: 'Say lie – ... L-i-i-e! Now say life. L-i-i-f-e! You see! Life is just a long drawn out lie with a sniffling sigh at the end' (p. 668). She addresses this to Marsden the novelist, arguing that he probably knows this already as someone who works 'with words'. In *Strange Interlude*, O'Neill tests words to their very limits, and in many ways proves that theatre is ill-equipped to match the great novels of the period, such as *The Sound and the Fury* or *Mrs Dalloway*, as a modernist expression of the life of the mind.

Theatre as Synecdoche

Strange Interlude envisages the theatre as a space in which it is possible to turn the inner outward, to make the private public. In later O'Neill plays, however, the converse is more prevalent. The stage becomes a synecdoche for the spaces beyond it, representing the breadth of American society as O'Neill understands it. He sees the USA as a failure, doomed to repeat its mistakes in a cycle of diminishing returns. This applies especially to the plays *The Iceman Cometh* (1946), *Hughie* (written in 1941, premiered in 1959), and *Long Day's Journey into Night* (written in 1941, premiered in 1956), which is analysed in greater detail at the end of this chapter. *Hughie* is a return to the one-act play, though it is unique in O'Neill's oeuvre in that there are only two characters, the 'Broadway sport' and 'Wise Guy' Erie, a 'cynical oracle of the One True Grapevine',[8] and the unnamed Night Clerk in the West Side hotel he patronises, whose role is to listen to and punctuate Erie's long monologues about his crooked past. Though the majority of the play comprises Erie's recollections, it is strongly suggested that his late-night anecdotes are merely an oft-repeated routine in a cycle of venality. To him, life is a 'racket' (p. 848), and every room a makeshift casino. All through the play, Erie talks with affection of the old night porter, Hughie, and the card-games he played with him, but by the end of the play it is clear as Erie rolls out the dice that the new night clerk will become the next Hughie, in the latest version of the salesman–punter dynamic at the heart of American relationships. The play anticipates some of the European dramas of the 1950s and 1960s, particularly those of Samuel Beckett (1906–89), whose plays use the theatre in a similarly claustrophobic way, and, like this late O'Neill play, offer no closure.*

This is even truer of *The Iceman Cometh*. It takes place entirely in Harry Hope's saloon bar, ironically named given that its motley patrons are hopeless causes. They await the arrival of their friend Hickey, who they believe will relieve the tedium of repetitive spats and drinking bouts. The characters hail from radically different backgrounds. There is an African-American ex-gaming house proprietor, an alumnus of Harvard Law School, an English ex-army officer; such variety would appear to represent the full complement of American social groups, but O'Neill shows the utopian dream of the diverse nation descending into alcoholism and idleness. The strong implication here is that America itself has become a saloon full of no-hopers. But it has also become a theatre. The characters know that they suspend reality by shutting themselves away from the city outside, but it is a space in which they can indulge their escapist 'pipe dreams': they choose to live within a fiction. When the long-awaited travelling salesman Hickey returns, he is a changed man. No longer a drunken dropout, he now advocates a life of self-belief and apparent asceticism with evangelical zeal. He uses Hope's barroom as a stage from which to preach to his begrudging disciples; he is almost messianic, promising that a better world lies outside its walls. In Act III, some of the characters attempt to quit Hope's, and walk through the saloon doors into the light, but their time outside is brief. Rocky excitedly observes, 'Jees, Harry's startin' across de street!' but then quickly notices him boomeranging back in panic.[9] Hope breathlessly relates his street trauma, which turns out to be a run-in with an 'automobile'; it is almost as if he has never encountered one before. These scenes are a comical, ironic take on the deterioration of the American belief in Manifest Destiny;† the bar-bums are a grotesque of the original founding fathers, as the pioneering spirit is reduced to nervous forays

---

* *Hughie* might especially anticipate Beckett's *Waiting for Godot* (1953) and *Endgame* (1957).

† For an outline of the concept of Manifest Destiny, see Part Two: 'A Cultural Overview'.

into downtown side-streets. Here, more than at any other time, the saloon bar becomes a synecdoche of the theatre itself. O'Neill does not represent any world external to the barroom: to go outside is to go offstage. The characters inside briefly become an audience to the actions of those outside, but it is impossible to make a stage beyond the stage. This increases the discomfort of an audience co-opted into the idle world of *The Iceman Cometh*'s characters: the trapped watch the trapped. O'Neill has indeed invented a new kind of American theatre, one which reverses many of the tropes of nineteenth-century US political rhetoric and poetry and twentieth-century fiction by introducing a strain of peculiarly American claustrophobia. Out of the literary genres, it is drama that can most competently express how the freedoms beyond the front door might actually be as oppressive as the inner life behind the facade.

Tennessee Williams and the Fourth Wall

The plays of Tennessee Williams (1911–83) would initially appear to have little in common with those of O'Neill. They are often unabashedly lyrical where O'Neill has only 'a touch of the poet', to quote the title of one of his plays. With the exception of *The Glass Menagerie* (1944) and *Camino Real* (1953), most of Williams's major plays refrain from experimental modes.* Nevertheless, he too is fascinated by the interplay between public and private personae, and the limits of drama's capabilities in representing it. Deception is a key concern. As Brick says in *Cat on a Hot Tin Roof* (1955), 'Mendacity is a system that we live in. Liquor is one way out an' death's the other';[10] it is a line that could easily have found its way into *The Iceman Cometh*. But deception is something that Williams recognises as highly necessary within theatre. The character of Tom Wingfield in *The Glass Menagerie* states, 'I am the opposite of a stage magician. He gives you illusion that has the appearance of truth.

* Much of his later work was experimental, incorporating elements of Bertolt Brecht's 'alienation' technique and Japanese Noh and Kabuki theatre. Some of these seldom-produced late plays have been collected, with a helpful introduction, in Annette J. Saddik, ed., *The Traveling Companion and Other Plays* (New York: New Directions, 2008).

I give you truth in the pleasant disguise of illusion.'[11] With his frail sister, dull job in a shoe factory and poetic aspirations, Tom is Williams's most autobiographical creation, and thus it is possible to read a statement of the playwright's own intent in the words of his avatar.* The truest drama is that which never loses sight of its own theatricality; much as the fool Touchstone puts it in Shakespeare's *As You Like It*, 'the truest poetry is the most feigning.'[12] Self-deception, then, might be the consequence of a failure to acknowledge or understand that all public identities are a type of performance.

However, if all public identities are performed to some degree, then the distinction between public and private can all too easily blur. Is there, after all, any space that is not public? Many of Williams's plays posit that there is no space that is not vulnerable to outside forces; privacy is frequently impossible. In theatre, this is in any case an eternal truth. It is a voyeuristic art form that depends on audiences eavesdropping, and intruding into the living rooms and bedrooms of the characters on stage. The so-called 'fourth wall', the invisible barrier between audience and actors that must be assumed on both sides for the suspension of disbelief, is the biggest theatrical illusion of all, and even in his most ostensibly realist plays, Williams renders it problematic, either by breaking through it, or questioning the impregnability of other walls on stage.

In *The Glass Menagerie*, Tom Wingfield addresses the audience directly, an exemplary case of 'breaking the fourth wall'; he is both a character in the play and its writer and narrator. Though there are earlier examples of this device being used, many critics of twentieth-century drama would credit the Italian dramatist Luigi Pirandello (1867–1936) with establishing its modern currency in the play *Six Characters in Search of an Author* (1921). Prior to Williams's *Glass Menagerie*, the playwright Thornton Wilder (1879–1975) had introduced it onto the American stage, in *Our Town* (1938), in which the Stage Manager creates the play as it progresses before the audience's eyes, and *The Skin of Our Teeth* (1942), in whose script it is written that characters must forget their lines. In *The Glass Menagerie*, the fourth wall is

* The name Tom is a further correspondence: Tom Williams became Tennessee in 1939.

broken so that the audience may accept that the action is set in the past, that 'the play is memory' (p. 235). Tom proceeds to switch from direct address to playing an active role in the recounted family history that makes up a majority of the remaining stage time. We encounter Laura, his shy and fragile sister, who prefers the company of her glass animal ornaments to that of peers or potential lovers, and their mother Amanda, anxiously obsessing over Laura's future, worried that her daughter is unemployable and unmarriageable.

This is the stifling world from which Tom recoils in the central narrative of the play, and in the final scene, the Tom of the past leaves his St Louis family by way of a fire escape, metamorphosing into the present-day Tom who narrates his own history. This explains the necessity of directly addressing the audience; in doing so, he can prove the play's 'truth', namely that he has indeed left home to become a writer, as he affirms at the end of the play, and that his presence on stage as he guides us through the autobiographical scenes is the evidence. By the play's close, he is a bystander, watching from the sidelines as Amanda and Laura perform a dumb-show. Williams effects a reversal here: Tom the narrator becomes Tom the audience, a peeping Tom, voyeuristically spying on his family's goodnights. He has escaped the theatre of the home, and broken through the fourth wall, but Amanda and Laura are doomed to remain trapped within it and behind it.

Performing Privacy

The Glass Menagerie sets a template for much subsequent American drama. Through the 1950s, 1960s and 1970s, many of the most critically and commercially successful serious plays centred on the living spaces of tense, tightly wound family units, often featuring domineering women, and rebellious sons or husbands who either dream of escape or re-enter a domestic setup with unease.[13] This applies to O'Neill's *Long Day's Journey into Night*, written in the early 1940s but first produced posthumously in 1956, Arthur Miller's *All My Sons* and *Death of a Salesman*, which are analysed further on in this chapter, to the work of Edward Albee (1928–), in *The American Dream* (1960) and *Who's Afraid of Virginia Woolf?* (1962), on and into the plays of

Sam Shepard (1943–), including especially *Buried Child* and *Curse of the Starving Class* (both 1978). In many ways, the American home and its discontents became more rigorously deconstructed in drama than in any other art form: US theatre had found its metier. By the time Williams was at his peak, Hollywood was going through a 'golden age'. Without the use of soundboards, expensive lighting or location shots, stage drama could not hope to tackle the grand narrative. It is telling that there few if any works of epic American theatre beyond O'Neill's update of Aeschylus, *Mourning Becomes Electra* (1931); the most recent play of note on such a grand scale, *Angels in America* (1991) by Tony Kushner (1956–), constantly reminds its audience that the stage is limited, calling for the angels' wires to be plainly visible.

It is apt, then, that in *The Glass Menagerie*, Tom's main means of escape from the pressures of family life is the movies, which allows him to indulge fantasies of alternative lives. It is almost as if cinema is Tom's passage out of the theatre of the family home; for the family home is indeed a theatre, cramped and filled with intrusive spectators, and he of course presents it to the audience directly as a stage. This is developed and extended in Williams's next great success, *A Streetcar Named Desire* (1947). In the restricted space of the Kowalski household, and in the wider New Orleans street, every act is public, even in the supposed privacy of the family home. Walls are thin, and doors are seldom bolted. The audience first meets Stanley Kowalski on the street, hollering at his wife Stella, who appears on the first-floor landing of their house. He throws her some meat, a primal gesture that pays no heed to domestic nicety or intimacy, carried out in full view of his neighbours. Privacy is alien to him, for he is uncultivated in the true sense. As Williams explains, he possesses an 'animal joy in his being', as the 'gaudy seed-bearer'.[14] For Stanley, there are no borders, nor are there barriers to his physicality; he likewise refuses to observe any prescribed protocols of social interaction.

Stanley's sister-in-law, Blanche Dubois, on the other hand, is initially at pains to maintain her privacy. Her arrival at the Kowalski house causes her distress; the close quarters are immediately a threat to her delicate sense of self, and quite unlike the Southern house of her past life, 'Belle Reve'. There are no doors between her sleeping space and the living room, and she expresses discomfort at the 'merciless glare' of the Kowalski light bulbs. In contrast to Stanley's 'animal joy', Blanche's behaviour is often self-conscious about the degree to which it is performed. She alters the lighting, covering the 'naked bulb' she so detests with a Chinese paper lantern. This is a function of her need to assume the outward signs of conventional feminine beauty, even propriety, in order to mask a more morally and psychologically ambiguous self. Women, she explains, must 'put on soft colours' to create some 'temporary magic' around them (p. 169). She arranges the lantern, her dresses, her entrance into the poker party, as a set designer, a costumier, an actress might. It thus turns out that her craving for privacy is a desire for a clearer demarcation between the spaces in which she can perform the outward persona of the Southern belle and those in which the tortured inner Blanche may be hidden. It could be argued that the lack of this distinction is what drives her to the brink of insanity, for her fate is to be raped by Stanley: the ultimate violation of privacy.

But in metaphorical terms, Stanley's destruction of Blanche's theatricality is as invasive and devastating as his sexual advance. His sneering putdown of her 'Mardi Gras outfit' and her construction of a stage scene where 'lo and behold the place has turned into Egypt and you are the Queen of the Nile', pitch the apparent realness of Stanley's world against the supposed fakery of Blanche's. His rhetorical question, 'What queen do you think you are?' (p. 213), even implies that there is something of the drag artiste about her; it is doubtful that a gay playwright such as Williams would use the word 'queen' without nodding towards this definition. Earlier episodes lead up to this moment. When Blanche croons 'It's only a paper moon' in the bath, revelling in artifice in what seems to be the only lockable room in the house, Stanley grows impatient with both his bladder and her balladry; the matter-of-fact banality of his need to urinate is directly juxtaposed with her stagey toilette. Most tellingly of all, in Scene Nine, Mitch, Blanche's brief love interest, rips the paper lantern off the lamp in an attempt to be 'realistic' with her, to which she retorts, 'I don't want realism!' (p. 213).

The most violent juxtaposition of all, then, is between the melodrama of Blanche and the almost oppressive realism of the Kowalski household.

A Streetcar Named Desire is a watershed in American drama because it manages to juggle both these forms, and in many ways becomes a play *about* the clash between them; a play that looks back through American theatrical history and forward into its future, and in consigning melodrama to the mental hospital, chooses the uncertainty of that future.

Williams and Miller: Public Falls, Private Grief

Later Tennessee Williams plays focus more and more on fallen men and the impact of the fallen on those around them. How might a public fall from grace be prevented from provoking a publicly acted-out grief? In *Cat on a Hot Tin Roof* (1956), the former athlete Brick literally falls from grace one night while attempting to jump hurdles under the influence of alcohol. His misguided run, a plan hatched in the freedom of darkness, results in injury, and a 'nice little item' in the '*Clarksdale Register.*'[15] Though figuratively, Brick appears to have been running away from something or someone – his wife Maggie, his father and/ or himself – he ends up with even less privacy, as a minor news story; and, walking around on crutches, he must carry with him a visible symbol of his own decline, a sort of stigmatic penance. Despite the fact that Maggie and Brick are living in his father's large plantation house, they are boxed into a corner, their precarious marriage squeezed into an appropriately thin-walled wing of the house, on which everyone intrudes or is imagined to be eavesdropping: Big Daddy claims to 'hate eavesdroppers' (p. 57), but his wife, Big Mama says elsewhere that she hates 'locked doors in a house' (p. 32). Furthermore, the family believe they have a right to know what goes on in Brick and Maggie's bedroom; even the children confront them with Maggie's childlessness. As with the idlers of *The Iceman Cometh*, Brick's only respite is in alcohol, which produces a 'click' inside his head. Unlike Tom in *The Glass Menagerie*, he escapes inwards; there is no fire escape, but there is a liquor cabinet.

Inward escape was the germ of what arguably became the most analysed of all mid-century American plays, *Death of a Salesman* (1948) by Arthur Miller (1915–2005). Miller originally intended to call it 'The

Inside of his Head', and to represent this head on stage, which would then open up to reveal the action within.[16] Though this device was never used, we are, in a sense, back in the realm of O'Neill's *Strange Interlude*, with the psyche of Willy Loman, its ideals and memories, running alongside the action of the present time in his interactions with his wife Linda and sons, Biff and Happy. However, where O'Neill has characters step aside from their dialogue to 'perform' spontaneous lines of thought, Miller lets the past and present and the interior and exterior action bleed into one another. Whilst not in realist mode, the more impressionistic episodes and dream sequences of the play can nevertheless be interpreted as realistic representations of the breakdown of the protagonist. For example, Willy has visions of his Uncle Ben, a shadowy figure who symbolises the early American pioneer spirit. Ben is a model of everything that Willy is not; a successful, wealthy businessman held in high esteem by his peers. He is a staged character, but only in the past of Willy's imagination. Early in the play, while playing dice with his neighbour Charley, Willy addresses the Ben in his head aloud; Charley asks him, 'Did you call me Ben?'[17] This opens a split on stage between the inside and outside of Willy's head, as he sustains conversations with Ben and Charley at the same time. 'Why shouldn't he talk to himself?' Linda asks her sons, when he 'driv[es] seven hundred miles home without having earned a cent' (p. 163). The indignity of being undervalued by a company indifferent to all he has apparently achieved for them, selling wares to clients who no longer recognise him, has caused him to break down. Lack of knowledge of Willy in the outside world has led him to lose knowledge of his own self; as Biff concludes towards the end of the play, 'the man didn't know who he was' (p. 222).

There is a chain of loss here, a diminishing of respect within Willy's profession and the wider society it serves, leading to diminished respect within his neighbourhood, then his family, and finally within his own heart and mind. For Miller, a sometime socialist, every individual had a stake in society, and his or her share of the attendant rights and responsibilities, but the capitalistic USA of the mid-twentieth century, suspicious of any kind of collectivism, did not often allow for this to be expressed. Uncle Ben's mantra, 'when I walked into the jungle I was seventeen. When I walked out I was twenty-one. And, by God, I was rich!' (p. 160) expresses the original myth of resourceful American individualism. However, the cruel irony remains that the urban jungle, if anything, is more uncompromising than the uncultivated land of the first colonies, and allows for a good deal less optimism and ambition. 'Gotta break your neck to see a star in this yard', mutters Willy, squashed into an identikit Brooklyn house whose mortgage has taken the best part of his working life to pay off. Rather than betokening limitless freedom, the towering built environment blocks Willy's physical line of sight and, more metaphorically, impedes visionary ideas; skyscrapers and corporation towers offer no opportunity for blue-sky thinking.

This dramatises the central problem within Miller's early work: societies comprise individuals of like mind, but when they are of like mind in their devotion to individual*ism*, then it is difficult to see where responsibility and culpability really lie. In *Death of a Salesman*, Willy Loman is presented to us as an everyman ('low-man'), known in the title of the play not by name but career, the marker by which wider social value is too often measured, and in his case a career of commission-based pay that records success solely in mercenary terms. Theatre provides the opportunity for making modern tragedy out of such material. When Linda makes an impassioned plea on Willy's behalf to their sons, telling them 'attention must be paid', even though 'he's not the finest character that ever lived', she is really acting as a mouthpiece for Miller, breaking the fourth wall to address the audience; and she is also stepping outside of the drama to act as a kind of chorus. The 'Requiem' at the end of the play, after Willy's suicidal car-crash, is a catharsis of sorts, as Willy's family and neighbours realise his death is a painfully necessary sacrifice that might bring about a less troubled future. The same could be said of the ending of *All My Sons* (1946), Miller's first success, in which Joe Keller, who has presided over the manufacture of faulty fighter-plane components that kill twenty-one pilots, turns a gun on himself in order to free his family from the taint of association. Just before he commits suicide, his son Chris becomes the voice of moral conscience, proposing that 'You can be better! Once and for all you can know there's a universe of people outside and you're responsible to it.'[18]

The Personal and the Political

Much of Miller's work has a strong sense of political, as well as moral purpose. *The Crucible* (1953) remains his most performed play. It is set during the Salem witch trials of the 1690s, when Puritan suspicions amongst neighbours and families spiralled to such a degree that they became a matter of life and death. In the 1950s, America was going through another period of intense and zealous finger pointing. In the wake of the Cold War, the nuclear threat and the national fear of communist infiltration, Senator Joseph McCarthy presided over federal investigations into individuals suspected of communist sympathies. McCarthyism was especially hostile to the arts, believing them to be a breeding ground for potential sedition, and the HUAC (House Un-American Activities Committee) was set up to question many high-profile figures. Elia Kazan was one such luminary; the original director of *A Streetcar Named Desire* and *Death of a Salesman* was questioned in 1952 and chose to divulge the names of other left-wing agitators in the industry, a way of lessening his own fate at the hands of the state. Miller was aggrieved at Kazan's decision to testify; when he himself came up for trial in 1956, he refused to attend.

A culture of mistrust began to form as the so-called Second Red Scare took hold. The fear was to a large extent xenophobic, a panic over the possibility of outside agents penetrating the American family. In order to combat the outside coming in, federal government insisted on the enemy within being outed. Private lives were exposed for the supposed public good. Much of the drama, indeed much of the literature of this period, was itself infiltrated by the language of McCarthyist paranoia; 'your talents are wasted as a housewife and mother, you really ought to be with the FBI,' says Maggie to her sister-in-law Mae in *Cat on a Hot Tin Roof*, after she realises her movements are being tracked (p. 51). *The Crucible* examines this culture of snooping and blame with the forensic eye of the anthropologist, and creates a new kind of drama in the process. The action is interrupted by long passages of prose explanation, giving details of historical background (the characters were all based on actual figures) and character motivation.

Whether a narrator is employed to read the passages is left at the director's discretion; but it is nevertheless an almost O'Neill-esque device which could potentially de-theatricalise the play. At the same time, it is highly conscious of itself as a document of future historical importance, a document not unlike those from the seventeenth century used by Miller in his research. Furthermore, it is a document of how theatrical politics itself was becoming, with its inexorable chains of blame and unravelling denouements, its stagey testimonies by suspected actors in front of voyeuristic audiences. The centrepiece of *The Crucible*, the trial of John Proctor, is both a straightforward representation of the events in puritan Salem and an implicit critique of the legal processes at work in the HUAC. *The Crucible* therefore puts the HUAC trials on trial; the theatre becomes a courtroom, both within the plot, and in a wider allegorical sense. America is shrunk to fit the stage, and is questioned under the glaring lights and the stares of the audience.

The critical and commercial success of *The Crucible* was a measure of how far US theatre had come in thirty or forty short years. Eugene O'Neill was so unsure of how to represent America on stage that he set his first ten or so plays at sea, in a no man's land romantically separate from the outside pressures of society. By 1953, a playwright such as Arthur Miller could argue persuasively for an American theatre ideally suited to the examination of public/private binaries, whose experiments in form, through the work of O'Neill and Williams, reflected America's own struggle to achieve the balance 'between order and freedom'.[19]

Extended Commentary: O'Neill, *Long Day's Journey Into Night* (1956)

In 1973, the drama critic Thomas Adler described Edward Albee's play *Who's Afraid of Virginia Woolf?* as a 'long night's journey into day.'[20] The implication of this clever reversal is that Albee's work marks a progress from the difficult family dramas that preceded it, into a new dawn. Yet *Who's Afraid of Virginia Woolf* was first performed in 1961, barely five years after the premiere of Eugene O'Neill's *Long Day's Journey Into Night*. Adler's play on words reveals as much about the centrality of O'Neill's posthumously premiered masterpiece to the American theatrical canon as it does Albee's claims to similar status. Even though *Long Day's Journey Into Night* was completed in 1940, O'Neill refused to publish it until after his death; it was too full of autobiographical incident, too personal for him to risk commercial or critical failure. It therefore cannot claim any influence on the great plays of the late 1940s and early 1950s, such as *The Glass Menagerie*, *Death of a Salesman* or *All My Sons*, yet it is in many ways the epitome of American domestic drama.

As in Miller's *All My Sons* and Williams's *The Glass Menagerie* and *Suddenly Last Summer* among others, *Long Day's Journey Into Night* centres around a dominant mother figure whose near-pathological delusions put domestic harmony at risk. In a detailed character assessment typical of O'Neill, Mary's 'most appealing quality is the simple, unaffected charm of a shy convent-girl youthfulness she has never lost – an innate unworldly innocence'.[21] She is immediately cast as the play's spectre, obsessed with a past she habitually and continually revises. Through her, O'Neill examines the ease with which individuals seek explanation for present wrongs within past history, and suggests that progress may be impossible in a world of endless, repetitive cycles. As Mary says, 'the past is the present, isn't it? It's the future, too. We all try to lie out of that, but life won't let us' (p. 50).

Here we encounter the ghost of an earlier O'Neill character, Nina Leeds from *Strange Interlude*, who urges us to read the 'lie' within 'life'. However, unlike Nina, who acknowledges the falsity of the everyday in an impassioned outburst, Mary is resigned to it, and passive in the face of it. Elsewhere she says, 'None of us can help the things life has done to us. They're done before you realize it, and once they're done they make you do other things until at last everything comes between you and what you'd like to be, and you've lost your true self for ever' (p. 33). This betrays an almost fatalistic attitude. Human beings have no influence over life, and are acted upon by it; they neither create nor shape it. History, then, is only a series of wrong turnings, and the human struggle is a battle against overpowering forces beyond the control of the individual. Mary's way of coping with this powerlessness is to lose her 'true self' by surrendering to morphine. The audience learns from the other characters in the play, Mary's husband Tyrone and their two living sons, Edmund and Jamie, that this forms a cycle of behaviour; since the death of her child, she has been in and out of sanatoria, and her addiction to opiates is ongoing.

Most crucially, however, the cycle appears to be one of diminution and decay. Just as Mary maps out life's inexorable decline towards the loss of 'your true self for ever', so does O'Neill plot *Long Day's Journey Into Night* through a course of diminishing returns. The play's title implies this. Although in experience day follows night, O'Neill is using the terms more metaphorically. A journey usually has an end, a purpose, but life's only endpoint is death; it is a voyage from light into dark, and the cyclical rituals with which humans mark their existence only move ever closer towards this ultimate demise. Dramatic devices are used to convey this. For example, each of the play's four acts begins with characters around the dining table, but there are fewer and fewer seated as the play progresses. Similarly, characters constantly allude to the fog that envelops their house, and with each act, the stage directions call for this fog to become denser. By Act Four, the house is not even lit, and Edmund and Jamie's attempts to switch on lamps and chandeliers are met with irritation by their father, Tyrone.

With devices such as these, O'Neill appears to have struck a balance between his 'novelistic' tendencies and the demands of the theatre. The progressive weakening of the light serves an immediate dramatic function, marking off the hours of the day; in Act Four, the near-darkness also signifies the miserliness of Tyrone, who is reluctant to pay the electricity company any more than is strictly necessary. However, the lapse into darkness and the thickening of the mist around the house also have philosophical implications. In Act Four, Edmund declaims that 'for a second you see – and seeing the secret, are the secret. For a second there is meaning! Then the hand lets the veil fall and you are alone, lost in the fog again, and you stumble on toward nowhere, for no good reason!' (p. 94). This statement, which seems to anticipate that of Pozzo in Samuel Beckett's *Waiting for Godot* (1953),* expresses both Edmund's attitude towards the futility of the human condition and O'Neill's towards the inadequacies of his own art in dealing with it. In this highly autobiographical play, 'Eugene' is the name of the Tyrone's dead child, a loss they still grieve, and a sense of the playwright's self-annihilation haunts the play. The character of Edmund is the most easily identifiable with O'Neill himself: a young, drifting, depressive artist-figure who rebels against his father's authority. It is thus difficult to read or hear his pronouncements on his own literary capabilities as anything other than an expression of the playwright's own professional doubts. When his father suggests he has a poet within him, Edmund replies:

> The *makings* of a poet. No, I'm afraid I'm like the guy who
> is always panhandling for a smoke. He hasn't even got the
> makings. He's only got the habit. I couldn't touch what I tried
> to tell you just now. I just stammered. That's the best I'll ever do
> ... Stammering is the native eloquence of us fog people. (p. 95)

Just as for only 'a second' there is meaning, so it is that artistic endeavour is also a struggle in the dark, with only the occasional flash of true insight. As if to demonstrate this, O'Neill spends the best part of the play's final act quoting other writers at length. Tyrone lectures his sons on the virtues of Shakespeare throughout *Long Day's Journey Into Night*, but as the action courses further towards its 'night', he is answered with extensive lines of the poets Charles Baudelaire (1821–67), Ernest Dowson (1867–1900) and Algernon Swinburne (1837–1909). Edmund thinks himself an inferior wordsmith, to the extent that when he does give a half-decent speech, he comments on it sarcastically, 'Not so bad, that last, eh? Original, not Baudelaire. Give me credit!' (p. 94); this could very well be O'Neill himself, ironically seeking critical approval.

---

* 'They give birth astride of a grave, the light gleams an instant, then it's night once more.' Samuel Beckett, *Waiting for Godot*, in *The Complete Dramatic Works* (London: Faber and Faber, 1990), pp. 7–88 (83).

However, in this play, even the greatest literature is not adequate to the task of communicating family tragedy. Shakespeare's supposed civilising influence is subverted; when Tyrone quotes Prospero from *The Tempest*, reminding Edmund that 'We are such stuff as dreams are made on',[22] Edmund retorts that 'we are such stuff as manure is made on' (p. 79), and when Mary appears on the staircase for her final words, doped into a stupor with morphine, Jamie announces sardonically, 'The Mad Scene. Enter Ophelia!' (p. 106). Where in many of his plays, O'Neill privileges the *nebentext* of the play, those parts of the published work that are not performed aloud on stage, here he allows his character to speak it. Likewise, although the volumes in the bookcase at the back of the stage are given in the detailed stage directions, they are also listed by Tyrone in a dismissive outburst about his son's reading habits; and so, despite displaying many of the attributes for which O'Neill has been criticised, *Long Day's Journey Into Night* sees him scrutinising and unravelling both his art and his life more than in any other work.

Long Day's Journey Into Night epitomises mid-century American drama. It centres on an ill woman, prone to self-dramatisation, a subject familiar to anyone acquainted with *All My Sons* or *A Streetcar Named Desire*. Trapped in a kind of domestic claustrophobia, the characters keep each other under constant surveillance, discussing repeatedly the signs of Edmund's incipient tuberculosis and Mary's renewed reliance on opiates; the emphasis on the watcher and the watched is again recognisable in some of Miller's and Williams's greatest plays. *Long Day's Journey Into Night* also looks forward to the American drama of the 1960s and 1970s. The ghost of the dead child stalks the works of Edward Albee (1928–), particularly *The American Dream* (1960) and *Who's Afraid of Virginia Woolf?* (1962), and the postmodern drama of Sam Shepard (1943–), especially *Buried Child* (1978). These works are indebted to O'Neill. Despite continuing to divide critical opinion, he found the American family, and by extension the American body politic, to be dysfunctional and in need of forensic theatrical dissection; the templates he set for doing so ensured that the US stage might rise to this difficult task.

Notes

1   See the official website of the Nobel Prize: http://nobelprize.org/nobel_prizes/literature/laureates/1936/oneill-speech.html.
2   William Dunlap, *History of the American Theatre* (London: Richard Bentley, 1833), p. 2.
3   See Roman Ingarden, *The Literary Work of Art: An Investigation on the Borderlines of Ontology, Logic, and Theory of Literature*, trans. George G. Grabowicz (Evanston: Northwestern University Press, 1973), pp. 208–9. The translator of this edition uses the terms 'main text' and 'side text' but the German forms are used most often.
4   See especially Kurt Eisen, *The Inner Strength of Opposites: O'Neill's Novelistic Drama and the Melodramatic Imagination* (Athens: University of Georgia Press, 1994).
5   See for example Matthew H. Wikander, 'O'Neill and the Cult of Sincerity', *The Cambridge Companion to Eugene O'Neill*, ed. Michael Manheim (Cambridge: Cambridge University Press, 1998), pp. 217–35.
6   Eugene O'Neill, interview with J. S. Wilson, quoted in Croswell Bowen, *The Curse of the Misbegotten: A Tale of the House of O'Neill* (London: Rupert Hat-Davis), pp. 312–13.
7   Eugene O'Neill, *Strange Interlude*, in *Complete Plays 1913–1920* (New York: Library of America, 1988), pp. 629–818 (634). In adopting this technique, the play also makes use of another key Modernist influence, that of Sigmund Freud and his psychoanalytical theories of the unconscious.
8   O'Neill, *Hughie*, in *Complete Plays 1913–1920*, pp. 829–51 (832).
9   O'Neill, *The Iceman Cometh*, in *Complete Plays 1913–1920*, pp. 561–711 (675).
10   Tennessee Williams, *Cat on a Hot Tin Roof* (1955. London: Penguin, 2001), p. 83.
11   Tennessee Williams, *The Glass Menagerie* (1945. London: Penguin, 2000), p. 234.
12   William Shakespeare, *As You Like It* III.iii.16, in *The Complete Works*, ed. Stanley Wells and Gary Taylor (Oxford: Clarendon Press, 1999), pp. 627–52 (642).
13   For a study of this trend, see Geoffrey S. Proehl, *Coming Home Again: American Family Drama and the Figure of the Prodigal* (Madison: Fairleigh Dickinson University Press, 1997).
14   Tennessee Williams, *A Streetcar Named Desire* (1947. London: Penguin, 2000), p. 128.
15   Tennessee Williams, *Cat on a Hot Tin Roof* (1956. London: Penguin, 2001), p. 20.

16   Arthur Miller, 'Introduction to the Collected Plays', in *Plays: One* (London: Methuen), pp. 3–55 (23).

17   Miller, *Death of a Salesman*, in *Plays: One*, pp. 130–222 (154).

18   Miller, *All My Sons*, in *Plays: One*, pp. 57–127 (126).

19   Miller, *The Crucible*, in *Plays: One*, pp. 223–329 (229).

20   Thomas P. Adler, 'Albee's "Who's Afraid of Virginia Woolf?": a long night's journey into day', *Education Theatre Journal* 25 (1973), pp. 66–70.

21   Eugene O'Neill, *Long Day's Journey Into Night* (1956. London: Nick Hern, 1999), p. 2.

22   Shakespeare, *The Tempest* IV.i.156–7, *The Complete Works*, pp. 1167–89 (1186).

Part Four
Critical Theories and Debates

American Cities

In 1908, Henry James (1843–1916) visited a country he had not been to for twenty-five years. It was his native America, now to be described from a tourist's perspective for *The American Scene* (1909). He first arrives in New York and finds it full of 'the same old sordid facts':[1] rushing traffic, loose cobbles and lazy policemen. Baltimore seems 'a cheerful little city of the dead' (p. 608), Washington the self-preoccupied 'City of Conversation' (p. 636) and in Boston he feels the ghostly presence of Emerson, Thoreau and Hawthorne. Yet he himself is also a kind of ghost here, a nineteenth-century gentleman of letters cast adrift in an alien landscape. In the same year as James published his travelogue, the Europe he had just left saw the publication of modernist manifestos calling for 'multicoloured, polyphonic tides of revolution in the modern capitals'.[2] Even James's nostalgic narrative captures some of this upheaval. His childhood home has been destroyed, nothing is quite where he remembers, and he smells a new sort of greed – 'there was money in the air, ever so much money', he remarks, ruefully (p. 514). Money, for Henry James, was nothing new, but here it becomes the one constant in a city that is otherwise in perpetual flux.

America was not alone in undergoing a period of sustained urbanisation at the turn of the century, but the question was of degree. From 1850 to 1900, Chicago's population doubled in size, creating the city of 'unspeakable squalor'[3] that Frank Norris (1870–1902) describes in *The Pit: A Story of Chicago* (1920). This Chicago has its own mind, its own subjectivity. In one passage, the heroine of the novel, Laura, imagines the city almost as a pioneer bestriding its environs for miles around:

> The Great Grey City, brooking no rival, imposed its dominion upon a reach of country larger than many a kingdom of the Old World. For thousands of miles beyond its confines was its influence felt. Out, far out, far away in the snow and shadow of northern Wisconsin forests, axes and saws bit the bark of century-old trees, stimulated by this city's energy. Just as far to the southward pick and drill leaped to the assault of veins of anthracite, moved by her central power. Her force turned the wheels of harvester and seeder a thousand miles distant in Iowa and Kansas. (p. 57)

The city reaches far beyond its own boundaries; it is a life-force that is so powerful that its conceptual reach far outpaces its physical limitations. However, it does at least exude a certain amount of romance. By contrast, there is very little but fetid, 'dreary' wood houses in the meatpacking stockyards of Upton Sinclair's *The Jungle* (1906). The Lithuanian immigrants who move to Chicago in the hope of a better life whisper the name of the city almost as a charm or spell, but the stench of the stockyards, 'elemental ... raw and crude ... rich, almost rancid, sensual and strong',[4] suggests not civilisation or progress, but a regression into the primeval: the disorientation of the 'urban jungle'.

The demography of the country was remapped in other ways, too. Immediately after the First World War, half a million black migrants moved from the South to the urban centres of Chicago and New York. As Richard Wright records in his semi-autobiographical *Native Son* (1940), the cramped conditions and derelict housing they found when they got there was often little improvement on the rural poverty they had left behind. The works of Ash Can painters such as Robert Henri also suggested that the modern city could be dirty, hostile and treacherous. Yet urban life was heralded by workers, economists and social theorists alike as the future of American culture, as this euphoric extract from intellectual progressive Randalph Bourne indicates:

Who can walk the lighted streets of a city at night and watch the flowing crowds, the shining youthful faces, the eager exhilaration of the sauntering life, or who can see the surge of humanity or a Sunday, without feeling the strange power of this mass-life? This mysterious power of the city which sucks out the life of the countryside, which welds individuals into a co-operative life, is not this the basal force of the age, and does it not suggest the stirrings of a new civilization, socialized and purified? In this garish, vulgar, primitive flow of Broadway, are not new gods being born?[5]

If, as Bourne suggests, the modern city forms gods and deities, it is also parasitic. The basal force of the age is at once fundamental, and debasing. Israel Zangwill's 1908 play *The Melting Pot* imagines the American city as a utopian crucible full of different ethnicities, religions and cultures living side by side. Yet, as James suggests, perhaps these individuals shared nothing at all other than a desire for money.

American literature of the twentieth century celebrates and exposes its cities in equal measure. The city offered iconic national symbolism, as in Hart Crane's poetry sequence *The Bridge* (1930).* It promised both a liberating anonymity and a terrifying isolation. Yet the literary history of the period also shows the importance of the city for providing networks and communities of writers. San Francisco in the 1950s and 1960s was not only the starting point for gay liberation or the hippie movement but also a new urban centre for poetry. Writers of the 'San Francisco Renaissance', from Jack Spicer (1925–65) and Kenneth Rexroth (1905–82) to Robert Duncan (1919–88) found both formal and practical succour in envisioning their work as a collective project. They published through the burgeoning underground presses growing up in the city, offering another reading of the American metropolis that sees it not through its literary representation but rather through the networks and friendships it builds and sustains. The 'New York

---

* See Part Three: 'Visionary Poetry' for a detailed discussion of the work of Hart Crane, including *The Bridge*.

Poets', from Frank O'Hara (1926–66)* to John Ashbery (1927–), offer another nexus of poetic lineage. More recent writing about American cities, responding to the 9/11 attacks of 2001, has given rise to further contradictions about the modern metropolis; the skyscraper, for most modern Americans a symbol of success, power and authority, has also proved to be the most vulnerable to attack.

Capital Desires

It was the skyscraper that helped define the modern city for early twentieth-century social theorists; 1913 saw the opening of the Woolworth building in New York, heralded at the time as a new cathedral of commerce. The phrase implies a newly secular or pluralist democracy that can unite itself around capital expenditure and gross domestic product. City architecture provided a useful analogue for other types of social theory, too. The first decades of the century saw a lively debate between the progressives, who believed America was an improvised experiment that would eventually arrive at a perfect state, and the 'City Beautiful' interventionists, who felt that careful town planning, social integration policies and a tight watch on immigration would build an orderly and prosperous country. Both groups drew heavily on examples or metaphors lifted from city living, pointing to America's urban centres as the only place to see the country's internal desires writ large. As Robert Park wrote in his 1929 essay, 'The City as Social Laboratory', in the city 'all the secret ambitions and all the suppressed desires find somewhere expression.' He talks of a city that 'magnifies, spreads out, and advertises human nature in all its various manifestations.' Park finds this aspect of the city fascinating, but goes further, arguing that it is this amorphous quality that makes the city 'of all places the one in which to discover the secrets of human hearts, and to study human nature and society'.[6]

---

* See Part Three: 'Visionary Poetry' for a detailed discussion of the work of Frank O'Hara.

Here the city opens out the country's secrets and darkest thoughts about itself. It becomes the sociologist's dream; its billboards and garish signs not only advertise consumer products but also human nature itself. The move to the city ushered in a technological age, a new world order 'bound to the technical and economic conditions of machine production which to-day determine the lives of all the individuals who are born into this mechanism', as economist Max Weber (1864–1920) wrote in *The Protestant Ethic and the Spirit of Capitalism* (1904–5).[7] Goods were imported, shipped in from Europe and Asia, or transported for miles on new railroad tracks. What had been homemade was now a commodity; the newly leisured class crowned by Thorstein Verblen's sociological study of 1899 favoured 'conspicuous consumption' over a Puritan work ethic.[8] America's 40 per cent growth in GDP from 1900 to 1929 offered the promise of apparently endless prosperity.

If the sociologist or economist could afford to be even-handed about the possibilities and dangers of the city, novelists of the period tended to take sides. Theodore Dreiser's (1871–1945) seminal naturalist novel *Sister Carrie* (1900) is a tale of seduction, but the young protagonist boarding her train for Chicago is undone not by a man, but by the city itself which, as the narrative warns us forbiddingly, 'has its cunning wiles, no less than the infinitely smaller and more human tempter.'[9] This turn-of-the-century metropolis runs on a cycle of money, desire and inequality, with 'a high and mighty air calculated to overawe and abash the common applicant, and to make the gulf between poverty and success seem both wide and deep'.[10] Dreiser makes this sprawling city a finely tuned map. Chicago's grid-like network of streets promises less the endless possibilities of the American road than order, enclosure and containment. The city provided Dreiser and novelists of the period with formal models, too. *Sister Carrie* is resolutely naturalist and deterministic; its central protagonist is given little in the way of agency. Her desires and needs are manufactured by her environment, while her success is determined by the city's whims rather than her own character. This type of novel, first popularised in France by writers such as Emile Zola and Honoré de Balzac, makes individuals the products of economic circumstance. Carrie begins with a desire for honest labour, but after working in a squalid shoe factory settles for the moral indelicacy of being a kept woman. Like the eponymous heroine of Willa Cather's *Lucy Gayheart* (1935), who delights in 'the city of fact' rather than the city of feeling,[11] Carrie's idealism only extends as far as getting and spending, of acquiring the money which everyone else seems to have and which she deduces she must desire. When even Chicago's anonymous locations begin to threaten her furtive romantic encounters, Carrie elopes with a married man to Canada. They eventually move to New York, taking pseudonyms to escape discovery. In Dreiser's novel, Carrie's fate is plotted schematically against that of her eventual husband Hurstwood, who finds in New York only poverty and degradation. Carrie's own success as an actress is mirrored in terrible symmetry by his failure. Readers are left in little doubt as to Dreiser's own views, and can take little delight in the shrill and shallow trappings of Carrie's success. Towards the end of the novel, Carrie meets Robert Ames, an intellectual who tries to persuade her that art, rather than materialism, might be the way to make her happy. But if this is a lesson Dreiser feels she must learn, she either cannot grasp it, or finds it soon forgotten. She is rich by the final chapter of the novel, but restless and unfulfilled.

The lure of the American city prior to the Wall Street crash perhaps explains its appeal for writers later on in the century. E. L. Doctorow (1931–) returns to the early part of the century in *Ragtime* (1975), but his sharp-eyed satire finds little room to indulge nostalgia for the certainties of the country before Depression: 'There were no negroes. There were no immigrants',[12] his narrator states, flat with irony. His own novel, interweaving the story of three families in New York with fictional representations of everyone from Houdini to Freud revels in the noise and energy of the period. The music of ragtime becomes the most useful analogy for his own syncopated, propulsive narrative energy; as the narrator tells us of Coalhouse Walker's piano-playing, 'this was a most robust composition, a vigorous music that roused the senses and never stood still for a moment', like 'light touching various places in space, accumulating in intricate patters until the entire room was made to glow with its own being' (pp. 183–4).

Only retrospectively, perhaps, did the American reading public see the value in insider's tales from the city rather than Dreiser's moralising rags-to-riches narratives. While Doctorow mined the 1920s for his *Ragtime, Call It Sleep* (1936) by Henry Roth (1906–55) had to wait thirty years for a reprint, when it suddenly became immensely popular. The novel describes 1920s New York through the eyes of David Schaerl, a boy growing up in a Jewish ghetto. From the very outset of the narrative, David is both central and marginal; his first observation as he stands below a kitchen sink too high for him to reach is that 'the world had been created without thought of him'.[13] The Yiddish words of his family rabbi puzzle and confuse him; as he and his mother make the journey from Poland to New York to meet a father he has never seen before, the Statue of Liberty appears both as a figure of wonder and as a vague menace: 'shadow flattened the torch she bore to a black cross against flawless light' (p. 10). She offers perfection, but it is perfection that seems obscured and unattainable.

In Sinclair Lewis's early novels, *Free Air* (1919) and *Main Street* (1920), his stance is both satiric and expansive. Although the incredible popular success of the latter perpetuated the image of Lewis sneering at small-town America – memorialised as 'Gopher Prairie' – the automobile trip that structures his first novel finds the protagonists revising their stance, and wondering whether the big cities they call home are in fact 'the real America'. Brooklyn-born Claire learns that 'there may be an almost tolerable existence without gardenias or the news about the latest Parisian imagists'.[14] Revisionist novels describing the early twentieth century not only question the promise of the city and its capitalist ethos but also suggest that the city itself might be less central that it appears.

The Modernist City

Sinclair Lewis's elision of urban America with 'news of the Paris imagists' is significant: American cities of the period were also radical centres of modernist experiment. As the Northern cities sometimes turned away dismissively from the Southern towns and regional centres that provided their growing population, their avant-garde artists looked with expectation to the international networks being formed by writers such as Gertrude Stein (1874–1946), T. S. Eliot (1888–1965) and Djuna Barnes (1892–1982). The poet Mina Loy (1882–1966) saw in urban life the possibility of female emancipation and formal experiment. Born in London but spending time in Florence and Paris before becoming an American citizen in the 1920s, she voiced the city and the female body, finding in them both a centre of pain, with an ever-increasing radius.[15] In this version of the American metropolis, New York is closer to Paris or London than Pittsburgh or Virginia. Its literature looks back to Edgar Allen Poe's urban *flâneur* in stories such as 'The Man in the Crowd' (1840), where nameless and anonymous spectators intermingle in a vast urban playground.

The work of John Dos Passos (1896–1970) is similarly innovative. He brought the stream-of-consciousness technique to the American city in works such as *Manhattan Transfer* (1925). The novel's interweaving of a series of urban vignettes shares something with German director Fritz Lang's *Metropolis* (1927). Lang's film explores a futuristic dystopia, where a nameless city buckles under the weight of capitalism and its iniquities. Dos Passos, who was born in Chicago to a father preoccupied with conglomerates, mergers and acquisitions, knew first-hand that company profit could be an expedient for subjecting employees to terrible working conditions. *Manhattan Transfer* is not an indictment of capitalism (in fact, Dos Passos would go on to support Senator McCarthy in the 1950s), but it questions the human cost of fast-paced urban life. Its formal innovations are inextricable from its representation of the city itself. As Dos Passos remarked in his essay 'Against American Literature' (1928), 'our books are like our cities; they are all the same'.[16] His work is both stylistically distinctive and determined to make New York unutterably different from any other urban centre in the country. The novel's innovation relies in part on its busy and urgent cuts between synchronous stories and unrelated characters, but the figurative language also offers its own novelty, revealing a very different city from the New York Henry

James might recognise. It is a disorientating world of metal and glass, where characters are always in thrall to their surroundings. This is acutely apparent in a description of a hot day in the city, where in the 'heavy heat, streets, stores, people in Sunday clothes, strawhats, sunshades, surfacecars, taxis, broke and crinkled brightly about [Ellen] grazing with sharp cutting glints as if she were walking through piles of metalshavings.' Even the sounds of the city are described viscerally as though 'groping continually through a tangle of gritty saw-edged brittle noise.'[17] Here, Dos Passos deliberately collapses the distinction between the figurative ('as if she were walking through piles of metalshavings') and the literal, as in the crinkling cars. The metaphors are always mixed or synaesthetic. Characters 'grope' though 'noise'; the interference of the city is invasive and discomforting, and it actually warps the way the body responds to it. In this brittle urban jungle, the individual consciousness cannot quite hold onto its sanity. Ellen compares her mind to 'a busted mechanical toy' (p. 400), while the words she speaks are contradicted by the other words that 'spilled confusedly inside her like a broken package of beads' (p. 244). Language itself is co-opted by the city in this novel, as billboards create a textual world full of signs. Characters walk through streets of 'scrambled alphabets' (p. 351). The degenerated language here calls to mind nothing so much as Babel, the city that was cursed by God to speak in tongues after its inhabitants tried to build a tower that reached to the heavens. This implicit apocalypse is prophesied by a drunken tramp towards the end of the novel, who reminds Joe and Skinny that 'God took seven minutes to destroy Babylon, and will raze New York to the ground in seven seconds' (p. 381). The rattling, buzzing, frenetic movement of the novel is both infectious and haunted by what might lie after, or beyond it.

Other writers responded with a series of alternatives to Dos Passos's bustling, giddy New York. In the short story 'He' (1927) by H. P. Lovecraft (1890–1937), the central, nameless character moves from New England to New York but finds only 'a sense of horror and oppression' and men 'without dreams'.[18] One night a stranger promises to show him the history of the city, and explains how the land was bartered from a Native American. A chilling scream evokes the spirit of the Native American who then wreaks vengeance on the city for forgetting its origins. Here, modern New York is the same dystopian world that Fritz Lang imagined in his film, determined to forego history and continuity. The poet Charles Sandburg (1878–1967) shared Dos Passos's sense that each American city needed its own literary identity, but offered a more traditional response in a series of poems commemorating his native Chicago. Rather than highlight the city's alienating qualities, Sandburg looked back to Walt Whitman, creating a loving and incantatory portrait of Chicago. This is a propulsive, nominal poetry, offering a series of kennings[*] to describe its particular characteristics.[19] Sandburg's Chicago is brawny, muscular and happy to get its hands dirty. Over fifty years later, the poet Mike Royko mocked Sandburg's wide-eyed affection for the city, finding it more appropriate to describe the city spinning in a futile cycle of financial exchange, the allusion highlighting the commemorative power of Sandburg's work.[20]

The American city offered a distinctly modernist poetics, as works by T. S. Eliot and Hart Crane showed. Yet William Carlos Williams, drawn to the local and the everyday, found New York too grand a setting for his signature long poem. His five-book work *Paterson* (1946–58) focuses instead on the eponymous city in New Jersey. Here was an urban centre that did not dwarf its inhabitants but, in Williams's words, 'provided an image large enough to embody the whole knowable world about me'.[21] The poem, which began as a single eight-line verse in 1926, grew into a work that was less epic in scope than generous. The poem emphasises local and individual detail. Although it uses the fragmented voices and collage-techniques that characterised modernist writing from Eliot to Dos Passos, Williams's city is neither 'unreal' nor menacing. Tellingly, the four books of the poem are structured around the river and waterfall that first made Paterson into a large settlement. The reassuring compass of natural geography underpins a world where there is still faith in a shared language.[22] As in Dreiser's *Sister Carrie*, the city here is a character, but rather than proving a malevolent force,

---

[*] A kenning is a compound of two words that substitute for a more well-known one. Kennings are particularly common in Old English literature, where synonyms for frequently used nouns must be used.

it provides an analogue both to the river that runs through it and to the life of the people who inhabit it. Here, the possibility of the city's fall or natural decay is not seen, as with Dos Passos, as something apocalyptic, but rather part of the natural cycle of beginning, seeking and falling away. The familiar urban furniture of churches, factories and telephone wires is joined with birds singing, in rich Chaucerian allusion (p. 266). The city in modernist poetry need not be a waste land.

Williams's benevolent cityscape proved an inspiration to the next generation of poetic experimenters. Charles Olson (1910–70) chose Gloucester in Massachusetts as the setting for *The Maximus Poems* (1960) and a topographical map of his adopted hometown provided the collection's cover art. This experimental work, which uses quotation, letters and historical documents to build up its verbal portrait of the city, looks to civic history as well as the avant-garde. Olson was prompted to begin the poetic cycle when he came across a nineteenth-century history of Gloucester. The poems tell the story of the city's first settlers, immigrants from Plymouth, London and the West Country. The crisis of the modern American city is solved here by turning back to its origin, as a small city, uncorrupted by the nation.[23] Olson's work also points to a developing strand in American literature at the time, a literary movement which might see the past not as a byword for sentimental nostalgia but a new kind of radicalism. For Olson, history is another type of text, like the 'scrambled alphabet' that Dos Passos celebrates in *Manhattan Transfer*. The then, as well as the now, can be the starting point for the future.

The Postmodern City

Where turn-of-the-century city planning had pivoted on a debate between the progressives and the City Beautiful, post-war American architecture posited a new design question. As the swiftly erected modernist tower blocks began to decay, architects such as Robert Venturi (1925–) wondered if functionalism and clean lines didn't leave out something important. In his book *Complexity and Contradiction in*

Modern Architecture (1966), he called for a new architecture that might include ornament, humour, or a playful engagement with the past. This new, postmodernist design might build a new kind of 'collage city', as Colin Rowe and Fred Koetter argued in their 1970 book of the same name.[24] The collage might offer something new to American writers of the city, too, as Olson's scrapbook aesthetic suggests. Novelists of the 1970s and 1980s rebuilt the literature of the American city, creating works that relied less on alienating anonymity and more on bizarre coincidence, arbitrary patterning and a parodic allusion to the past. Like the new architecture, which embraced styles from the past that modernists would have dismissed as vulgar, this would be an urban literature less anxious about its formal inheritance, gaining artistic mileage from the dizzying range of traditions included in its texts.

For a series of postmodern novelists, the detective story provided a key template for the rewriting of the American city. The choice of genre is significant; unlike modernist writers, who sought to differentiate themselves from the cheap and disposable bestsellers of the period, writers such as Thomas Pynchon (1937–), Don DeLillo (1936–) and Tama Janovitz (1957–) revel in the collapsing of high and low forms. In their work, the formulaic qualities of the detective novel are in place, but the riddling complexity of the seemingly arbitrary narrative prevents the readers from arriving at an answer. In a modern world characterised by the contingent, the serendipitous and the random, the certainties of fiction suggest conspiracy theory rather than realism. How could two characters in the vast metropolis of New York ever meet accidentally, or find their lives had anything to do with each other? These novelists play on our expectations of a novel versus our experience of urban living, challenging us to question our reasoning, or even our sense that things might happen for a reason.

Thomas Pynchon's *V.* (1963) chronicles the life of discharged US soldier Benny Profane. On returning to New York and reconnecting with a group of bohemian artists known as the Whole Sick Crew, he meets the mysterious old man Herbert Stencil, who is searching for the 'V.' of the novel's title. Like a whodunit, the narrative offers a series of clues as to what 'V.' might symbolise. Herbert Stencil's name suggests an important meta-textual clue, and several of the flashbacks involve characters beginning with V, from Victoria Wren, murdered in the Egyptian section of the novel, to Veronica, the name given to a rat who haunts the sewers of Manhattan. The extended passages describing New York's sewers points to Pynchon's re-imagining of the city space. Here is a new kind of natural habitat. The novel also resembles a kind of cryptic crossword clue, full of implicit and explicit meanings. The competing flashbacks often seem unrelated to the narrative, but challenge the reader to make links, even as they question our ability to do so. One character imagines history as a garment 'rippled with gathers in its fabric'. In this metaphor, history is neither linear nor chronological, but is built around a series of folds where time might expand, jump, or shift. Living in a 'gather' rather than a 'crest', the modern city-dweller cannot tell if everything is entirely arbitrary or wholly meaningful.[25]

A similarly baffling contingency operates in Tama Janowitz's *A Cannibal in Manhattan* (1988), which follows a reformed cannibal Mgungu from an imaginary island to New York, where he marries a New York heiress. His journey to the mainland suggests the original journey to the New World. However, this is not the story of the savage tamed, but the penitent man turned back to crime. While he pours out passion for Thoreau and the wide-eyed promise of America, his wife tells him to look savage and act cynical. By the novel's conclusion, he has turned back to cannibalism, his vice offering a metaphor for the postmodern city and its literature, always recycling, repeating and engorging themselves on the edible detritus of history. The difference between this urban reversion and that of Upton Sinclair's jungle is that in the postmodern city, there is always the chance that the opposite will happen; because there is no linear narrative, or 'metanarrative' as the French postmodern theorist Jean-François Lyotard (1924–98) might put it, there may be no progress, but there is no true regress either.[26] Such fragmentation and self-perpetuating cyclicality is also crucial to Paul Auster's (1947–) *New York Trilogy*, the name given to the sequence of novels encompassing *City of Glass* (1985), *Ghosts* (1986) and *The Locked Room* (1987). As the narrator reminds us early on, New York is 'the most forlorn of places, the most abject ... the disarray is universal'.[27]

City of Glass, the first novel in the trilogy, begins with someone dialling a wrong number. This mixture of coincidence and subconscious purpose defines the movement of the narrative. Meanwhile, the protagonist, Daniel Quinn, is a novelist who likes reading detective stories for their economic sense of cause and effect: 'everything becomes essence; the centre of the book shifts with each event that propels it forward' (p. 8). The tension between these two ways of reading the city – the clean efficiency of everything having a purpose versus the terror of the unknown – defines Auster's novelistic world. As the novel progresses, the gap between the real and the imagined becomes blurred; the inadvertent caller is one Paul Auster, who works for a private detective agency. Is this a representation of the real author? What is the relationship between Paul Auster and the narrator, who promises us he has 'refrained from any interpretations' (p. 132)? Here, the 'inexhaustible space' (p. 3) of New York offers an endless range of possible readings. New York becomes an apparently blank page, the noisy letters of Dos Passos's 'scrambled alphabet' apparently scrubbed out. Auster's *Moon Palace* (1988) is another work that presents us with a self-consciously textual representation of New York that questions its own efficacy; the central character describes building furniture in his apartment entirely out of books he has inherited. The 'inexhaustible space' of the city is then perhaps illusive; in the work of Auster we feel the textual relationship to the past, as the character and the novel seek out a partial story of inheritance.

The fluid and porous encounters which take place in the postmodern American city, then, are always haunted by questions of identity and origin. As urban spaces fractured into more and more micro-communities – bohemian quarters, gay villages, minutely differentiated ethnic groupings – the city becomes a string of villages all asserting their own identities and origins, to the extent that if the postmodern metropolis has a coherent identity of its own, it can only be one of glorious plurality. This is what has led some theorists of space to declare the city the ultimate expression of the postmodern. For Kevin Robins, the move from the grand narratives of modernist abstraction to these smaller, more contingent, more individualised narratives-within-narratives makes the postmodern city 'an attempt to re-imagine urbanity'; it is about 'recovering a lost sense of territorial identity, urban community and public space'.[28] Sequences such as the *Tales of the City* series by Armistead Maupin (1944 –), set in the bohemian quarters of San Francisco, map out this 're-imagined urbanity', forming elastic community identities within the apparently random matrix of the shifting postmodern cityscape.

The City and Millennial Apocalypse

The postmodern city is, nevertheless, not all about the embrace of fragmentation. There are also apocalyptic narratives to be told too. Ever since cities grew exponentially at the turn of the twentieth century, they have been identified with potentially calamitous events in the popular imagination; this is particularly true of Hollywood, which has over the years attacked New York in particular with monsters, aliens, giant gorillas and gremlins. Because of their scale, metropolises are sites of mass panic. In the 1990s, this pre-millennial paranoia was a common feature in the literature of the American city. For example, Don DeLillo's *Underworld* (1997) returns for its titular image to Pynchon's New York sewers, but there are deeper questions of root and source here too. The protagonist, Nick Shay, is a waste management expert, and the novel asks what we might do with the political as well as the personal refuse of the past. Things can be buried, but their fallout continues to leech into the ground beneath our feet; the Cuban Missile Crisis and the atomic weapons testing of the 1960s both loom large over the characters' lives. The mysterious disappearance of Nick's father also offers up the text as a kind of detective novel, prompting the reader to ask not just who killed his father, but what the relationship might be between the internal and external worlds represented in the work.

Apocalyptic New York reaches a kind of fever pitch in *Angels in America* (1991), a two-part play by Tony Kushner (1956–). Kushner's Manhattan sits uneasily with itself and its own past. The AIDS epidemic is beginning to spread; the city, with its random interconnections, literally becomes a vector of infection. There are also more cosmic matters going awry. The hole in the ozone layer is getting larger, and the sky appears to be turning mauve. Nevertheless, apocalypse is not all fire, brimstone and punishment, it also offers opportunities for prophecy and miracles. Having been promised the 'threshold of revelation',[29] the HIV-positive Prior Walter is visited by an angel, who crashes through his ceiling at the end of the first play (which is entitled, rather tellingly, *Millennium Approaches*). This is an instance of postmodern 'magic realism', though the audience is both required to suspend their disbelief, and revel in the artifice; Kushner notes in the stage directions that no attempt must be made to cover up the wires on which the angel hovers. Prior Walter allows us to see the spectacle for all its kitsch or camp value: '*Very* Steven Spielberg', he declares, as 'a sound, like a plummeting meteor, tears down from very, very far above the earth, hurtling at an incredible velocity towards the bedroom' (p. 90).

In the second part, whose title *Perestroika* invokes the recent historical context of the play,* Prior himself has the chance to become a prophet, and to enter into a higher, cosmic realm. However, he makes the crucial decision to stay in New York among his friends and lovers, an extended, postmodern family of sorts. In the epilogue to the play, the major characters discuss the end of the Cold War in Central Park, standing around the Bethesda fountain, which symbolises continuity and replenishment throughout *Angels in America*. Prior Walter steps out of the scene to address the audience, reminding us of his love for the park: 'this is my favourite place in New York City. No, in the whole universe' (p. 97). What he seems to value is its ability to combine the ordinary and the extraordinary. The fountain is turned off because it is winter – ice in the pipes, he confides to the audience. This practical note does not jar; postmodern New York has the ability

---

* *Perestroika* is a Russian term, meaning 'restructuring', used by the last President of the USSR, Mikhail Gorbachev (1931–) to describe the far-reaching reforms implemented in the last five years of the Soviet Union. *Angels in America* dates from 1991, the year that the USSR collapsed, and two years after the fall of the Berlin Wall marked a symbolic end to the Cold War.

to juggle the grandiose with the banal, and it is the way that these two realities run in parallel that allows Prior Walter 'more life' at the end of the play. New York has averted its millennial disaster, but only because of its extraordinary resilience.

Rebuilding the City

While the urban literature of the 1990s suggested a pre-millennial anxiety about apocalypse, destruction, or the end of history, the events of 9/11, the first ever civilian attack on American soil, irrevocably changed the way America thought about its cities, and what they might symbolise. Subsequent works, even those not directly referencing the World Trade Centre attacks, are haunted by its presence; it has left a dust cloud in its wake. In this sense, 9/11 put an end to the playfully shoulder-shrugging moral causality of postmodernism. Even if the techniques used by writers such as Pynchon and Auster continued to influence writers of the 2000s, the relativism they implied could not be supported without ethical questions being asked; Julia Keller in *The Chicago Tribune* wrote a piece on how 'after the attacks, postmodernism loses its glib grip'.[30] Even in the apparently postmodern novel *Chronic City* (2010), Jonathan Lethem (1964–) takes care that his narrator does not share some of his narcotically influenced friend Perkus's wilder ideas about New York being a simulacrum, a 'virtual reality' or 'concocted environment'; while Perkus believes the metropolis has slipped into a 'temporal lacuna' and needs Manhattan to be 'both a falsehood and in ruins', Chase, the narrator, believes that 'by recent measures the city was orderly, flush with money, a little boring, even'.[31] Post-9/11, New York, and indeed the American city at large, has to find points of reconnection, and engage with the ordinary, the mundane, even, in order to survive the aftermath of its trauma.

In one of her last essays, 'Regarding the Pain of Others' (2003), the writer Susan Sontag (1933–2004) notes that 'a cityscape is not made of flesh. Still, sheared-off buildings are almost as eloquent as bodies in the street'; she goes on to mention the examples of Kabul in Afghanistan,

Sarajevo in Bosnia, and Ground Zero, the patch of land left decimated by the fall of the Twin Towers.[32] The poet Mark Doty (1953–) takes this further, observing that 'Three thousand people disappear on September 11. The city continues in some way to carry those bodies, to carry not just all those names and photographs, but the dust of those bodies. We breathe it in.'[33] Doty is speaking both metaphorically and literally here; it is a physical fact that people inhaled the debris of buildings *and* humans on 11 September 2001, but his point is also that nobody in New York on that day could fail to be conscious of the interconnectedness of individual fates. Some post-9/11 novels have registered an urgent desire to regain a sense of the city as a family, or a continuous history. One of the most striking examples is *Extremely Loud and Incredibly Close* (2005), the second novel of Jonathan Safran Foer (1977–). Oskar Schell, the narrator, is a rather exceptional young boy who has lost his father to the rubble. He embarks upon a quest to explain the story behind a key he retrieves from his father's effects; the quest almost becomes a postmodern nightmare for a variety of reasons. The archetypal set-up of the postmodern novel of the American city – the missing father and the search for identity – is here replayed with an increased urgency and fervour. Foer's work is full of narrative ingenuity and graphical innovations which seek to mirror Schell's bewilderment, and his sense of a loss that goes beyond something that can be explained or articulated. Blank pages, photos, overwritten paragraphs and a 'notebook' create a collaged text that is almost overwhelmed by words and questions, as Schell, finding a key in a vase, attempts to finds out everything there is to know about New York, and so to discover what has been taken from him. One of Oskar's most haunting precocious questions is: 'What if skyscrapers had roots?'[34] Those high buildings which seem to stretch to the sky also prove perilous; their destruction seems senseless, and without logic. The novel's final irony is perhaps that the text that Foer is writing in order to make sense of 9/11, and the notebook that his narrator is keeping, is less an answer to this loss than a reason for it. As Schell suggests with anguish, the contents of the offices, '[a]ll … those notepads, and Xeroxes, and printed e-mails, and photographs of kids, and books, and dollar bills in wallets, and documents in files … all of them were fuel' (p. 325). Here the city's textual presence ends up destroying itself. Even as Schell realises that his father's precious written keepsakes made the towers burn more quickly, he acknowledges the need to create more text to explain it. Nevertheless, along the way, he creates some surprise connections, and makes some unlikely friends; his desire to piece the city and its inhabitants back together again turns out to be infectious.

Other post-9/11 novels deal with different aspects of the aftermath. Don DeLillo's *Falling Man* (2007) takes as its central image the famous photograph of an office worker plummeting to his death from one of the towers, but the novel does not concern him; rather, it is an everyman tale about Keith Neudecker, and how he readjusts to 'normal' life in the wake of his brush with death (he escapes the attacks with minor injuries). John Updike's novel *Terrorist* (2006) attempts to respond more directly to the legacy of the 'War on Terror', tracing the life of an Islamic terrorist from his apparently benign upbringing in New Jersey to increasingly militant religious views and an eventual act of treason against his own country. This marked a departure for a novelist whose stock-in-trade had been portraits of disillusioned suburbia; the hostile critical reception suggested both an imaginative failure on Updike's part and a country still not able to imagine that its greatest threat might come from its own shores. While Updike's work is a brave failure, it tellingly looks to the literary history of the American city for its locale. Ahmad, the puritanical protagonist at the centre of the novel, is raised in the comfortable world of Paterson, New Jersey, the very same city that William Carlos Williams chose as the symbol of American community and kinship. Perhaps reviewers' bafflement at the novel came not primarily from Ahmad's final destructive act but from its seemingly docile origins. Nevertheless, readers of the future may ultimately look to novels such as Foer's to examine where the American city stood at the dawn of the twenty-first century. Like all great American literature of the city, it emphasises the ability of the metropolis to refashion itself against all the odds.

Notes

1   Henry James, *The American Scene* (1909) in *Henry James: Collected Travel Writings* (New York: Library of America, 1993), p. 357.

2   F. T. Marinetti. 'Manifesto of Futurism' (1909), *The Norton Anthology of American Literature Volume D 1914–1945* (New York: Norton, 2007), p. 101.

3   Frank Norris, *The Pit: A Story of Chicago* (New York: Penguin, 1994), p. 54.

4   Upton Sinclair, *The Jungle* (1906. New York: Penguin, 1985), p. 32.

5   Randalph Bourne, *The Radical Will: Selected Writings, 1911–1918* ed. Olaf Hansen (New York: Urizen, 1977), p. 522.

6   Robert Park, 'The City as Social Laboratory' (1929), in *On Social Control and Collective Behaviour*, ed. Ralph H. Turner (Chicago: University of Chicago Press, 1967), p. 45.

7   Max Weber, *The Protestant Ethic and the Spirit of Capitalism* (Oxford: Oxford University Press, 2010), p. 174.

8   See Thorstein Veblen, *The Theory of the Leisure Class* (Oxford: Oxford University Press, 2009).

9   Theodore Dreiser, *Sister Carrie* (Oxford: Oxford University Press, 1991), p. 1.

10   Dreiser, *Sister Carrie*, p. 15.

11   Willa Cather, *Lucy Gayheart* (New York: Penguin, 1999), p. 34.

12   E. L. Doctorow, *Ragtime* (New York: Random House, 1975), p. 4.

13   Henry Roth, *Call It Sleep* (New York: Cooper Square, 1965), p. 15.

14   Sinclair Lewis, *Free Air* (London: University of Nebraska Press, 1993), p. 102.

15   Mina Loy, 'Parturition', *The Norton Anthology of American Literature Volume D 1914–1945* (New York: Norton, 2007), p. 1457.

16   John Dos Passos, 'Against American Literature' (1928), *Travel Books & Other Writings* (New York: Library of America, 2003), p. 587.

17   John Dos Passos, *Manhattan Transfer* (London: Houghton Mifflin, 1953), p. 136.

18   H. P. Lovecraft, 'He', *Dagon and Other Macabre Tales* (Sauk City: Arkham House, 1987), pp. 230–1.

19   Carl Sandburg, 'Chicago' (1916), *The Complete Poems of Carl Sandburg* (London: Harcourt Brace, 1969), p. 3.

20   Mike Royko, 'San-Fran-York on the Lake', *I May Be Wrong, But I Doubt It* (Chicago: Henry Regnery, 1968), pp. 3–6.

21 William Carlos Williams, press release written for the publication of *Paterson* in 1951; reprinted in Christopher Beach, *The Cambridge Companion to Twentieth-Century American Poetry* (Cambridge: Cambridge University Press, 2003), p. 110.

22 William Carlos Williams, *Paterson* in *Selected Poems* (London: Penguin, 1976), p. 232.

23 Charles Olson, 'Letter 3', *The Charles Olson Reader* (Manchester: Carcanet, 2005), p. 53.

24 See Robert Venturi, *Contradiction and Complexity in Modern Architecture* (New York: Museum of Modern Art, 1966) and Colin Rowe and Fred Koetter's *Collage City* (Cambridge: MIT, 1978).

25 Thomas Pynchon, *V.* (London: Vintage, 2007), p. 132.

26 See Jean-François Lyotard, *The Postmodern Condition: A Report on Knowledge* (1979. Manchester: Manchester University Press, 1984).

27 Paul Auster, *New York Trilogy* (London: Penguin, 1990), p. 76.

28 Kevin Robins, 'Prisoners of the City: What Ever Could a Postmodern City Be?', in Eric Carter, James Donald and Judith Squires, eds, *Space and Place: Theories of Identity and Location* (London: Lawrence and Wishart, 1993), pp. 303–10 (304).

29 Tony Kushner, *Angels in America Part One: Millennium Approaches* (London: Nick Her, 1993), p. 22.

30 Julia Keller, 'After the Attacks, Postmodernism Loses Its Glib Grip', *Chicago Tribune*, 27 September, 2001.

31 Jonathan Lethem, *Chronic City* (London: Faber & Faber, 2010), pp. 457–8.

32 Susan Sontag, *Regarding the Pain of Others* (London: Hamish Hamilton, 2003), p. 7.

33 Mark Doty, interview with Christopher Hennessy, in Hennessy, *Outside the Lines: Talking with Contemporary Gay Poets* (Ann Arbor: University of Michigan Press, 2005), p. 83.

34 Jonathan Safran Foer, *Extremely Loud and Incredibly Close* (London: Penguin, 2005), p. 323.

American Masculinities

'Whoso would be a man, must be a non-conformist'; so runs one of the many dicta of 'Self-Reliance' (1841), arguably the most influential of all works published by the poet and essayist Ralph Waldo Emerson (1803–22).[1] The mythical male archetypes of the American cultural imagination are more often than not rebels and iconoclasts. From frontiersmen such as Daniel Boone, 'Buffalo' Bill Cody and Davy Crockett to the outlaws, Billy the Kid and Jesse James; from the lonely private detectives of Raymond Chandler and Dashiell Hammett's novels, such as Philip Marlowe and Sam Spade, to James Dean and Neal Cassady, countercultural 'rebels without a cause', the American male has been besieged with role models of self-determination whose defining characteristics are resistance to status quos and social norms. In time, this resistance has become a norm in itself, particularly in many cultural representations. While the 'all-American hero', usually of athletic prowess as well as unimpeachable morals, is a recognisable archetype, the anti-hero is just as integral to the collective imagination; for every Superman, there is a Holden Caulfield, the rebellious protagonist of J. D. Salinger's *The Catcher in the Rye*.

Conventional American heroism is often associated with the frontier, pioneer spirit and 'manifest destiny'.* Except in the world of team sports, it is synonymous with autonomy. The attraction of the

* See Part Two: 'A Cultural Overview' for a more detailed explanation of these concepts.

mythical cowboy lies in his independence. He makes his own rules and lives by them; his acreage is his kingdom. In this crucial regard, paradigms of manhood and masculinity in nineteenth-century America were very different to those of old-world Europeans. In England, 'gentlemanliness' was the model to which many young men aspired, particularly among the educated middle-classes; to be a gentleman was to conform to a set of recognisable values, to reach the pinnacle of a particular social hierarchy. The American male had different priorities that were not always compatible with this idea of 'society'; in Emerson's words, 'society everywhere is in a conspiracy against the manhood of every one of its members'. Early into its self-construction, the USA embraced the philosophy and culture of individualism; the French political historian Alexis de Tocqueville (1805–59) discusses it in his landmark work, *Democracy in America* (1835–40), noting that this fundamentally American characteristic 'disposes each citizen to cut himself off from the mass of his fellow men', leaving 'the larger society to take care of itself'. Though he is cautious about the potential implications for community feeling, Tocqueville accepts that individualism is a natural consequence of the democracy and religious freedoms that underpin the founding of the American constitution.[2] For Emerson, this is the very spirit of America, and he makes explicit its dependence on a certain type of masculinity; individualism is seen to be responsible for a healthy, self-determined masculinity, and in turn this masculinity upholds the greater good of individualism.

The Strenuous Life

In contrast to many British versions of manliness, then, American masculinity has usually been predicated on independent-mindedness and non-conformism. To paraphrase the famous 1969 Frank Sinatra song, it is often vital that American men be seen doing things their way. As early as 1832, the prominent statesman Henry Clay lauded the 'self-made men' of Kentucky in a senate speech, and before long the 'self-made man' was one of the major motifs of the American national narrative, spawning nineteenth-century biographies and hagiographies such as John Frost's *Self Made Men in America* (1848) and Charles Seymore's *Self Made Men* (1858). To be self-'made' was to be of independently acquired wealth, implying that individualism was not only good for the soul, body and intellect, but also a chief factor in the economic growth of the nation; the measurement of the man, then, was both his degree of personal freedom and the means by which he earned it. Such economic expansion mirrored the pioneering spirit that had seen American men claim the land and profit by it in the nineteenth century. This permutation of individualism can be read in early twentieth-century novels such as *The Financier* (1912) by Theodore Dreiser (1871–1945), which relates the ups and downs of the businessman Frank Cowperwood. Cowperwood judges successful masculinity by its ability to expand its reach; his eagerness to make money is akin to the American desire to tame the land and bring it under ownership. The apparent naturalness of such materialism is first figured in Cowperwood's childhood observation of a fish-tank, in which a lobster takes a squid as its prey; this is a world in which the bigger fish swallow the lesser. But there is also a distinct machismo in his attitude to acquisition. When his wife Lillian gives birth to a son, Dreiser writes that 'he liked it, the idea of self-duplication'.[3] Here there is little difference between fathering a child and Cowperwood's first business venture, buying soap from the market and selling it at a higher price to a grocer for quick profit. Dog-eat-dog capitalism is equated with a kind of biological determinism, which depends on men supplanting their enemies, and sowing their own seeds in their place.

In *The Financier*, Dreiser is responding to an archetype, one to some degree established by the political discourse of the time. In 1899, the future US president, Theodore Roosevelt, gave a speech to the Hamilton Club in Chicago, on what he called 'the strenuous life'. Roosevelt was sternly opposed to leisure and inherited wealth, marks of the 'over-civilised man' whose implicit effeminacy is a betrayal of the pride of his nation: this idler is 'a cumberer of the earth's surface'.[4] The published version praises instead 'those virile qualities necessary to win in the stern strife of actual life', arguing that the Civil War was a positive experience because it showed 'iron in the blood' and America's readiness to square up to catastrophe. He expands upon this in 'The American Boy' (1900), in which patriotism is even more explicitly linked to testosterone levels: the 'great growth in the love of athletic sports', he notes, has had 'an excellent effect in increasing manliness' and the willingness to show 'pluck, endurance and physical address' produces 'the kind of American man of whom America can be really proud'.[5] The essay concludes with a much-quoted maxim: 'In short, in life, as in a football game, the principle to follow is: Hit the line hard; don't foul and don't shirk, but hit the line hard!'*

Early twentieth-century American literature still promoted such masculine ideals with a certain amount of optimism and energy. Nevertheless, American writers were seldom as unambiguous as Roosevelt in their examination of the apparent connections between male physical prowess and moral superiority. One of the most prominent novelists of the early twentieth century, Jack London (1876–1916), achieved popularity for his rugged adventure fiction, particularly two novels written from the perspective of dogs, *The Call of the Wild* (1903) and *White Fang* (1906), but it is *The Sea-Wolf* (1904) that is especially telling. In this novel, a bookish man of leisure, Humphrey Van Weyden, is rescued from his boat by the captain of seal-hunting schooner, Wolf Larsen. Larsen is the epitome of self-made toughness, but the power of his body is also primal. His name is characteristic of London's fiction; he is almost half-animal, his strength that of 'the creatures we imagine our tree-dwelling prototypes to have been', full of 'the potency of motion, the elemental stuff'.[6] The regime Van Weyden enters on the *Ghost* when he becomes Larsen's cabin boy is a world away from his previous life as a 'gentleman'. The rather aristocratic Humphrey becomes the more primitive 'Hump', the object both of Larsen's protective, almost homoerotic interest, and his lackey, his 'manhood' subject to 'slurs' (p. 632). Larsen is 'an individualist of the most pronounced type' (p. 540), which clashes with Van Weyden's humanism: 'I may have

* See Part Two: 'A Cultural Overview' for further discussion of this.

learned to stand on my own legs', says the latter, 'but I have yet to stamp upon others with them', to which Larsen replies, 'Your education is only half completed, then' (p. 632). Van Weyden is the novel's ultimate victor, but the significance of his ascendancy can be read in two possible ways: he either unites intellect with physical strength, thus creating a new kind of heroism, or alternatively, he is proof that the survival of the American man depends on a rediscovery of primal muscularity.

The Legacy of War

As the British writer Andrew Sinclair has noted, 'individualism and Nietzschean belief in the strength of the will' are usually more apparent than London's self-avowed socialism.[7] From a twenty-first century perspective, London's novels often look very much like advertisements for Roosevelt's 'strenuous life'. This 'strenuous life' was in fact part of a wider objective – to advance a type of American cultural imperialism; the individual was still part of a greater good. However, the anti-hero that emerged as one of the definitive male archetypes of the twentieth century could arguably be traced to the resistance of this greater good; he is often a reluctant arbiter between liberty and the forces, external or internal, that threaten to compromise it. These crisis points occurred continually in the USA throughout the twentieth century, and questions of American masculinity have often been central to their cultural and literary resonance.

On 6 April 1917, President Woodrow Wilson abandoned the American policy of non-intervention in Europe, and declared war on Germany. Over 2 million men were drafted to fight, including many writers and intellectuals. Some enlisted voluntarily, though many grew to regret it; among them were the novelists John Dos Passos (1896–1970) and Ernest Hemingway (1899–1961) and the poet and novelist E. E. Cummings (1894–1962). Dos Passos volunteered with the Norton-Harjes Ambulance Corps during 1917, and some of his experiences are depicted in his first novel, *One Man's Initiation:*

1917 (1920); much of this short work deals with the culture-shock of arriving in Europe. However, it is *Three Soldiers* (1921) that examines the effect of war upon the minds and bodies of men in most detail. The novel focuses not on the active theatre of war so much as tensions within the US army itself, and the eponymous servicemen offer contrasting views of life in the forces. All three have enlisted willingly, rather than being drafted. Chrisfield is a volatile young man, who in his irritation kills one of his own, an American lieutenant; the Italian-American Fuselli is a sycophant who believes primarily in the glory of the military life for its own sake, and is desperate to be promoted from private to corporal. The novel comes to settle more on the progress of John Andrews, a composer from New York. His initial reason for enlisting is defiantly anti-individualistic, a subversion of Theodore Roosevelt's rhetoric; he is 'sick of revolt, of thought, of carrying his individuality like a banner', instead desiring only to lose himself in the crowd, 'to be but one organism'.[8] By the end of the novel, he has been wounded, and appears unable to escape the military machine because of bureaucratic red tape. It turns out that the 'Hun' is not the real enemy. Rather, it is a system invented and overseen by the American establishment itself; so much for the self-made men of the New World.

E. E. Cummings is even more scathing in his criticism of an America that wants her men to be heroic, but only in a narrow, top-down definition of the term. One of Cummings's most widely known poems, 'i sing of Olaf glad and big' (1931) apparently pays tribute to a man he met in training at Camp Devens in Massachusetts, who preferred to read Thomas Browne's *Religio Medici* than take up his gun.[9] This conscientious objector was sent to an army prison, at which it was highly likely that he was beaten. 'i sing of Olaf glad and big' treats him as a true anti-hero. Cummings's characteristic use of lower-case letters sees his capitalised name dignified alongside those of God and Christ, a privilege not granted to his colonel or the president of the United States. Olaf curses the flag, and is repaid with a type of bullying that specifically belittles his masculinity, with overtones of sodomy; the officers 'egged the firstclassprivates on / his rectum wickedly to tease / by means of skilfully applied / bayonets roasted hot with heat'.[10]

The officers are described as 'a yearning nation's blueeyed pride', almost a kind of Aryan super-race in which Americans have entrusted their hopes, but the end of the poem witnesses Olaf trumping their conventional heroic credentials: 'unless statistics lie, he was / more brave than me: more blond than you'. Olaf's courage is anti-courage, the exact opposite of how the commanders of the military, and the head of state himself, would define it. To go against the received wisdom of the establishment is true bravery; blondness may usually be associated with the clean-cut conventional hero, but here such boyish appeal is invoked by Cummings only to point to the redundancy of such archetypes.

His earlier novel, *The Enormous Room* (1922), which focuses on the author's experiences as a volunteer for the same American Red Cross ambulance corps as John Dos Passos prior to conscription, similarly promotes individualism in the face of institutionalisation. When Cummings is detained at a camp in the Norman town of La Ferté-Macé on suspicion of treasonable correspondence, he is forced to live and eat meagrely with a motley group of oddballs and outcasts. Though their experiences are sometimes hellish, they retain their eccentricity. Anticipating some of the more existentialist literature of the 1950s, Cummings at various points restates his need to exist apart, and even the tiniest room with the smallest amount of privacy might suffice: 'I was myself', he writes, in a standalone sentence.[11]

While Cummings and Dos Passos were praised for their war testimonies, Ernest Hemingway's *A Farewell to Arms* (1929) is undoubtedly the most acclaimed and well known of all American First World War novels. Hemingway had already published *The Torrents of Spring* (1926), *Fiesta: The Sun Also Rises* (1926) and the short stories of *In Our Time* (1925) and *Men Without Women* (1927), both of which are concerned with finding a language that might anatomise masculinity. In the posthumously published memoir *A Moveable Feast* (1964), the chapter 'Miss Stein Instructs' relates the advice of the novelist Gertrude Stein (1874–1946), a friend and mentor to Hemingway during his time in Paris. Her views on writing mingle with her warnings against homosexuality;[*] the juxtaposition reveals Hemingway's anxieties about

---

[*] Stein's antipathy is specifically towards male homosexuality; she was a lesbian herself.

the potential effeminacy of writing as a vocation. He goes to some lengths to justify the singular, influential minimalism for which he is famous, implicitly linking it to the tough, muscular honesty of his own maleness. He cautions himself against writing 'elaborately' and emphasises his manliness outside of the creative context, divulging that after writing, 'it was necessary to get exercise, to be tired in the body, and it was very good to make love with whom you loved'.[12] As the critic John Dudley has argued, the myth of authorship in the nineteenth century 'often carried suggestions of effeminacy', but the twentieth century witnessed the rise of the 'virile, robust man of action', a rise in which Hemingway played a pivotal role.[13]

The dispassionate, undemonstrative voice of Frederic Henry in *A Farewell to Arms* is similar to that of Jake Barnes in *Fiesta: The Sun Also Rises*. However, where the earlier novel depicts the leisurely drifting of expats in Paris, who journey to Spain to watch bullfighting chiefly in order to *do* something, *A Farewell to Arms* is full of incident. Frederic Henry is a lieutenant in the Italian army's ambulance corps, and is a man of action in that he appears to live entirely in the present; the novel never elaborates on his history, and he never explains his motives for volunteering. He is anything but a patriot, registering great ambivalence towards both countries and the cultural identities on which they depend. Concepts make him suspicious; he feels that 'abstract words such as honour, glory, courage, or hallow were obscene beside the concrete names of villages, the numbers of roads, the names of rivers'.[14] This is a manifestation of a kind of anti-intellectualism. Elsewhere, Frederic muses, 'I was not made to think. I was made to eat ... Eat and drink and sleep with Catherine' (p. 206). This is, of course, self-contradictory; he also quotes the poet Andrew Marvell at one point. It is a little too easy to equate Frederic Henry with Hemingway himself, but he does neatly express one of the most prominent dichotomies of the novelist's self-construction. *A Moveable Feast* traces the progress of Hemingway the reader, and his encounters with literary luminaries such as Ford Madox Ford and Gertrude Stein. Nevertheless, his voice frequently seems anti-literary; his masculine credentials are directly tied to his ability to play down his own intellectualism.

In 1939, the literary critic Philip Rahv characterised American literature at large as being caught between the 'paleface' and the 'redskin'. The former is a 'highbrow' for whom American culture is 'a source of endless ambiguities' (the 'drawing-room fictions' of Henry James are offered as exemplary), while the latter 'glories in his Americanism', looking West rather than East.[15] Rahv saw the 'redskin' triumphing over the 'paleface' in twentieth-century American literature; he bemoans the disappearance of 'high' culture in breathlessly racist overtones. Hemingway's voice could certainly be said to have 'triumphed'. Its echoes can be found in the writings of the Beat Generation, in J. D. Salinger's *The Catcher in the Rye* and the so-called 'dirty realism' of 1980s writers such as Richard Ford and Raymond Carver. Rahv's opinion of Hemingway, 'that perennial boy-man', may have been withering, but Hemingway's guidance on how the American male writer might tread the fine line between literariness and impulsive masculinity has been incalculable.

Men Out of Work

Nevertheless, the more rugged of Hemingway's tales were as increasingly escapist in a 1930s context. The 1929 stock market crash brought the Great Depression in its wake, and the American male faced his next crisis, namely whether it was possible to maintain established models of masculinity in the face of unemployment, destitution and the destruction of decades of tradition. The Depression forced many American men to reconsider their relationship to land and nation. The hardest-hit were the agrarians – sharecroppers and tenant farmers – whose precarious roots became painfully and swiftly apparent. The 1930s novels of John Steinbeck (1902–68) all respond to these shifting parameters. Though not set during the Depression, Steinbeck's second major work, *To a God Unknown* (1933), is clearly of its time. It is driven by an aching nostalgia for the fallen land of pioneers, charting Joseph Wayne's emblematic migration from New England to California. His story has explicit biblical echoes, for, just as Adam

210

named the animals, Joseph 'spoke with the sanction of the grass, the soil, the beasts wild and domesticated'.[16] However, it is clear that this cannot end in fertility and prosperity; Joseph's fate, as a symbolic 'first man', is to slash his wrists during an elemental rainstorm, his blood leeching into the soil. Depression or no depression, nature regains control when mankind fails to master it. *Of Mice and Men* (1937) is equally ambivalent about male physical authority and the relationship between mankind and the land. Lennie and George dream of owning their own ranch. George, the savvier of the two, constantly reassures his clumsy, mentally disabled friend that they intend to 'look after' each other; they are drifters, and thus have no family except themselves.[17] However, the novella does not promote a kind of homosocial marriage.* The prospects of a long-lasting bond between the two men are destroyed when Lennie, unaware of the power of his own brute strength, kills the wife of Curley, the son of the owner of the ranch on which Lennie and George work; she offers him her hair to stroke, but screams on realising how strong he is, and in the ensuing confusion, he breaks her neck. Knowing that Lennie will be killed by Curley's lynch-mob, George shoots him out of mercy. Throughout the novella, Lennie enthuses about the rabbits he will be able to tend once he and George establish their ranch; by the end, the image of Lennie himself is of an animal, put out of its misery in a supposedly humane fashion.

Though they live through uncompromising times, Steinbeck's men still make ethical choices and sacrifices. Much of his work, though, is also motivated by socialist beliefs; individualism makes for precarious futures and, taken to the market capitalist extremes so viciously critiqued in *The Grapes of Wrath* (1939), can actually, paradoxically, *deny* the individual voice or agency. Some Depression novelists take this even further. The novels of Erskine Caldwell (1903–87) have always caused controversy, their literary merits debated, and their obscenity

---

* In sociology and cultural studies, homosociality indicates a close same-sex relationship that is passionate but non-sexual. It might be seen in so-called 'buddy movies' (also known as 'bromances') and features extensively in the queer theory of Eve Kosofsky Sedgwick, particularly in the book, *Between Men: English Literature and Male Homosocial Desire* (1985).

censured. Nevertheless, they are key documents of their time; *Tobacco Road* (1932) and *God's Little Acre* (1933) in particular are unflinching in their representation of the depths to which impoverished families plummeted during the crisis. Aside from the Southern grotesques and sexual sensationalism, Caldwell asks some valuable questions about the state of the American man in the 1930s. Both Jeeter Lester in *Tobacco Road* and Ty Ty Walden in *God's Little Acre* stubbornly refuse to leave the land they have planted and tilled for decades, in order to seek prosperity in another line of work. Jeeter's wife is suffering from pellagra,* and most of his children have fled to the city, but he will not be uprooted because 'the Lord made the land, and he put me here to raise crops on it'. To desert would be to betray his family heritage, for his 'Daddy' and grandfather worked the land before him. Any alternative to this patrilineage would be an affront not only to Jeeter's family, but also his gender; he refuses to find work in the cotton mills because 'winding strings on spools' is 'for the women folks'.[18] Jeeter's relationship with his own masculinity, then, matters more than whether or not he can feed the next generation of Lesters, a case of male pride literally turning sterile.

The Domesticated Man

In reality, by the 1930s, fewer and fewer men were working the land. In his influential study of the emerging metropolitan office class, *White Collar* (1951), the sociologist C. Wright Mills (1916–62) looks back over the Depression period as one in which the urban economy sealed its advantage over the rural. City monopolists squeezed production in order to keep prices up; though in any case, by the Second World War, vast swathes of land were severely depleted from decades of over-farming. It was becoming less and less likely that success could be gained from the fat of the land; urbanism dictated that the 'white collar' clerk was rapidly becoming the new American anti-hero, the

* Pellagra is a vitamin deficiency disease usually caused by a chronic lack of vitamin B3 in the diet.

'little man' struggling to retain an individual identity amidst the faceless corporation.[19] By 1951, Wright Mills could confidently state that

> By examining white-collar life, it is possible to learn something about what is becoming more typically 'American' than the frontier character probably ever was. What must be grasped is the picture of society as a great salesroom, an enormous file, an incorporated brain, a new universe of management and manipulation. (p. xv)

The self-made man was being threatened by the system; this sociological and demographic turn would come to define the literature and culture of American masculinities beyond the Second World War, from the everyman travails of Willy Loman in Arthur Miller's play *Death of a Salesman* (1949) to Sloan Wilson's novel *The Man in the Grey Flannel Suit* (1955), in which the eponymous character must adjust to the transition from war-hero to company middle-man. The pressures on the post-war male became more tied to material security and status symbols than ever before, as summarised by the sociologist Talcott Parsons in 1959: 'virtually the only way to be a real man in our society is to have an adequate job and earn a living'.[20]

Many worried that the rise of the white-collar worker had an emasculating influence. Men were much more likely to work alongside women in the office. Their athletic potential went unrealised at the desk. And once again, the progress of the male family line was jeopardised; as C. Wright Mills notes, the small businessman's sons and the farmer's could often look forward to inheriting property, and thus status, but 'the floorwalker's sons or the assistant manager's cannot expect to inherit such family position' (p. 252). This explains some of the paranoia behind Willy Loman's misplaced faith in his son Biff in *Death of a Salesman*, the son whose peak came early at school in a baseball game, only to regress into restlessness and sporadic employment. It also lies behind the malaise of the title character in *Rabbit, Run* (1960), the first in a series of five novels by John Updike (1932–2009) which chart the ups and downs of American culture through another everyman, Harry

'Rabbit' Angstrom.[21] In *Rabbit, Run*, the reader encounters Angstrom, currently a salesman for the MagiPeeler, a labour-saving kitchen device; even the object he must promote is designed for housewives, a sign that women were often the real targets and beneficiaries of the domestic consumer boom. Angstrom used to be a basketball star, and in the novel's opening sequence, he is seen trying to join some youths in their game, a poignant reminder that any sense of male destiny predicated on sportsmanship is transitory and unstable. His marriage is faltering, and he takes to the road, hoping that his motor adventure will help him regain a sense of himself as an American male. However, his southward trajectory from Pennsylvania offers no wilderness, no primal site of pioneer spirit. He spies a farmer, and grows to resent the 'smugness' and 'solidity' of this man with his 'work-worn hands'. The experience causes the former athlete to grow physically clumsy, as if his 'shoelaces [were] too long' or there were 'a stick between his feet'.[22] Rabbit's anxieties are bound up with a suspicion that his masculinity is waning; it is an almost pathological understanding of maleness in crisis which reverberates through much post-war American fiction, on and into the work of Richard Ford (1944–), for example, whose Frank Bascombe novels offer useful comparisons to the Rabbit series.

Fears of Feminisation

Conventional American masculinity was threatened by other influences in the 1950s. There was a mounting unease about the possible 'feminisation' of the male. While offering young men the opportunity to restock their reserves of masculine pride and re-establish the heroic primacy of the American male, the Second World War also advanced the emancipation of women to some degree. Women contributed hugely to the effort at home. 'Government Girls' were hired in major federal departments; the Red Cross and nurse corps offered women a variety of key roles, and there were even opportunities for female civilians to fly aircraft, in organisations such as the WASP (Women Airforce Service Pilots) and WAFS (Women's Auxiliary Ferrying Squadron). Women correspondents also stepped out onto the frontlines, notably Lee Miller, war photographer and writer for *Vogue*, and Martha Gellhorn, whose *Collier's* dispatches were renowned for their apparently un-feminine objectivity, seemingly so at odds with the beautiful, glamorous woman who penned them. Gellhorn was the third wife of Ernest Hemingway, for many the epitome of the macho American writer, and his influence on her war reports, as well as on novels such as *A Stricken Field* (1940) and *The Face of War* (1959) proved that a woman writer could succeed in previously male-dominated spheres of literary endeavour.

More conservative writers and thinkers were apprehensive about the blurring of gender lines, and believed women to be exerting too much influence on men. Among all the 'enemies within' in 1950s America – the suspected communists infiltrating government, cinema and literature, the emergent homosexual, the 'rebel without a cause' – there was also the mother. The male fear of female domination found its most histrionic expression in the tract *Generation of Vipers* by Philip Wylie (1902–71), originally published in 1942, though reissued in 1954 because, according to Wylie, its predictions had come true to a degree 'bordering on insanity'.[23] His most notorious coinage, subject to frequent charges of misogyny, was 'Momism': the fetishising of the domineering American mother by her emasculated sons. Some of his ammunition came from the Austrian psychoanalyst Sigmund Freud (1856–1939), whose theories reached a height of popularity in 1950s and 1960s America; but he also saw the phenomenon around him in everyday life, declaring breathlessly that 'I cannot think, offhand, of any civilisation except ours in which an entire division of living men has been used, during wartime, or at any time, to spell out the word "mom" on a drill field' (p. 197). Overbearing mothers are certainly a feature of much post-war American literature and film. Philip Roth's take on this archetype in his 1969 novel, *Portnoy's Complaint*, is played for comedy. The loud Jewish mother of the title character is a figure of fear, necessitating the psychotherapeutic confession around which the novel is based. Having called her son's penis his 'little thing' at an impressionable age, she is implicitly blamed for his addiction to masturbation, which despite being recounted with a certain witty bravado ('I am the Raskolnikov of jerking off', says Portnoy at one point, invoking the murderous anti-hero of Dostoevsky's *Crime and Punishment*), actually turns out to be a pathological weakness.[24]

The supposed prevalence of the domineering mother was even used to explain in part the culture of teenage rebellion that is now so strongly identified with the 1950s. The film *Rebel Without a Cause* (1955), directed by Nicholas Ray, depicts the turbulent life of the seventeen-year-old Jim Stark, who refuses to conform to societal norms and commits acts of delinquency. In many ways, he is the latest in the line of self-determined young men, except he has no direction, no purpose. One possible reason for this is the emasculation of his father, who is seen performing household chores in an apron, to the demands of Stark's mother. The film confirmed the iconic status of James Dean, whose combination of outsider toughness and almost feminine vulnerability was typical of the new breed of male Hollywood idols. Dean, Marlon Brando and Montgomery Clift all had bisexual affairs, and had an androgynous appeal. Clearly, masculinities in 1950s America were in a period of great transition.

Coming Out

The war also offered opportunities for gay men to confound prejudice and make a valuable contribution to the army effort. During the First World War, homosexual soldiers could be tried for sodomy and sentenced to fifteen years' imprisonment, but by the 1940s, the official line was to refer offenders to the army psychiatrist. Conscripts were supposedly screened, subjected to questions about their sex lives and interests, but in practice the military were not always so discriminating, especially when the need for servicemen was so great. In any case, same-sex congress often had little to do with the supposedly discernible homosexual 'type'. Apparently well-adjusted men, comfortable with their own gender and sexual orientation, could nevertheless engage in gay sexual activity if social or financial expediency dictated it. In one of the most famous novels to deal with the war, *From Here to Eternity*

(1951), James Jones originally included scenes with explicit references to same-sex practices; in the manuscript, the character of Maggio takes money as a gigolo for older Hawaiian men, and discusses the limits of what he will do for financial reward. Jones's publisher, Scribner, were uneasy, and censored the most risqué passages; Jones later argued that many soldiers treated homosexuality with a matter-of-fact shrug, and that it was disingenuous to exclude it from realist accounts of the war.

It is possible to detect similar undertones in other celebrated military novels of the period. For example, General Cummings in Norman Mailer's *The Naked and the Dead* (1949) is a latent homosexual. He flirts obliquely with his aide, Hearn, carries silk handkerchiefs and orders fresh flowers to be brought to his tent, which are markers of the kind of effeminacy that the draft board might mistakenly and stereotypically equate with gay inclinations. He is also a sadist, ordering his troops to go through unnecessary and sometimes humiliating trials. Mailer infers that this is an expression of Cummings's repressed sexual 'urges', urges that sometimes keep him awake at night. Feelings of sexual inadequacy cause him to seek to dominate his men as a way of reasserting his own masculinity; his argument runs that men do not seek approval from women, but that they measure their capabilities solely against those of their male peers. This was also Mailer's view; though he was uncomfortable with homosexuality, he was nevertheless aware of its place in the formation of masculine identity. In his 1954 essay, 'The Homosexual Villain', he uses examples from his own work, including General Cummings and Leroy the secret police agent in *Barbary Shore* (1951), to comment on the archetype of the queer crook, but he also acknowledges that male homophobia is really a reflection of sexual insecurity, and that masculinity is usually only a topic of debate when it is threatened in some way. He writes that 'there is probably no sensitive heterosexual alive who is not preoccupied at one time or another with his latent homosexuality'.[25] Far from constructing gay males as preening queens and sissies, Mailer acknowledges the potential for homosexuality within all men, though this of course falls well short of complete acceptance. Nevertheless, this view could only have come from the experiences of wartime service, where huge numbers of men were separated from regular female contact for months on end, repeatedly forced to confront their maleness, and, in some cases, the presence of gay servicemen within their ranks, performing their duties with a vigour and commitment equal to that of their straight peers.

The City and the Pillar (1946), the first major novel by Gore Vidal (1925–), is even more candid about this shift in male consciousness. The protagonist, Jim, is athletic and patriotic, a regular all-American guy who just happens to be attracted to members of his own sex. He develops a crush on the high school sports star, Bob, and the two become friends the summer after graduation. Friendship leads to some homoerotic bonding in a deserted cabin out in the countryside, and a brief sexual encounter. Over the coming years, Jim continually revisits the cabin in nostalgic fantasies, dreaming of what it might be like to settle down with his first love for good. His hopes remain unfulfilled; when he finally rediscovers Bob, now married, the two go drinking in New York and share a hotel room. Bob talks of some of the 'queers' he has met in the army, but Jim misinterprets the direction of their conversation and advances on him. When Bob registers alarm, Jim is destroyed; unable to cope with the destruction of his ideal, he chokes Bob to death.* Jim moves in homosexual circles in New York and Hollywood, but his broader identity is not tied to the subculture. It could be argued that what really breaks his heart at the end of the novel is the implied equivalence Bob draws between their adolescent sexuality and the more socially unacceptable practices of the adult homosexual. The nature of their relationship as youths is a form of innocence, and the attempt to regain that innocence only corrupts it. It would appear that love between males is a sin only when it is named.

At a predominantly homosexual party, Jim listens to two men deep in conversation about this dichotomy. One of them contends that the war has caused 'a great revelation'. 'Normal-looking young soldiers' have had their inhibitions 'broken down' so that 'for the first time they have the opportunity to dredge their own subconscious of mysterious longings ... returning to that primitive state when, once upon a time, we were both man and woman complete in ourselves.'[26]

---

* This is the case in the original version of the novel, but in the 1965 revision, Vidal has Jim rape Bob instead of killing him.

The 'mysterious longings' here would seem to have little to do with the trappings of a proto-gay subculture; rather, they are a reconnection with a well-established form of American masculinity, founded on unabashed, 'primitive' homoeroticism, the bonding of bodies and souls espoused in the poetry of Walt Whitman or in Herman Melville's short stories and novels. These early, foundational American texts of the nineteenth century depicted 'manly love' as a kind of Eden, a 'paradise of bachelors',[27] and for many the war experience and its aftermath reopened the gates to this promised land. Writers became more and more emboldened to discuss gay sexuality in their work; the 1940s and 1950s would see a steady increase in high-profile homosexual writers, including the novelists Truman Capote, James Baldwin and Gore Vidal, the poets Robert Duncan, Jack Spicer and Frank O'Hara, and the dramatists Tennessee Williams, William Inge and Edward Albee. Duncan even wrote a polemic of sorts, 'The Homosexual in Society' (1944), in which he took the risky decision to divulge his own sexual orientation in order to distance himself from the 'cultish' homosexual subculture and argue for a more integrated role for gay men in public life. John Cheever could declare that 1948 was 'the year that everyone in the United States was worried about homosexuality': 'Is he? Was he? Did they? Am I? seemed to be at the back of everyone's mind'.[28] One text especially caused alarm: *Sexual Behaviour in the Human Male* (1948), a now-discredited but historically important report by the psychologist Alfred Kinsey, which claimed that 37 per cent of adult males had had at least one same-sex experience.

Further on into the 1950s, the 'Beat Generation' of writers would continue the celebration of 'manly love', both sexually in the case of Allen Ginsberg's poetry and William Burroughs's novels, and, in the work of Jack Kerouac, more platonically, though the relationships between men in his novels were by no means devoid of erotic frissons. Kerouac was troubled by his own bisexual tendencies, and tended to erase much of the queerness of the Beat movement from the final drafts of his novels, but it can clearly be detected between the lines. In *On the Road* (1957), the famous *roman a clef* written during the 1940s and 1950s that charts Kerouac's brotherly relationship with Neil Cassady and their travels together across the USA, the love between the two men occasionally veers into distinctly romantic territory, particularly in Part Three. Dean Moriarty (Cassady's fictional alias) has just been thrown out by one of his women, Camille, and he and Sal Paradise (Kerouac's own pseudonym) hatch a plan to move to Italy together. Dean suddenly flashes Sal a look: 'he never took his eyes off mine for a long time', narrates Sal, and 'I looked back at him and blushed.'[29] This is clearly a flirtation, a testing of the sexual tension between the two men, and it affects them both profoundly. With tears in his eyes, Sal urges Dean to come to New York with him; he asks him what was behind the 'look', but Dean is too bashful to say. Instead, they watch a Greek wedding play itself out underneath their San Franciscan vantage, and Dean resolves, in 'a very shy and sweet voice', to leave with Sal for Italy, the two of them 'broken-down heroes of the Western night' (p. 173). The 'hero[ism]' of the men is the product of their boyish infatuation with each other, and recalls other borderline homoerotic relationships between earlier literary 'heroes', such as Ishmael and Queequeg in Melville's *Moby-Dick* (1851) or Huck and Jim in Mark Twain's *Adventures of Huckleberry Finn* (1885). This is as much part of *On the Road*'s American mythology as its open highways and westward travelogues.

It could be argued, in fact, that much subsequent gay literature, from the time of the Stonewall Riots of 1969, in which gay men stood up to police persecution in New York, to the liberation movements of the 1970s, kept up the American tradition of the self-reliant, non-conformist male. It was also able to play itself out in the all-male fantasy land that much American literature had always implied, the 'masculine wilderness of the American novel' that seeks to exclude women, in the view of the feminist writer Carolyn Heilbrun.[30] Novels such as Andrew Holleran's *Dancer From the Dance* (1978) and Larry Kramer's *Faggots* (also 1978) emphasised the counterculture of the holiday resort, Fire Island, once beloved of the gay poet Frank O'Hara, and now an uninhibited party hangout. Equally important were the *Tales of the City* series by Armistead Maupin (1944–) and the novels of Edmund White (1940–), both of whom went on to chronicle the trauma of AIDS in the 1980s and 1990s, and respond to shifting values in the gay communities of San Francisco and New York.

Feminist, Queer and Beyond

As well as the rise of gay liberation movements, American masculinity had to absorb other waves of social change in the 1960s and 1970s. The Vietnam War, the most divisive conflict since the Yankees fought the Confederates in the 1860s, once more challenged the patriotism and patience of young Americans, though as the critic Susan Jeffords has noted, it did also 'remasculinize' the American male.[31] The anti-war protest movements attracted a coalition of outcasts and rebels, and were closely identified with the 'hippies' of the late 1960s counterculture, whose fluid sexual identities and often androgynous outward appearances showed further blurring of the boundaries between the genders.

The rise of feminism through the 1960s and 1970s also challenged the American male's self-perception as never before. In 1970, the feminist critic and activist Kate Millett (1934 –) published *Sexual Politics*, which read writers such as Henry Miller and D. H. Lawrence through current theories of patriarchy. Norman Mailer, a writer who comes in for particular opprobrium, was sufficiently incensed by Millett's book to publish his own response, *The Prisoner of Sex* (1971), in which he denounces the Women's Movement as 'the most prominent phenomenon of the summer season' and waspishly declares 'the land of Millett' to be 'a barren and mediocre terrain', implying that she is less than a 'real' woman for being a substandard intellectual.[32] These hiccups are not necessarily typical of male writers' responses to the first wave of feminism. Vestiges of misogyny remain throughout American literature; but even those novelists who write extensively about divorce and marriage troubles, such as John Updike and Richard Ford, discuss the disconnects between the sexes in post-feminist ways.

During the 1980s, feminism had become established enough to spark its own versions among men; male pro-feminists (akin to the 'New Man' in the United Kingdom) sought to take on some of the roles traditionally associated with women, and advance the causes of feminism through activism. Nevertheless, there were backlashes. The hungry market-capitalist culture of 1980s cliché, immortalised in films such as *Wall Street* (1987) and the Tom Wolfe novel *The*

Bonfire of the Vanities (also 1987), marked the resurgence of the self-made man, liberated into financial speculation by President Reagan's deregulations and tax cuts. This was a world of bonds, in two senses; financial product, created, marketed and sold almost entirely by men, whose mutual patter, buoyed dichotomously by both competition and 'male bonding', could be unabashed in its sexism. One of the chief observers of this newly aggressive white-collar world was the playwright and screenwriter David Mamet (1947–). His work is awash with expletives and simmering verbal violence. In the play *Glengarry Glen Ross* (1982), four estate agents are set into competition by their boss to find profitable 'leads'; the victor wins a Cadillac, the runner-up a set of steak knives, and the two losers are fired. This survival of the fittest charade is denounced by the salesman Ross, who complains 'when they *build* your business, then you can't … *enslave* them, treat them like *children* [and] leave them to fend for themselves'.[33] The implication is that this hyper-masculine contest of wills actually emasculates the men it is supposed to empower.

Elsewhere, Mamet has expressed his distaste for the term 'male bonding', though he does praise 'the joy of male companionship'.[34] This return to the lifestyle summarised by Mamet as 'The Lodge, Hunting, Fishing' was also practised by the 'Mythopoetic' Men's Movement; inspired by the work of the poet Robert Bly (1926–), in particular his 1990 publication *Iron John: A Book About Men*, this movement advocated a rediscovery of the spirituality of men's relationships with each other and the land. Nevertheless, many of these reactions against feminism were and continue to be highly self-aware, particularly in that they acknowledge they are performative. The queer and feminist theorist, Judith Butler (1956–), argues in the much-quoted *Gender Trouble* (1990) that far from being essential, gender identities are constructed through a series of repeated acts over time.[35] While it is a mistake to conflate 'performativity' in this instance with what we might understand as 'performance', there has nevertheless been a marked awareness, even embrace, of maleness as an act in much American literature of the 1990s and 2000s.

The work of two novelists, Bret Easton Ellis (1964–) and Chuck Palahniuk (1962–), is exemplary here. In the 1990s, Easton Ellis's notorious *American Psycho* (1991) was the object of much reactionary hostility, with its often luridly sexual, graphic violence. Patrick Bateman is an investment banker, one of the new breed of macho Wall Street 'yuppies'.* He obsessively catalogues all the details of the consumer society around him – Haagen Dazs ice-creams, Genesis albums and such – which even gives him a certain nerdy street-credibility. Yet as the novel progresses, the reader encounters a series of gruesome murders; he rapes women, saws off their limbs and, most horrifyingly, engages in a bout of cannibalism. It would appear that Bateman's outward life is completely divorced from his inner; the two represent a hyper-masculinity taken to its most extreme limit. Nevertheless, the reader is left wondering by the end whether or not the violence actually takes place, or whether it is a fantasy; details do not always tally, leaving the 'truth' of the plot ambiguous. Similarly, Chuck Palahniuk's novel *Fight Club* (1996; made into a film in 1999) depicts a respectable office worker caught in the middle of an identity crisis. Though he outwardly carries many of the hallmarks of the 1990s American male, he joins the 'fight club' in order to regain something primal; a kind of male bonding à la the 'mythopoetic men's movement' that depends upon bare-knuckle combat in a secret location, a reminder of the ritual performativity of manhood. The narrator offers a partial explanation of this behaviour in contemporary sociology that would not be out of place in Philip Wylie's *Generation of Vipers* ('what you see at fight club is a generation of men raised by women')[36] but it also embraces the homoerotic; Tyler Durden, the leader of the club, is idealised by the narrator, and there is even a kiss. It is revealed, however, that Tyler is in fact himself the narrator, and that he is suffering from a kind of split personality disorder. Though he seems to desire a return to the machismo of the traditional American anti-hero, this is in fact the consequence of a wider fracture in masculine identity.

---

* 'Yuppie' is formed from the acronym YUP (Young Urban Professional), which became widely used in the 1980s to describe young self-made businessmen and women in urban centres.

Since the 1990s, writers have continued to play with archetypes and stereotypes, subverting them with irreverence. Jeffrey Eugenides's *Middlesex* (2002) tells the story of an inter-sexed character, Cal Stephanides, who is a woman for the first half of the novel, and a man in the second, making valuable points about the constructed nature of gender; the girl, Callie, fakes period pains because she thinks they will make her seem more womanly, while the man, Cal, must learn to write more like a man, with less 'girls' school propriety'.[37] In 1997, even cowboys turned queer; Annie Proulx's short story 'Brokeback Mountain', made into an Oscar-winning film in 2005, used the most stereotypical frontier myth of all to show how tragedy can ensue from social expectations of what the 'masculine' might signify. In many ways, then, it seems that the plurality of American masculinities will only continue to replenish itself well into the twenty-first century.

Notes

1   Ralph Waldo Emerson, 'Self-Reliance' (1841), in *The Oxford Authors: Ralph Waldo Emerson*, ed. Richard Poirier (Oxford: Oxford University Press, 1990), pp. 131–51 (133).

2   Alexis de Tocqueville, *Democracy in America* (1840. New York: Library of America, 2004), p. 585. See also Steven Lukes, who argues that individualism is a 'symbolic catchword of immense ideological significance', fundamentally linked to the key American values of 'free enterprise, and the American Dream'. Lukes, *Individualism* (Oxford: Blackwell, 1973), p. 26.

3   Theodore Dreiser, *The Financier* (1912. London: Constable & Co., 1936), pp. 68–9.

4   Theodore Roosevelt, 'The Strenuous Life', *The Strenuous Life: Essays and Addresses* (London: Thomas Nelson & Sons, 1911), pp. 11–33 (13).

5   Roosevelt, 'The American Boy', *The Strenuous Life*, pp. 181–91 (182).

6   Jack London, *The Sea-Wolf* (1904) in *Novels and Stories* (New York: Library of America, 1982), pp. 479–771 (494).

7   Andrew Sinclair, introduction to London, *Martin Eden* (1909. New York: Penguin, 1993), p. 10.

8   John Dos Passos, *Three Soldiers* (1921. New York: Random House, 1932), p. 22.

9 See Christopher Sawyer-Laucanno, *E.E. Cummings: A Biography* (London: Methuen, 2005), pp. 142–3.

10 E. E. Cummings, 'i sing of Olaf glad and big', *Complete Poems 1910–1962*, ed. George James Firmage (London: Granada, 1981), p. 340.

11 E. E. Cummings, *The Enormous Room* (1922. Harmondsworth: Penguin, 1971).

12 Ernest Hemingway, *A Moveable Feast: The Restored Edition* (London: Jonathan Cape, 2010), p. 58.

13 John Dudley, *A Man's Game: Masculinity and the Anti-Aesthetics of American Literary Naturalism* (Tuscaloosa: University of Alabama Press, 2004), p. 5.

14 Ernest Hemingway, *A Farewell to Arms* (London: Arrow, 1994), p. 165.

15 Philip Rahv, 'Paleface and Redskin', *The Kenyon Review* 1:3 (Summer 1939), pp. 251–6 (251).

16 John Steinbeck, *To a God Unknown* (1933. London: Heinemann, 1979), p. 27.

17 John Steinbeck, *Of Mice and Men* (1937. New York: Penguin, 1986), p. 14.

18 Erskine Caldwell, *Tobacco Road* (1932. Athens: University of Georgia Press, 1995), p. 117.

19 C. Wright Mills, *White Collar: The American Middle Classes* (New York: Oxford University Press, 1951), p. xii.

20 Talcott Parsons, 'The Social Structure of the Family', *The Family: Its Function and Destiny*, ed. Ruth Nanda Anshen (New York: Harper & Brothers, 1959), p. 271.

21 Updike's other 'Rabbit' novels are: *Rabbit Redux* (1971), *Rabbit is Rich* (1981), *Rabbit at Rest* (1990) and the novella *Rabbit Remembered* (2001).

22 John Updike, *Rabbit, Run* (1960. London: Penguin, 2006), p. 23.

23 Philip Wylie, *Generation of Vipers* (1942. London: Frederick Muller, 1955), p. ix.

24 Philip Roth, *Portnoy's Complaint* (1969), in *Novels: 1967–72* (New York: Library of America, 2005), pp. 277–468 (291).

25 Norman Mailer, 'The Homosexual Villain' (1954), in *Advertisements for Myself* (Cambridge, MA: Harvard University Press, 1992), pp. 222–7 (226).

26 Gore Vidal, *The City and the Pillar* (1946. London: John Lehmann, 1949), pp. 202–3.

27 See especially Walt Whitman, *Democratic Vistas* (1871. Iowa City: University of Iowa Press, 2010); Herman Melville, 'Paradise of Bachelors and the Tartarus of Maids' (1855), in *Billy Budd, Sailor, and Selected Tales*, ed. Robert Milder (Oxford: Oxford University Press, 1998), pp. 74–96.

28 John Cheever, *The Journals* (London: Jonathan Cape, 1991).
29 Jack Kerouac, *On the Road* (London: Penguin, 2001), p. 172.
30 See Carolyn Heilbrun, 'The Masculine Wilderness in the American Novel', *Saturday Review*, 29 January, 1972, pp. 41–4.
31 See Susan Jeffords, *The Remasculinization of America: Gender and the Vietnam War* (Bloomington: Indiana University Press, 1989).
32 Norman Mailer, *The Prisoner of Sex* (London: Weidenfeld and Nicolson, 1971), p. 73.
33 David Mamet, *Glengarry Glen Ross* (London: Methuen, 1984), p. 16.
34 David Mamet, 'In the Company of Men' (1989), in *A Whore's Profession: Notes and Essays* (London: Faber & Faber, 1994), pp. 279–83 (283).
35 See Judith Butler, *Gender Trouble: Feminism and the Subversion of Identity* (London: Routledge, 2006).
36 Chuck Palahniuk, *Fight Club* (1996. London: Vintage, 2006), p. 50.
37 Jeffrey Eugenides, *Middlesex* (London: Bloomsbury, 2002), p. 418.

Home and Away

In 1903, the Wright brothers made the first successful plane flight; in this bigger, faster, more efficient world, the American journalist and historian Henry Adams (1838–1918) wondered how the next generation would anchor itself, and where it would find its home or point of origin; 'the child born in 1900', he declared, would be born into 'a new world which would not be a unity but a multiple'.[1] His autobiography, *The Education of Henry Adams* (1907), shows a turn-of-the-century American man of letters in perpetual flight, from Paris to Berlin to New York. The world is dynamic, and continually on the move: modernity requires its citizens to be mobile, and perpetually unsettled. In one sense, this disruptive change might explain why the archetypal twentieth-century citizen is American, a native of the land where, as Emerson had pointed out fifty years earlier, 'everything looks new and recent … our towns are still rude, – the make-shifts of emigrants, – and the whole architecture tent-like'.[2] Yet this national definition, which finds a people characterised simultaneously by their determination to establish a home and the desire to move onwards, also suggests the tensions implicit in such a vision. George Bailey's dilemma in the Frank Capra film *It's a Wonderful Life* (1946) is, in this sense, proverbial: are the three most exciting sounds in the world 'anchor chains, train motors, and train whistles' or the regularity of 'breakfast is served, lunch is served, dinner is served'?[3] American literature of the twentieth century is both dispossessed and pioneering. It celebrates home comforts only to look further out to the horizon; it satirises the stability of picket fences and tidy domesticity but defends that same territory with a fierce single-mindedness if it appears to be under threat. 'There's no place like home' is the title of an 1892 work by American landscape artist Thomas Hicks. Yet although this phrase is later gifted to a homesick Dorothy in Frank L. Baum's novel, *The Wizard of Oz* (1900), the painting itself offers little solace. Like the grey world of Kansas from which Dorothy longs to escape, the painting shows a farmer and his wife staring grimly in opposite directions in front of an unlit fireplace. This home is singular only in its relentless turn inward, and in its suspicion of difference.

The last hundred years have seen American homes that are both so makeshift that they blow away, as in Steinbeck's Dust Bowl,[*] or so heavily policed by gates and fences, as in Tom Wolfe's New York, that they might be mistaken for prisons. Metaphors of home have also had a particularly powerful currency in American rhetoric, from the 'final frontier' that created the myth of the Space Race in the 1960s to the focus on Homeland Security following the 9/11 attacks. The home is both domestic and global, simultaneously suggesting containment and relentless expansion. Its perpetual attraction to American culture suggests, as Alexis de Tocqueville wrote in 1835, a society which

> comprises all the nations of the world – English, French, German: people differing from one another in language, in beliefs, in opinions; in a word a society possessing no roots, no memories, no prejudices, no routine, no common ideas, no national character, yet with a happiness a hundred times greater than our own ... What is the connecting link between these so different elements? How are they welded into one people?[4]

---

[*] The 'Dust Bowl' was a period of destructive dust storms across the prairies of the Great Plains of the Midwest, caused by intensive crop rotation and drought. It coincided with the Depression, making life precarious or even impossible for many tenant farmers in the early 1930s.

American literature of the period has worked both to create a home – a 'connecting link' for these disparate groups of people – and to question its efficacy; in doing so, it also sets up a competing series of trends or traditions which provide shelter, a sense of belonging, or a point of departure for the writers that look to its inheritance.

The Pioneer

In 1913, Willa Cather (1873–1947) made the unusual decision to set her second novel in the Midwest. For a writer courting literary respectability, this was a perverse move; as one anonymous critic responded, 'I don't care how well she writes, I don't give a damn about Nebraska!'[5] If her interest in the Great Plains suggested an idiosyncratic turn to the local and the regional, her work was pioneering in other ways too. The three novels that would make up her 'plains' trilogy – *O Pioneers!* (1915), *The Song of the Lark* (1915) and *My Antonia* (1918) – are full of determined and resolute women and immigrants. If the West was settled by the cowboys, it was managed and turned to profit through figures such as Alexandra Bergson in *O Pioneers!*, the Swedish-American girl who sees the potential for a profitable farm where her brothers see only a 'cluster of low drab buildings huddled on the gray prairie, under a gray sky'.[6] These are fragile and foreign places to make a home; Cather's Nebraska towns are always struggling not be blown away, her houses tilting with the wind as if 'straying off by themselves'. An analogy can be made between the frail farmsteads of her novels and her own characters: in each successive novel, Cather tries to anchor her women grudgingly into a romance plot. *O Pioneers!* finds Alexandra making an unconvincing alliance with her childhood friend Carl, yet the most meaningful relationship in these novels is between the heroine and the enigmatic land itself.

A strange mixture of pragmatism and mysticism informs the response of characters such as Alexandra Bergson to this peculiar land, the 'horse that no one knows how to break to harness, that runs wild and kicks things to pieces' (p. 148). Even when, later in her career, Cather turns to the shimmering city lights of Chicago or, as in the Pulitzer Prize-winning novel *One of Ours* (1922), follows her small-town protagonist Claude Wheeler to the battlefields of France, it is always the local and the domestic that provides solace and stability. As his mother mourns Wheeler's death at the end of *One of Ours*, she finds comfort that it came in heroic combat abroad rather than a shell-shocked suicide on his return. Until his death, like many of Cather's protagonists, Wheeler is allowed to 'hope extravagantly', and is spared any 'desolating disappointment'.[7] In the novel's closing image, his mother imagines his spirit not in heaven but hovering somewhere above the kitchen stove. In Cather's Midwest, at least, a home once established is never forgotten. Her imaginative recreation of the frontier creates it own sense of home, in both literary and geographical terms. Nearly a century later, when the disillusioned Midwestern family of Jonathan Franzen's *The Corrections* (2001) gather for an acrimonious Christmas dinner, the matriarch, Enid Lambert, finds a halting moment of repose thinking back to the 'close-knit frontier communities of oaks and maples'.[8] If there is any writer in modern literature who offers that world, it is Cather, with her series of determined immigrants and homesteads.

Cather's refusal to acknowledge the Great Depression in her later work, or engage with political decisions shaping the very world she described drew consternation from critics in the 1930s. It was John Steinbeck (1902–68) who would show how the Midwesterners might cope with a crop that didn't prosper, or explore how political as well as personal factors might threaten the longevity of the American home. From his earliest work, Steinbeck countered the idealism of the frontier with the pragmatics of colonial expansion. In *The Pastures of Heaven* (1932), a Spanish corporal discovers a rich and fertile valley which becomes the setting for the twelve interconnected stories that make up the novel. Yet tellingly, the corporal's discovery is prompted not by opportunism but by a very suspect sort of serendipity: he is chasing runaway American Indian slaves. Steinbeck's first major success came with *Tortilla Flat* (1935), which focuses on a group of homeless men after the First World War. Steinbeck draws on the chivalric quest narrative but for ironic appeal: these men are anchorless, nomadic, and without a final destination.

Steinbeck's Pulitzer Prize-winning *The Grapes of Wrath* (1939) is partly a novel about escape, venerating in poetic prose Route 66, 'the mother road', 'the path of a people in flight'.[9] It follows the 'Okies' of the Great Depression, as their Dust Bowl farms are repossessed or destroyed after the Wall Street Crash of 1929. Here Steinbeck draws on his own experience as a Depression-era journalist, documenting with often moralising urgency the appalling conditions facing the nomadic people travelling to California in hope of a better life. Yet the novel also picks apart the wilful optimism of the pioneer, and questions the limits of individualism. The characters are criticised for their ignorance as well as celebrated for their stamina. Although the book centres on one family, the Joads, the course of the novel divides and splits their blood loyalty; the closest they come to contentment is in the makeshift camps run by their fellow refugees. This is the moment that the pioneers embodied by Alexandra Bergson in Cather's novel must ask for help, or offer to share food with a neighbour. The novel's clear-eyed presentation of the corrupt state-run farms of California led to the book being banned in several Californian counties, and burned in Salinas Valley. Yet the novel's assessment of the American dream was perhaps even more revolutionary than its indictment of the state governors. In the poetic interchapters that are woven through the Joads's story, Steinbeck not only points out that the golden promise of California was in fact plundered from the Mexicans during the Mexican–American war of 1846–8 – 'they guarded with guns the land they had stolen' (p. 213) – but suggests that the individual must be supported by the state. Steinbeck's novel observes the legacy of President Roosevelt's New Deal, which found the US government attempting to regulate the markets after the country reached 25 per cent unemployment and witnessed the closure of all national banks. If the Joads begin to see the trickle of state aid later in on the novel, it is just as often misappropriated by greedy middle men. The novel's final scene finds Rose of Sharon, who has lost her baby, suckling a sick starving man. The scene might suggest a terrifying inversion, but it is also an almost biblical image of renewal. The young mother has spent much of the journey west fantasising about the commodities that would be hers in a land of plenty: 'we'll live in town an' go to the pitchers whenever, an' – well, I'm going to have a 'lectirc iron' (p. 172). The political and environmental catastrophes that wreak their havoc on the Joads's aspirations also rescue them from the banal goal of material acquisition. The homes in *The Grapes of Wrath* are migratory, transient and fragile, but the nightly ritual of the travellers setting up their camps for the evening also replays in miniature the perennial American tradition. Here, during the most inhospitable of journeys, is a tentative sort of comfort.

The stabilising possibilities of home are also explored in the novels of Thomas Wolfe (1900–38), particularly in his first, *Look Homeward, Angel* (1930). The opening paragraph makes an explicit link between the great journey of the pilgrims to America, and the more arbitrary, contingent sense of settlement that underpins all subsequent American journeys:

> A destiny that leads the English to the Dutch is strange
> enough; but one that leads from Epsom into Pennsylvania,
> and thence into the hills that shut in Altamont over the proud
> coral cry of the cock, and the soft stone smile of an angel,
> is touched by that dark miracle of chance which makes new
> magic in a dusty world.[10]

The early stages of this 'dusty' journey are unsure, as the pioneers' son, Oliver Gaunt, traverses the great continent in an aimless drift, and eventually gives way to alcoholism. Yet his central faith in the 'new magic' of home and his love for his children eventually see him reform. Home becomes less a final destination here than a continual negotiation. Writers such as Wolfe and Cather do not evade the difficulties and contradictions of forging a home, but the prairie optimism of their works suggests a place sanctified by the perilous journey to get there. Only in Steinbeck do we see a writer beginning to question the limits of idealism, and offer an American vision defined not by continual expansion, but restlessness, resettlement and itinerancy.

Houses of Horror

As second- and third-generation immigrants began to forget that first journey, or find their family histories of manifest destiny forgotten or diluted, the sturdy narratives of home became ironic, confused, or parodic. As Berndt Ostendoof and Stephan Palmie have pointed out, the shifting and diversifying demographic of twentieth-century America brought both internal division and conformity: 'ethnic fragmentation increased as everyday culture became unified', bringing 'a radical reinterpretation of the traditional American compromise between the individual, the group, and the polity represented in the national motto *e pluribus unum*'.*[11] The sense of home as a soured plot is writ large in works such as *Revolutionary Road* (1961), by the novelist Richard Yates (1926–92). The name of the suburban housing estate that gives the novel its title suggests iconoclasm and innovation, the spirit of the founding fathers; but the lives of the protagonists Frank and April Wheeler are marked only by retrenchment and suffocation. They are smart, intelligent and dangerously self-aware about the perils of conformity. At first, they see their new home as a challenge: 'a sparse, skilful arrangement of furniture would counteract the prim suburban look of this too-symmetrical living room', the knowing estate agent assures them.[12] The necessary corrections they make to their home suggest a couple who might hold the inevitable at bay. Frank laughs off his cripplingly dull job in the city, as they make plans for a bohemian life in Europe. Yet as pregnancy, promotion and alcoholism inflict their scars upon them, their home becomes a burden rather than a sanctuary. April's final self-destructive act at the novel's climax is marked by an eerie insistence that her home should be as orderly as her life is chaotic: before she sits down to write what she suspects might be a suicide note, she attempts a final, thorough clean of the house. The supporting couples that survive the dull certainty of the perfect home do so only through damage limitation; the novel ends with the indifferent husband Howard Givings turning off his hearing

---

* *E pluribus unum* is the motto found on the seal of the United States; it translates as 'out of many, one'.

aid so as to escape the inane chatter of his wife as she speculates on the new couple moving in to the Wheelers' old house. The road is revolutionary here only because of the terrifying circularity and stasis of its inhabitants. It is a road which leads nowhere.

The conformity of the suburban idyll sometimes prompts writers into disruptive comedy, domestic tragedy or, in the case of Donald Barthelme (1931–89), the absurd. His surreal postmodernism upsets the social etiquette and petty rituals of the middle-class characters he describes. Like a zanier version of John Cheever (whose suburban short stories are examined in Part Three: 'The American Short Story'), Barthelme constructs worlds just on the edge of sanity, as in his short story 'Sakrete' (1987),[13] narrated by a man increasingly obsessed with the garbage cans going missing on his suburban street. His discomfort turns first to mistrust, as he accuses conspicuous neighbours, and then madness, as he enlists his son to poison the rats he is convinced are responsible. Seemingly passing moments or chance encounters unravel a carefully constructed facade of domestic contentment. A similar trajectory, if in a more realist narrative mode, underpins the work of Joyce Carol Oates (1938–). In *American Appetites* (1989), Oates questions the legitimacy of ambition and material aspiration, as the affluent world of Ian and Glynis McCullough is shattered by a bizarre phone call Ian receives at work. The border of the family property might be carefully patrolled, but the outside world is chaos: Ian is paralysed by the thought that 'unrelated individuals, wholly unaware of one another, nonetheless cooperated in a collective destiny.'[14]

Other suburban novels instead emphasise its unreality. In *The Virgin Suicides* (1993), Jeffrey Eugenides (1960–) reconstructs Grosse Pointe, Michigan, an affluent adjunct of Detroit, in which a Greek chorus of teenage boys (the third-person plural narrator(s) of the novel) watch the comings and goings of their neighbours' house with lurid fascination. On one level, their fixation on the five Lisbon sisters is an ingenious take on the gossip and garden-fence surveillance already associated with the suburbs in the popular imagination. However, as any viewer of the television series *Desperate Housewives* might attest, too often gossip is only a way of processing or attempting to neutralise the extraordinary events that occur in ostensibly mundane, identikit surroundings. The Lisbon girls are fascinating because they are incarcerated by their parents and denied any meaningful communication with the outside world. Their suburban home is an experiment in stopping time, an attempt to preserve a kind of prelapsarian innocence which instead causes a grand, tragic fall; the serial suicides of all five daughters. Eugenides's novel is an example of the 'suburban gothic'.[15] However, much of its feverish depiction of suburbia is down to the narrators' inability to fix it; it is almost so familiar as to be weirdly unfamiliar, particularly when recounted twenty years on. The 'molting trees' and 'overexposed grass' of the early 1970s (impressionistically captured by Sofia Coppola in her 1999 film adaptation) teeter on the edge of warped surrealism; it is only long after the suicides, when the narrators return to Grosse Pointe, that the felling of the sidewalk trees reveals 'how blinding the outside was becoming, our entire neighbourhood like an overexposed photograph'.[16] 'We got to see how truly unimaginative our suburb was', writes the narrative voice, 'everything laid out on a grid whose bland uniformity the trees had hidden'.

Some neighbours of the Lisbons conclude that the suicides bespeak something dark at the heart of the nation. Mr Hedlie links it to the 'dying of an empire', likening America in the early 1970s to decadent Vienna; nevertheless, Detroit's race riots are somewhere offstage, and when the boys hear 'gunshots coming from the ghetto', their fathers insist that the noise is 'only cars backfiring' (p. 36). For Philip Roth, tangible political realities eradicate the possibility of a perfect home in more direct ways. *American Pastoral* (1997) charts the unravelling of Seymour Levov's apparently serene family life when his daughter, Merry, sets off a bomb in a local post office in protest at the American involvement in the Vietnam War. The political unrest of the 1960s leading up to the 1973 Watergate scandal becomes the rug that is ripped from under the feet of the complacent suburban everyman. Here is America's brand of 'indigenous berserk', as the characters become 'history's plaything'.[17] This is another lost Eden, a key motif in much American writing. Characters long to be reunited with their first home, to rewind to a time before the fall; but just as the figures of Steinbeck's *East of Eden* (1952) come to realise that, like Adam in Genesis, they have been banished and are destined to plough unproductive land, so do suburban families experience their own Original Sins and paradises lost. *American Pastoral*'s conclusion elegises this loss: 'Yes, the breach had been pounded in their fortification, even out here in secure Old Rimrock, and now that it was opened it would not be closed again. They'll never recover' (p. 423). The title of Roth's novel becomes shaded with irony; their lives have been 'pastoral' only in that they have constituted a stylised performance of innocence. Many critiques of suburbia employ the same titular formula as Roth, inferring that the picket-fences and backyard pools are metonyms of the United States at large; whatever is wrong in suburbia can be used to diagnose problems at a national level, as Oates's aforementioned *American Appetites* or Sam Mendes's 1999 film *American Beauty* attest.

If notions of the perfect American home tend to focus on the 1950s, and the affluent suburbia typified in the work of novelists such as John Updike and Richard Yates, perspectives from earlier in the century and further afield suggest a constant fascination with the domestic. The mass increase in population in the early decades of the twentieth century saw a renewed interest in appropriating and ordering the home. *Ladies' Home Journal*, a popular women's magazine founded in 1883, increased its readership tenfold in this period: the popularity of works such as *Foods and Household Management* (1914) by Helen Kinne and Anna Maria Cooley suggested a horde of anxious housewives looking for guidance on how to keep the immaculate home. True to the Puritan roots of American culture, their textbook is keen to emphasise that the world of fast-food and convenience, far from making things easier for the homemaker, creates a terrible confusion and disorientating choice: 'every large city, and every large town, is a market of the world'.[18] The open, global borders of the world, as Henry Adams suggested, create an anxiety about what might constitute the local, the regional, or the domestic. Heroines from the period, like the eponymous character of Ellen Glasgow's *Virginia* (1913), bend themselves ready to the tasks of mending their husbands' clothes, or the glorious monotony of pouring out the coffee. Glasgow's ironic narrative finds a curious fascination in the way an exquisite Southern belle, reared inevitably for a dull marriage, struggles to see her destiny as adventurous and romantic. Only once

Virginia's child leaves, and she returns once again to the familial home, does she begin to see her own front door as 'the door of a prison', and tremble at 'the staircase which she would go up and down for the rest of her life'.[19] The promise of a perfectly kept home dwindles into inertia and indifference. Glasgow's heroine is named after the state that raised her; its conquest from the Native Americans promises untrammelled possibility, yet to her it offers only incarceration.

For this reason, the twentieth-century American home is less often the final prize at the end of a quest narrative than a scene of horror or attrition; the longed-for domestic setting in American literature is frequently haunted, possessed, or uncanny. It that opens Toni Morrison's *Beloved* (1987) is a central character. It has a number – 124 – rather than a name, but that doesn't stop it being 'spiteful'.[20] The novel, rather than building a home, deconstructs one. The spirit of slavery and its legacy haunts the house and its inhabitants, slamming doors, breaking windows and terrorising guests. The fractured, fragmented narrative, like the home itself, is shattered; it can be rebuilt, but never put back together in a coherent order. Here, the grand Southern house with its army of black servants is inverted and reconstituted into a nightmare two generations later. The past becomes literally uninhabitable, yet impossible to leave behind. *Other Voices, Other Rooms* (1948), the first novel of Truman Capote (1924–84), presents a similarly Janus-faced dwelling. When the protagonist, Joel Knox loses his mother, he is sent to live in rural Alabama with a father he has never met. The decaying mansion at first suggests a faded gentility and splendour, full of rusty alarm clocks and 'yawning' parlours,[21] yet the home is closer to Gothic horror than refuge. With his father inexplicably absent, the orphaned Joel plans his escape to the nearest hotel, or to 'go to California and pick grapes' (p. 133), but, as with Steinbeck, the dream of the West remains illusory. He is forced to return when he contracts pneumonia, and is nursed back to health by his transvestite cousin Randolph. His alcoholic cousin performs the role of both mother and father but in cruel parody; when the comforts of home are absent, it is restaged and mimicked. Like the spiteful haunting of 124 in Morrison's novel, Capote's family home is a kind of grotesque purgatory. It is a place you are exiled from but to which you can never return. If 'there's no place like home' proved one of the century's most enduring domestic maxims, Thomas Wolfe offered perhaps a most accurate epigram with his posthumous novel *You Can't Go Home Again* (1947). The novel centres on a provincial writer, George Webber, whose fiction memorialises his hometown, Libya Hill. Yet whilst he becomes a celebrated author, he is vilified by local people for his apparent distortions and misrepresentations of their way of life. The novel ends with him gripped by the conviction that his work has 'killed the thing which is most gloriously American';[22] by desecrating his home, he has become an exile.

In the most isolated or far-flung communities, then, a quiet tragedy plays itself out around the American home. Nowhere is the tragedy quieter or more painful than in the work of Marilynne Robinson (1943–), whose three lyrical novels *Housekeeping* (1980), *Gilead* (2004) and *Home* (2008) all excavate the loneliness of the family home. Here, familial bonds are paramount; even if apparently broken, they still track their escapees mercilessly. In Robinson's fiction, prodigal sons return only to leave again without explanation. Women banish the ghosts of the past only to set up homes that are always haunted. Robinson's first novel *Housekeeping* tells the story of Ruth and Lucille, two orphaned sisters who come to live with their eccentric Aunt Sylvie. For Lucille, Sylvie's idiosyncrasies will prove too great, and the sisters are eventually estranged. The novel ends with a final fleeing from the house that neither Sylvie nor Ruth can ever quite hold in subservience. Here the home is defined less by its doors or parameters than the viewer's perspective on it. As Ruth's narrative records, sitting at night in a lighted house suggests a kind of temporary border – 'we will pull the shades' from those who would seek to watch us – but once she abandons the house for the life of the hobo, she makes the 'absolute discovery' of loneliness.[23]

Frontiers and Borders

As the evening prowlers of Robinson's fictional metaphor suggest, the comfort of the home can only be defined by the threats it holds at bay. In Robert Frost's poem 'House Fear' (1920),[24] every time the anxious couple return to their lonely house they rattle the locks and keys in their front door noisily to give any spectral intruders time to escape. The safety of their home can never be experienced or enjoyed if they are contained within it; the couple must make a ritual departure and return to remind them both that the home is theirs, and that it is protecting them from something. The home has been used more widely in twentieth-century American literature as a synecdoche for a significant border, defining itself by what it leaves out. We might trace this in the series of Cold War-era domestic dramas of playwrights such as Tennessee Williams and Arthur Miller, echoing the fear of the outsider in the tense family triangles depicted on stage.*

Theorists Gilles Deleuze (1925–95) and Felix Guattari (1930–92) have pointed out that the borders between two apparently discrete nations, objects or substances are never clear:

> one can never posit a dualism or a dichotomy, even in the rudimentary form of the good and bad. You may make a rupture, draw a line of flight, yet there is still a danger that you will re-encounter organizations that restratify everything, formations that restore power to a signifier, attributions that reconstitute a subject … Groups and individuals contain microfascisms just waiting to crystallize.[25]

These 'microfascisms' form many of the divisions and ruptures in the apparently safe space of the American home and more widely, in the negotiation of American identity. *Accordion Crimes* (1996), by the novelist Annie Proulx (1935–), traces the stories of twentieth-century American immigrants. It follows their search for a home through the linked story of a battered accordion, which is passed from family to family by means nefarious, macabre and often grotesque. The first section of this episodic novel traces the journey of a Sicilian labourer who comes to America to find work. His sense of home depends on defining American as other, the new world he often regrets making his

* For a detailed discussion of intrusions into privacy on the American stage, see Part Three: 'The American Stage'.

own. Yet subsequent generations find this binary definition increasingly complex. In the 1930s, German-Americans in Wisconsin realise that the impending war makes it necessary for them to sever their notion of an original home. Quoting President Roosevelt, one character complains,

> 'some Americans needs hyphens in their names because only
> part of them have come over. But when the whole man has
> come over, heart and thought and all, the hyphen drops of
> its own weight out of his name'. And what else drops? Jesus,
> Jesus and Christ, a beautiful language, Bach, Handel, Mozart,
> Schiller drops, Goethe drops, Kant and Hegel, Wagner,
> Wagner drops. Schubert, he drops.[26]

Here, the national imperative to become fully American isolates the individual from their native culture, literature and music. Wider political changes mean that their American flag demands greater allegiance than their ancestry. By the time of the third-generation immigrant, when Proulx's narrative buzzes with the teeming stories of various descendants, notions of American choice have become crippling; one character nearly collapses in a supermarket from the dizzying range of alternative cat food varieties. By encouraging immigrants to abandon their native culture, Proulx suggests, the country has bred a nation that is in the habit of abandoning everything. By the novel's final stories, the landscape of America itself is an alien place, a momentary sensation between an air-conditioned car and an air-conditioned mall. As one character wryly remarks: 'there's no place in North America farther than twenty miles from a road ... It was in *National Geographic*' (p. 531). The original pioneering wilderness is now experienced only through a magazine.

The patrolled and paranoid spaces of the gated community in T. Coraghessan Boyle's *The Tortilla Curtain* (1997) also suggest the dangerously porous quality of the American border. This novel, looking back to *The Grapes of Wrath*, came in direct response to Proposition 187, a law passed in November 1994 in California denying illegal immigrants basic rights to healthcare or education.[27] Through a series of parallels, Boyle questions the relationship between the law-abiding American citizen and the illegal immigrant. The novel centres on Delaney, an ecologically minded WASP (Women Airforce Service Pilot) who runs over an illegal Mexican immigrant tellingly named Cándido. While Delaney attempts to forget the incident, Boyle's interweaving chapters and inexorable plot line mean they are now bound together. The reader is forced to weigh up this relationship in a series of plot echoes: an immigrant steals food to survive, one of Delaney's rich neighbours evades his taxes; Cándido cannot work after the accident and is forced to send his pregnant wife to hustle for work, and Delaney plays the house-husband while his wife develops a real estate empire. The image of the coyote recurs throughout the novel, Boyle drawing attention to the animal's ability to be both wild and tame. Yet perhaps the most compelling and threatening quality of the coyote is its indifference to borders. It is hearing the word 'borders' that first shatters Delaney's sense of smug suburban complacency: he takes 'an involuntary step backwards' as he has a sudden vision of 'all those dark discontented faces rising up from the streetcorners and freeway on-ramps to mob his brain, all of them crying out their human wants through mouths of rotten teeth'.[28] As Delaney comes to discover, a country defined by a 'golden door'* cannot shut up its gates without a dangerous leakage. Here, racial panic ruptures his sense of easy liberalism. The gated community does not offer freedom from danger, but rather operates a dangerous ideology of making fellow citizens appear 'outsiders'.[29]

Jonathan Franzen's novel *Freedom* (2010) is similarly concerned with the perilous implications of making a home, and of balancing the competing personal and political costs of various types of freedom. The novel begins with a portrait of the seemingly conventional Berglund family; their phonic similarity to Cather's Alexandra Bergson is not incidental. Descended from Sweden, they are the 'young pioneers of Ramsey Hill',[30] and move to a run-down area of St Paul in Minnesota. Ten years of burglaries and home improvement later, they

* This phrase comes from the poem 'New Colossus' (1884) by Emma Lazarus, inscribed on the Statue of Liberty.

have constructed a valuable piece of a real estate, and helped foster a 'good' neighbourhood. Yet as the family seemingly self-implodes in the opening chapter, Franzen unpicks the 'goodness' of those same neighbours, embroiled as they are in passive-aggressive competitions over whose children are more successful. The analogy between this created community and the larger question of how America deals with its neighbours is drawn several times in the novel. Towards the narrative climax, Joey, the Berglund's only son, must allow an illegal shipment of truck parts to Iraq to allow his family to put itself back together again. Joey becomes involved in vehicle trading when his halcyon college days are interrupted by 9/11; suddenly the world no longer seems benign or welcoming. Seeing the burning towers on television, Joey still leaves to attend his morning lecture before realising, when he finds the hall empty, 'a really serious glitch had occurred' (p. 232). The Berglunds's friend Richard is similarly afflicted; when he becomes a successful singer, interviewers ask him not about his music, but about his support for the Iraq War. This collapsing of personal, national and political borders doesn't allow characters to abnegate responsibility; they are never free to abstain. Like the paranoid couple in Frost's poem, the American family home must keep prodding away at its own edges, only measuring the value of what it has achieved by destroying it or leaving it altogether.

Escaping the Home

As quickly as American culture could construct its homes and communities, then, its writers recognised the terrifying constraints they might place on those who want out. *Her*, a novel by the poet H. D. (Hilda Doolittle, 1886–1961), written in 1927 and published posthumously in 1984, finds its protagonist stifled and isolated in her family home in Pennsylvania, returning there after an unsuccessful career at college. Home becomes the 'final test she failed in'; only after her escape to Europe can she become 'at one with herself, with the world, with all outer circumstance'.[31] H. D.'s novel is echoed

in another posthumous *künstlerroman*, *The Bell Jar* (1962),[*] which
sees Sylvia Plath (1932–63) depict her protagonist's despair in a final
suicide attempt, trying to bury herself in her mother's basement; the
contained and patrolled spaces of the respectful American home seem
antithetical to creative endeavour.

The perceived antagonism between the home and the liberated
American voice is embodied in 1950s 'beat' writing, and the series
of novels, poems, and films that would come to define road culture.
Although, as discussed earlier in this chapter, the lure of the road
was felt as keenly by Henry Adams or Ralph Waldo Emerson as Jack
Kerouac, the work of writers such as Allen Ginsberg and William
Burroughs carved out a distinctive countercultural response to the
apparently stultifying conformity of post-war American culture. The
word 'beat' is itself much mythologised, its meaning falling half-way
between 'dead-beat' and 'beatific'; the conflation of the down-and-out
and the visionary haunts the work of these writers. Joyce Johnson has
defined 'beat' as 'an evanescent moment of exalted exhaustion',[32] and
the sense of disappointment implicit here is also significant. Inspired
by bebop music, Jack Kerouac (1922–69) wrote his second novel *On
the Road* (1957) as one continuous sentence on a long roll of teletype.
It tells the story, through Sal Paradise, of Dean Moriarty, the archetypal
beat hipster, engaging on a series of road trips punctuated by alcohol,
women and poetry. Moriarty is both magnetic and enigmatic, as is the
quality of 'IT' he comes to embody for Sal:

> the only people for me are the mad ones, the ones who
> are mad to live, mad to talk, mad to be saved, desirous of
> everything at the same time, the ones who never yawn or say a
> commonplace thing, but burn burn burn like fabulous yellow
> roman candles.[33]

Notwithstanding such effusiveness, Kerouac's work also shows the
contradictions and paradoxes of this apparent liberation. The text
itself, with its unpunctuated sentences and apparently automatic

---

[*] A *künstlerroman* is a novel that traces the development of an artist.

composition, favours spontaneous utterance, yet subsequent archival work has suggested Kerouac thoroughly revised his text. While the novel seemingly heralds the rejection of religious orthodoxy or moral prudishness, Kerouac's notion of beat was strongly influenced by his Catholicism; it is no accident that the burning fire of the beatnik is compared to a 'roman candle' in the extract quoted opposite. Because the novel presents us with a series of journeys, often interrupted, abandoned, or cancelled, it is also a text of disillusionment. As Carlo reminds Dean mid-journey, 'the balloon won't sustain you much longer … you'll all go flying to the West Coast and come staggering back in search of your stone' (p. 117). The characters in *On the Road* spend more time running than returning, and never quite escape the past. Subsequent Kerouac novels register increasing scepticism about the fugitive life; for example, *Big Sur* (1962) is 'beat' at its bleakest, a semi-autobiographical chronicle of depression that sees Kerouac (aka Duluoz) journeying back and forth from the eponymous terrain of coastal Californian highlands to San Francisco, unable to settle or find his self in either.

Similar tensions characterise the works that the Beats inspired, whether in 'road movies' from *Thelma and Louise* (1993) to *Lost Highway* (1997) that promise exhilarating freedom but are also 'songs of the doomed',[34] or novels such as those of John Updike's Rabbit series (1960–2001), which show the impossibility of running away. Initially, the open road always promises the glamour of escape, of easy riders, gleaming mirrors and limitless country broken only by the occasional dead coyote or gas station. The counterculture has fed off this mythology since the 1950s and 1960s, ranging from the travels of Ken Kesey's 'Merry Pranksters', immortalised in Tom Wolfe's *The Electric Kool-Aid Acid Test* (1968), to the 'Gonzo journalism' of Hunter S. Thompson (1937–2005), whose zany travelogues take in the rootless bikers of *Hell's Angels* (1966), his own lysergic 'trips' in *Fear and Loathing in Las Vegas* (1971), and presidential electioneering in *Fear and Loathing on the Campaign Trail '72* (1973). Robert M. Pirsig (1928–) sees travelling the open road as a way of opening up philosophical enquiry and conversation in *Zen and the Art of Motorcycle Maintenance* (1974), while more recently, Dave Eggers (1970–) has taken the fantasy of escape to another level in the novel *You Shall Know Our Velocity* (2002), in which the protagonist Will comes into $80,000 and decides to spend it travelling the world, giving sums away to the people he believes most deserve financial aid. Nevertheless, the road can easily become a lifestyle choice, just like the gated house or the automatic garage door. As the French cultural theorist Jean Baudrillard (1929–2007) notes, the road can only be appreciated retrospectively, as a spectator sport. The immensity of the Texan hills is best seen in widescreen or in mechanical reproduction: 'we'd have to play it all from end to end at home in a darkened room, rediscover the magic of the freeways and the distance and the ice-cold alcohol in the desert and the speed and live it all again on the video at home in real time'.[35] The epiphany promised by the road, as Kris Lackey notes, is often partial, or even 'unearned, transitory, and inconsequential'.[36] Instead, the road brings with it 'something very much like homesickness', as Willa Cather notes in her short story 'The Bohemian Girl' (1912).[37] The automobile, too, can become a claustrophobic home of sorts, a space akin to the problematic enclosures it ostensibly escapes, as in Theodore Roethke's 1941 poem 'Highway: Michigan'; he depicts 'the progress of the jaded' jockeying for position as they leave town, motorists who are 'the prisoners of speed / who flee in what their hands have made'.[38]

In 1965, the American Dream, in Norman Mailer's eponymous novel, is characterised by strip joints and alcohol. It promises transience rather than emancipation, and its location is defined by artificially controlled, air-conditioned hotels: 'life in a submarine'. The closest it gets to community is the six-line highway, speeding by in 'your own piece of the mass production'.[39] The American writer is then always native yet always displaced, defined by both individualism and the need to pledge allegiance. In the poem 'From an Old House in America' (1974), Adrienne Rich (1929–) has her speaker returning to a decaying ranch house, placing her hands on the hand-prints left on an old doorframe to remember past generations of settlers, homemakers and itinerants. These are the stories of abandoned women, of mean and terrible marriages, or evictions. In the act of ventriloquising these subjects and stories, Rich finds isolation, reluctance and dispossession, but also a stubborn sort of belonging as her speaker identifies with a place she didn't choose, yet has become part of herself.[40] For twentieth-century writers, the Puritan descendants or second-generation immigrants who see America as a home rather than a destination, the domestic space is both the symbol of freedom and the curtailment of it.

The frailty of the search for home has recently reached nuclear proportions in *The Road* (2006), a Pulitzer Prize-winning novel by Cormac McCarthy (1933–). The novel imagines a post-apocalyptic world where a father and son must wander a desolate and barren America in search of food. Here the road is a place of dangerous visibility, where they might fall prey to cannibals, thieves, or murderers. The journey West, so often a visionary route in American literature, is confused in McCarthy's novel. The man and his son finally reach the coast only to be baffled by what they expected to find there beyond a grey, polluted ocean. McCarthy makes clear that they are making a specifically American journey – they are 'like pilgrims in a fable'[41] in a world that 'used to be called the states' (p. 43), but only occasional references to an old road map hint at their location. The remnants of the world they encounter remind us of America's colonial history, like the deserted Spanish ship they find on the shoreline with its hardware smelted in 'some bloomery in Cadiz or Bristol' (p. 290), but in other ways it is terrifyingly alien. Literature and storytelling provide no comfort – as the boy tells his father, 'in the stories we're helping people and we don't help people' (p. 287). Language becomes an empty signifier, a 'scared idiom shorn of its referents and so of its reality' (p. 93). Yet, paradoxically, it is only language that keeps the novel turning. With its brutal scenes of torture and its portrait of a world turned upside down, the narrative's only solace comes in the lyrical passage describing the world that has been lost. The final image in the novel is a memory of a trout swimming in a stream. The patterns on its back are compared to 'maps of the world in its becoming' (p. 241). This closing promise of renewal, in the most apparently bleak of situations, suggests both a terror more acute that any Henry Adams might have imagined at the turn of the century, and also a hope more vital.

Notes

1   Henry Adams, *The Education of Henry Adams* (Oxford: Oxford University Press, 1999), p. 382.
2   Ralph Waldo Emerson, 'The Progress of Culture' (1867), in *Selected Prose* (New York: Library of America, 1985), p. 443.
3   *It's A Wonderful Life* (dir. Frank Capra; 1946).
4   Alexis de Tocqueville, *Democracy in America* (New York: Knopf, 1945), p. 45.
5   As quoted in Susie Thomas, *Willa Cather* (New York: Barnes and Noble, 1988), p. 54.
6   Willa Cather, *O Pioneers!* in *Cather: Early Novels and Stories* (New York: Library of America, 1987), p. 139.
7   Cather, *One of Ours* in *Early Novels and Stories*, p. 1296.
8   Jonathan Franzen, *The Corrections* (London: Fourth Estate, 2002), p. 556.
9   John Steinbeck, *The Grapes of Wrath* (1939. London: Penguin, 2000), p. 172.
10   Thomas Wolfe, *Look Homeward, Angel* (1930. London: Heinemann, 1966), p. 1.
11   Berndt Ostendoof and Stephan Palmie, 'Immigration and Ethnicity', in Mick Gidley, ed., *Modern American Culture: An Introduction* (London: Longman, 1993), pp. 141–164 (160).
12   Richard Yates, *Revolutionary Road* (London: Methuen, 2001), p. 30.
13   Donald Barthelme. 'Sakrete', *Forty Stories* (London: Penguin, 2005).
14   Joyce Carol Oates, *American Appetites* (London: Picador, 1989), p. 3.
15   See Bernice M. Murphy, *The Suburban Gothic in American Popular Culture* (Basingstoke: Palgrave Macmillan, 2009).
16   Jeffrey Eugenides, *The Virgin Suicides* (1993. London: Abacus, 2001), pp. 6 and 243.
17   Philip Roth, *American Pastoral* (London: Jonathan Cape, 1997), p. 86.
18   Helen Kinne and Anna Maria Cooley, *Food and Household Management* (New York: Macmillan, 1914), p. 3.
19   Ellen Glasgow, *Virginia* (1913. London: Virago, 1981), p. 392.
20   Toni Morrison, *Beloved* (New York: Knopf, 1987), p. 1.
21   Truman Capote, *Other Voices, Other Rooms* (London: Penguin, 2004), p. 42.
22   Thomas Wolfe, *You Can't Go Home Again* (London: Heineman, 1968), p. 600.
23   Marilynne Robinson, *Housekeeping* (New York: Farrar, Strous, Giroux, 1980), p. 158.

24   Robert Frost, 'House Fear', *Collected Poems, Prose & Plays* (New York: Library of America, 1995), p. 123.

25   Gilles Deleuze and Felix Guattari, *A Thousand Plateaus* (London: University of Minnesota Press, 1987), reprinted in *Literary Theory: An Anthology*, ed. Julie Rivkin and Michael Ryan (Oxford: Blackwell, 1998), p. 517.

26   Annie Proulx, *Accordion Crimes* (London: Harper, 2006), p. 102.

27   For more details on this law, see Adalberto Aguirre, *Racial and Ethnic Diversity in America* (New York: ABC-CLIO, 2003), p. 56.

28   T. Coraghessan Boyle, *The Tortilla Curtain* (London: Bloomsbury, 1997), p. 101.

29   Edward J. Blakely and Mary Gail Snyder, *Fortress America: Gated Communities in the United States* (New York: Brookings Institution Press, 1999), p. 3.

30   Jonathan Franzen, *Freedom* (London: 4th Estate, 2010), p. 3.

31   H. D., *Her* (London: Virago. 1984), pp. 5 and 224.

32   Joyce Johnson, *Minor Characters: A Beat Memoir* (London: Penguin, 2000), p. 45.

33   Jack Kerouac, *On the Road: The Original Scroll* (London: Penguin, 2006), p. 45.

34   Michael Atkinson, *Ghosts in the Machine: Speculating on the Dark Heart of Pop Cinema* (New York: Limelight Editions, 1999), p. 16.

35   Jean Baudrillard, *America*, trans. Chris Turner (London: Verso. 1998), p. 23.

36   Kris Lackey, *RoadFrames: The American Highway Narrative* (London: University of Nebraska Press, 1997), p. 16.

37   Cather, 'The Bohemian Girl', in *Stories, Poems, and Other Writings* (New York: Library of America, 1992), p. 93.

38   Theodore Roethke, 'Highway: Michigan', in *Selected Poems*, ed. Edward Hirsch (New York: Library of America, 2005), p. 5.

39   Norman Mailer, *The American Dream* (London: Andre Deutsch, 1965), pp. 269 and 270.

40   Adrienne Rich, 'From an Old House in America', *The Fact of A Doorframe: Poems Selected and New 1950–1984* (New York: Norton, 1984), p. 216.

41   Cormac McCarthy, *The Road* (London: Picador, 2006), p. 1.

African-American Writing

'The problem of the twentieth century is the problem of the color-line': though they were written right at the beginning of the century, these words could not have been more prophetic.[1] When W. E. B. Du Bois (1868–1963) wrote *The Souls of Black Folk* (1903), the 'colour line' was a shameful reality. The black population were nominally freed from slavery after the Civil War, only to be met with segregation, poverty and the constant threat of violence. The South was still reeling from defeat in the war, and its reaction to this loss was to subject its freedmen to a form of apartheid. The United States sought to reassert itself as a nation with common, inalienable rights and values after the Reconstruction; one of the most important constitutional acts, the Fifteenth Amendment (1870), declared it illegal to deny the vote to an individual on grounds of race or former slave status. In reality, the intentions of Northern politicians had very little practical effect on the lives of many black people in the South. In the 1890s and 1910s, a series of laws was passed in Southern states to effectively disenfranchise the black population by introducing poll taxes and literacy requirements for the vote. These so-called 'Jim Crow' laws were technically constitutional, even though they effectively made the Fifteenth Amendment meaningless.* The same period saw the

---

* 'Jim Crow' was a pejorative term for a black African American, derived from the music hall act of Thomas D. Rice in the 1830s.

Supreme Court uphold the Plessy v. Ferguson case in 1896. A black railroad passenger, Homer Plessy, refused to sit in the 'coloured' car, arguing that such segregation violated the constitution; his plea was overruled by the judge, Howard Ferguson, who upheld the right of the state of Louisiana to regulate private businesses on its own terms. This landmark case gave other states the authority to maintain 'separate but equal' facilities and services, which were designed to give African Americans the bare minimum of constitutional protection, while stymieing any possibility of integration. When black people attempted to assimilate, or 'cross the colour line', they might well have been met by the lynch-mob; vigilante groups, including the notorious Ku Klux Klan , active in the 1870s and then again in the 1920s, policed their neighbourhoods and acted out violent statements of white supremacy. It was not until the Civil Rights Movement of the 1950s and 1960s that reforms were initiated and proper freedoms safeguarded. Even today, while legislated segregation is a thing of the past, there remain *de facto* ghettoes across urban America, and there are still equalities to be won and maintained.

The 'colour line' of which Du Bois writes, then, was an issue that went to the very heart of American self-definition, and exposed some of the contradictions and hypocrisies underlying the sanctity and legitimacy of the Constitution. Questions of self-definition are emphasised in *The Souls of Black Folk*, especially concerning the dichotomy of being both black and 'American'. The Declaration of Independence famously decreed that every human being had the right to 'life, liberty and the pursuit of happiness'; this was the supposed birthright of all American citizens. By the time of Du Bois's writing, African Americans were officially 'citizens' but many black lives fell far short of the principles outlined in the Declaration. To be an American is to be a free man; could the 'Negro' be considered an American at all? Perhaps in response to the 'separate but equal' policies around him, Du Bois argues that the two categories are almost self-contradictory, and describes his experience as an African American as a kind of 'double-consciousness', a 'sense of always looking at one's self through the eyes of others, of measuring one's soul by the tape of a world that looks on in amused contempt and pity.' He communicates the constant strain of being 'an American, a Negro; two souls, two thoughts, two unreconciled strivings; two warring ideals in one dark body', as 'dogged strength alone' keeps it from being 'torn asunder' (pp. 10–11).

'Double-consciousness' haunts *The Souls of Black Folk*, because 'the history of the American Negro is the history of this strife'. Yet Du Bois does not simply advocate assimilation; the key to progress depends upon appreciating and accepting difference, and allowing this into an understanding of what it is to be American: the 'Negro ... would not Africanize America', nor would he 'bleach his Negro soul in a flood of white Americanism'. Rather, 'he simply wishes to make it possible for a man to be both a Negro and an American' (p. 11). The desirability of American citizenship, and a belief in American ideals as a force for good, underpins Du Bois's proposals here. While his ideas were adopted by many black intellectuals, the assumption that recognition as an 'American' is an integral part of achieving equality and justice was continually questioned by people of African heritage over the coming years. Through the twentieth century, the writers and subjects of black American literature would alternately seek to unify their 'double consciousness', and assert their own uniqueness and difference, disavow their nationality, or even repudiate the concept of nationality altogether. If 'double consciousness' is 'the history of the American Negro', then the history of African-American literature in the twentieth century was an ongoing debate about whether or not this duality should be reconciled.

The 'Art Approach'

For W. E. B. Du Bois, it was clear that artistic endeavour was crucial to the empowerment of African Americans. He declared it was his ambition 'to make a name in literature and thus to raise my race'.[2] The title of *The Souls of Black Folk* takes it as read that African Americans have 'souls', but in the nineteenth century, racist thinking often pictured the black man in particular as a savage, barely a human being; many white

Americans questioned whether black people had souls at all. If art and literature are an expression of the soul, then the flourishing of African-American examples would be necessary proof of the humanness of black experience to white doubters.

The minister and author William H. Ferris noted in 1913 that Du Bois was 'one of the few men in history who was hurled on the throne of leadership by the dynamic force of the written word'.[3] In Du Bois's case, the written word was synonymous with education, the most powerful tool in the fight for compassion and equal rights. His stance here was quite different to that of other black leaders. It especially diverged from the tone set by Booker T. Washington (1856–1915), who with his own memoir-cum-manifesto, *Up From Slavery* (1901), had become the African-American voice that whites most accepted, even admired. Washington believed that the freedmen must work to better themselves in part through education, but also through physical graft and industry. He favoured the appeasement of white ex-slave-owners, and advocated gradualism over radical change. While this made him a popular figure with some, for others his philosophies became as much a part of the problem as a solution. The difference between Du Bois's emphasis on intellect and rhetoric, and Washington's belief in gradual practical change, is neatly dramatised in a 1966 poem by Dudley Randall (1914–2000), 'Booker T. and W. E. B.'. It imagines a conversation between the two, in which Washington ridicules the education of a slave when there is work to be done on the land; Du Bois counters him, arguing for the right to education and improvement.[4] Washington then states his faith in the acquisition of property as a way of getting ahead, but Du Bois contends that in the face of white prejudice money becomes meaningless: wealth cannot neuter anti-black violence.

Whether or not he really believed 'chemistry and Greek' to be a waste of time, Booker T. Washington rather ironically helped advance Du Bois's theory, that the more African Americans proved their abilities in the field of literature, the more their political cause would be advanced. This had already been evidenced during the nineteenth century, when the autobiographical writings of the escaped slave and subsequent activist and orator Frederick Douglass (1818–95) played an instrumental part in the progress of abolitionism.* By the 1910s and early 1920s, poetry was being singled out by black intellectuals as the art that was both most suited to African-American experience and most likely to attract the attentions of powerful white thinkers. Black poetry of a sort had already found an audience in the case of the works of Paul Laurence Dunbar (1872–1906) and were immensely popular, thanks to the patronage of white writers such as William Dean Howells. However, Dunbar was sceptical about such patronage, and it has since complicated his reputation; whites found his poems in Negro dialect appealing partly because they reinforced the stereotype of the placid black workman indelibly associated with slavery, while his standard English poems were generally neglected.

It was not until the early 1920s that the multifariousness of African-American poetry began to register in the white consciousness. One of the chief figures in this movement was James Weldon Johnson (1871–1938). Johnson had much in common with W. E. B. Du Bois; he too was elected to a prestigious university professorship (Du Bois was at Harvard, Johnson at New York University), and like Du Bois, he was heavily involved with the National Association for the Advancement of Colored People (NAACP). In 1921, he edited a landmark anthology, *The Book of American Negro Poetry*, the preface of which restates Du Bois's conviction that art might lead to emancipation:

A people may become great through many means, but there is only one measure by which its greatness is recognized and acknowledged. The final measure of the greatness of all peoples is the amount and standard of literature and art they have produced. The world does not know that a people is great until that people produces great literature and art. No people that has produced great literature and art has ever been looked upon by the world as distinctly inferior.[5]

---

* See Rowland Hughes, *York Notes Companions: 19th Century American Literature* (London: Pearson Longman & York Press, 2011) for a discussion of Douglass's autobiography.

Johnson's system of cultural evaluation may seem rather highbrow, but it certainly proved timely. By 1928, he could write that the 'newer approach' to racism 'requires a minimum of pleas, or propaganda, or philanthropy'; it centres instead on 'intellectual and artistic achievement', forming what he calls 'the art approach to the Negro problem'.[6] That evidence could be found for this 'approach' is testament to Johnson's own campaigns, but it could chiefly be explained by a movement across the arts in the 1920s and 1930s known as the Harlem Renaissance.

The Harlem Renaissance

The period of the Harlem Renaissance has been much analysed and much mythologised. Indeed, it was the subject of keen discussion as it happened, being largely a self-defining movement; artists were also critics of and commentators on the work of their peers. At the very centre of this dynamic culture was Langston Hughes (1902–67), a poet, prose writer and figurehead of African-American letters. As Hughes puts it straightforwardly in his autobiography *The Big Sea* (1940), 'the 1920s were the years of Manhattan's Black Renaissance'.[7] He goes on to describe the voguish clubs, parties and whist drives of 1920s Harlem, and the reader might be forgiven for imagining a black equivalent of the flapper and cocktail culture familiar from the works of F. Scott Fitzgerald. The two trends were certainly not unrelated, for an explosion in the popularity of jazz music was common to both; however, where many other literary movements of the 1920s ended in self-destruction, the Black Renaissance created audiences and opened up modes of expression whose influence reached way beyond their time.

In *The Big Sea*, Hughes describes his first foray into Manhattan's foremost African-American district with enthusiasm, almost wonder; his anticipation prevents him from 'put[ting] on paper the thrill of that underground ride to Harlem', and the sensation of finding 'hundreds of coloured people' on emerging from the subway (p. 81). The migration of Southern black families to Northern cities was the chief demographic phenomenon of early twentieth-century America. African Americans left the South in order to escape bigotry and violence and climb out of endemic poverty; Northern cities such as New York, Chicago and Detroit offered greater employment opportunities and, many believed, better futures for black children. The reality was rather different; by the time of the various civil rights and black protest movements of the 1960s, inner city ghettoes had eclipsed the rural South as the most visible sites of black deprivation and social division. Nevertheless, in the 1920s, Chicago's Southside, and especially New York's Harlem, had a great deal of metropolitan allure; so much, in fact, that prominent white celebrities might be encountered at 'rent parties' or glimpsed listening to Duke Ellington's band at the Cotton Club, even if his fellow African Americans were barred from such venues on account of their race.

Jazz and the blues are everywhere in Langston Hughes's poetry. His early verse in particular seeks to capture some of the rhythms and pungent harmonies of African-American music. Poems such as 'Dream Variations', 'The Weary Blues', 'Midwinter Blues' and 'Lonesome Place' either share their structures with the classic twelve-bar blues (in poetic form, translated into six stanzas of *ababab* rhyme) or directly express the joy and noise of dancing, singing or playing (see especially 'Lenox Avenue: Midnight').[8] However, such musicality is not mere abandonment or abstraction; as with all black art of the time, it has a strong political dimension, with jazz positioned as a form of lively opposition to a monochromatic, white-dominated world.[9] In Hughes's work, then, to sing is to assert a voice; it is to claim the right for that voice to be heard. In 'I, Too', he channels the ghost of Walt Whitman, whose 'Song of Myself' (1855) is one of the great statements of American individualism, claiming his right to speak for, and to, America too (p. 46). Though he writes as a black man who is forced to eat in the kitchen, he promises to grow strong from his experience and demand a place at the dining table. To sing America is to embody it, to be it; it is through singing that the speaker achieves a stake in his country. It is a motif that resounds through African-American literature, well beyond Hughes's work. We encounter it in the poem 'Heritage' by another Renaissance writer, Countee Cullen (1903–46), in which Africa is a prelapsarian paradise, that must be replicated in the New World; and during the 1960s, it would resurface in The Beatles' song 'Blackbird'

(1968),[10] and most prominently in the title of the first part of Maya Angelou's autobiography, *I Know Why the Caged Bird Sings* (1969).

In 'I, Too', Hughes also reminds white Americans that blackness cannot be erased from their heritage or history. A later poem, 'Theme for English B', from his 1951 sequence, *Montage of a Dream Deferred*, reiterates this reminder, making the white page on which he writes a metaphor for America, and its bringing together of different races under one banner (p. 410). Hughes believes in America; his ideals are expressed through a kind of pluralist patriotism. Other Harlem Renaissance writers were equally keen to imagine an America in which the black population might lay to rest the 'double consciousness' outlined by Du Bois. Alain Locke (1885–1954) was a hugely important figure in the movement, its 'Matthew Arnold', according to the critic Christopher Bisgby.[11] Locke edited a key anthology of prose and poetry in 1925, *The New Negro*. In the title essay, he writes of the northward migration of Southern blacks, proposing that 'with each successive wave of it, the movement of the Negro becomes more and more a mass movement toward the larger and the more democratic chance – in the Negro's case a deliberate flight not only from countryside to city, but from medieval America to modern'.[12] The Harlem Renaissance might not only be considered modern, but modernist; in its embrace of the music and art of the era, and its links to the nascent black cultural movement in Paris known as 'Négritude',* it offered a more authentic alternative to the 'primitivism' underlying many modernist works of art.†[13] While not explicitly aligning the works of the 'New Negro' to American modernism, Alain Locke implies that the voice of black New York is the voice of the now. There is no such thing as 'medieval

---

* 'Négritude' was an artistic movement initiated by black francophone writers in the 1930s, who used Marxist theories to rediscover their African roots outside of French cultural hegemony. Paris looms large in the imagination of African-American writers too; both James Weldon Johnson's *Autobiography of an Ex-Coloured Man* and Langston Hughes's *The Big Sea* feature sequences in the city.
† 'Primitivism' refers to any artistic movement which emphasises the supposedly 'primitive', or the incorporation of non-Western forms into Western art. Examples of specifically modernist primitivism include the Pablo Picasso painting *Les Démoiselles d'Avignon* (1907) and Igor Stravinsky's ballet *The Rite of Spring* (1913).

America', for the United States did not exist as a nation in the Middle Ages; the white South, then, is the imaginary America, while the black metropolis is a fulfilment of the modernity that is the USA's destiny.

The most modernist statement in Harlem Renaissance literature is the novel *Cane* (1923), by Jean Toomer (1894–1967). Toomer was born into a mixed-race family line with a history of both black slavery and white prosperity; indeed, he was often taken to be white. Much as Toomer occupied a liminal position between one race and another, so does *Cane* resist easy categorisation, comprising poems, prose character vignettes and almost play-like dialogue sequences. The polyphony of the work might imply a utopian fusion of black and white; an America achieved. Indeed, when asked to give biographical details by his publishers in 1922, Toomer declared 'from my own point of view I am naturally and inevitably an American'.[14] Nevertheless, the characters of *Cane* do not realise the revolutionary promise of Toomer's prose. They break out of the South, journeying to the North. Toomer's descriptions of Washington are intoxicating, but therein lies its danger. It is a 'beehive', a site of hyperactive busyness, but also a city in which to get 'drunk with silver honey'; the allure of materialism, of the money that implicitly rhymes with 'honey', is stronger than any more meaningful urban experience.[15] The third and final section of the novel returns to the South, suggesting that the North has failed its black migrants. There is no integration to be had in Chicago or Washington; just a different kind of alienation, not so dissimilar to that found by white writers in the big population centres.*

The Harlem Renaissance was thus not entirely a 'rebirth'; it could in fact be read as a false start. Some writers associated with the movement were cautious about its equal fascination with America and Africa, its potential to be drawn too much into the world of white patronage, and thus white values. The novelist Nella Larsen (1891–1964) writes in *Passing* (1929) of the trend for mixed-race people to 'pass' as whites. Clare Kendry marries a bigoted white man, John Bellew, who is unaware of her part-black heritage. When she meets an old black friend, Irene, after many years, she appears to proselytise for passing,

---

* See Part Three: 'The American City', for further discussion of this alienation.

saying 'You know, 'Rene, I've often wondered why more coloured girls like you ... never "passed" over. It's such a frightfully easy thing to do. If one's the type, all that's needed is a little nerve'.[16] Against her better judgement, Irene is intrigued by 'this hazardous business of "passing", this breaking away from all that was familiar and friendly to take one's chances in another environment' (p. 157). However, her relationship with Clare becomes convoluted. She suspects her of trying to poach her black husband, and grows increasingly exasperated at Clare's dishonesty with her own spouse about her racial background. Irene is 'caught between two allegiances, different, yet the same'. If she tells Bellew the truth, 'the race' is vindicated, but Clare is crushed, but if she keeps her silence, then 'the race' is 'crushed', and possibly herself with it; 'nothing, she imagined, was ever more completely sardonic' (p. 225). In the end, Clare falls to her death from a window; it is left to the reader to conjecture whether Irene pushes her, or she plummets accidentally. Whatever the cause, the consequence is unambiguous. 'Passing' oneself off as a different race can very well lead to another type of 'passing'; if not an actual death, then a spiritual or psychological one.

However, the most racially ambivalent of all Harlem Renaissance writers remains Zora Neale Hurston (1891–1960). Despite compiling collections of Southern black folktales, and collaborating with other Harlem writers, her work has been accused of neglecting the political and social duties of the oppressed African-American writer, particularly in times of radicalisation. Though her most read work, the lyrical Floridian novel *Their Eyes Were Watching God* (1937), is, like Larsen's novels, interested in the racial tensions between African Americans of different mixed heritages, it is just as much concerned with female subjectivity and sexual identity. While the next generation of black writers, such as Richard Wright and Ralph Ellison, complained that Hurston courted too much favour by playing to whites' stereotypes of blacks (a process that finds its own analogy in the novel when the black protagonist Janie is acquitted of murder by an all-white jury), Hurston attracted significant reappraisals in the 1970s and 1980s for being ahead of her time in discussing the discrepancies between the interior lives of African-American women and the roles they are expected to play.

In her 1928 essay, 'How it Feels to Be Colored Me', Hurston writes that at 'certain times I have no race, I am <u>me</u>. When I set my hat at a certain angle and saunter down Seventh Avenue, Harlem City, feeling as snooty as the lions in front of the Forty-Second Street Library, for instance … The cosmic Zora emerges. I belong to no race nor time. I am the eternal feminine with its string of beads.' Disavowing the idea of 'double-consciousness' she declares that she has 'no separate feelings about being an American citizen and colored. I am merely a fragment of the Great Soul that surges within the boundaries. My country, right or wrong.'[17] If for Hurston, to be 'me' is to be 'the eternal feminine', then her gender is even more central to her subjectivity than the colour of her skin. It is perhaps because of this that she feels she can successfully override Du Bois's 'double consciousness'. She recognises no segregation between her Americanness and her race; there are no Jim Crow laws policing identity. Instead, there are performative acts; the wearing of a hat at a certain angle, or the cultivating of a 'cosmic' persona. At a time when 'performing' race was tantamount to minstrelsy or the practice of music-hall 'blackface', the theatricality of Hurston's position on race is daring, but it sat uneasily with the tenor of the black writing that would emerge in the 1940s and 1950s.

The 'Second Black Renaissance'

The British critic Christopher Bigsby identifies the 1940s to the 1960s and beyond as a 'second black renaissance', made possible by the Harlem breakthrough of the 1920s, but in tone, motivation and style often radically different from its precursors. Like many critics, and indeed many African-American writers, he sees the novelist and essayist Richard Wright (1908–60) as the black literary figurehead of the mid-twentieth century; in terms of his influence, connection to other black writers, and standing within American culture at large, he was the natural successor to Langston Hughes. His first novel, *Native Son* (1940), was a sensation in its time. It relates the downward spiral of a black man, Bigger Thomas, who suffocates a Communist white girl to death in a moment of panic. This incident eventually leads to a place on Death Row, and the novel ends with Bigger awaiting electrocution. Throughout the book, black rats are used by Wright to symbolise the position of the urban African American; frequently regarded as little other than vermin, black people are subjected to vicious racism just as much as they ever were in the South. However, by the novel's conclusion, Bigger has discovered that he is a 'man', and this accords him enough self-respect to await his fate with a degree of resignation and dignity.

Similarly, in his memoir *Black Boy* (1945), Wright discusses the progress of an African-American's consciousness. It is a kind of *kunstlerroman* about the development of an artist; through cultivating his artistic sensibilities, Wright becomes a man. In this, it goes further than James Weldon Johnson's *Autobiography* or Langston Hughes's *The Big Sea*. It explores the intricacies of Wright's psychology with extraordinary depth, but also shows overwhelmingly that literary appreciation is a means of intellectual empowerment; even if the African-American man is treated like an animal (which is particularly true of the earlier Southern episodes before Wright moves to Chicago), his interior life makes a virtue of his humanity. Wright's pensiveness causes many whites to be suspicious of him; they ask him why he doesn't smile or laugh like 'other niggers'. His introversion is threatening to them, and is often taken for insolence; it costs him several jobs. The problem is that the white people around him expect him to perform his blackness in order to conform to their stereotype. He writes that he was 'living in a culture and not a civilization and I could learn how that culture worked only by living with it ... I had to feel and think out each tiny item of racial experience in the light of the whole race problem, and to each item I brought the whole of my life.' He records the stultifying effect of self-consciously performing for a white audience: 'In the past I had always said too much, now I found that it was difficult to say anything at all. I could not react as the world in which I lived expected me to; that world was too baffling, too uncertain.'[18] The divide within the African-American subject has shifted away from the 'double consciousness' of the American citizen and the black man, and into much more existential, even existentialist, terrain;* now it is a conflict between the inner soul and the outward pressures of society.

Several prominent African-American novels of the 1940s and 1950s took their cue from Wright's work, discussing the alienation of black city dwellers whose initial hopes of a better life in New York or Chicago had dwindled a generation or two along the line. This dwindling is summarised by Langston Hughes in his 1951 poem, 'Harlem (2)',[19] one of whose lines would go on to become the title of an influential 1959 play by the African-American dramatist Lorraine Hansberry (1930–65), *A Raisin in the Sun*. This work tells the story of a black family who move to an all-white suburb of Chicago after coming into some money, and the attempts of their white neighbours to expel them, and was written from Hansberry's own family experience, which ended in a landmark court case outlawing the 'restrictive covenants' implemented by realtors as a way of segregating urban housing stock. American fiction in general took a turn towards the alienated, disenfranchised or downtrodden in the 1950s and early 1960s; it was the era of Holden Caulfield, the rebellious teenage outcast in J. D. Salinger's novel *The Catcher in the Rye* (1951), the eponymous heroin addict of William Burroughs's *Junky* (1953) and the semi-suicidal Esther of Sylvia Plath's *The Bell Jar* (1963). The title of Richard Wright's novel *The Outsider* (1953) is a virtual rerun of the French existentialist philosopher and novelist Albert Camus's 1942 cult classic *L'Etranger* (often translated as 'The Outsider', rather than the more literal 'stranger'). It shares a sense of morbid despair with much non-black fiction of the time, but posits racism as a further reason for this despair; much of its tension also comes from its intellectualism, which puts its protagonist Cross Damon at odds with his fellow African Americans, as well as whites.

---

* The definition of existentialism continues to be fluid, but it is most associated with a group of French thinkers from the mid-twentieth century, especially Jean-Paul Sartre (1905–80) and Simone de Beauvoir (1908–86), who believed there was no such thing as the essential self, only a series of life choices that determined a person's identity or subjectivity.

Invisible Man (1952), by Wright's protégé Ralph Ellison (1914–94), is the finest achievement in this subgenre of African-American writing. Like Wright, Ellison was an intensely literary man, perhaps to be expected of a writer named after Ralph Waldo Emerson. The epigraphs to his novel, from T. S. Eliot and Herman Melville, establish *Invisible Man*'s allusiveness; there are subsequently references to and correspondences with Homer's *Odyssey*, Dante, Poe's gothic tales and the H. G. Wells novel with which Ellison's work shares its title.[20] The unnamed narrator-protagonist calls to mind that of Fyodor Dostoevsky's *Notes from Underground* (1864), itself a proto-existentialist novel. However, the practical displacement of race means that the narrator's alienation is socially produced: as he says, 'I am invisible, understand, simply because people refuse to see me.'[21] Like Wright's outsider, Ellison's invisible man joins a leftist organisation, in this instance known as 'The Brotherhood'; this proved controversial, given that the novel was published at the apex of McCarthyism.* The novel sees him trying to advance the progress of history, or arrest its typical motion. 'Beware of those who speak of the *spiral* of history', he warns early in the novel; 'they are preparing a boomerang. Keep a steel helmet handy' (p. 9). While his flirtation with communism does not secure any practical advantages, it does remind him that the world is full of possibilities; he does not actually give up hope. Near the beginning of the novel, he writes, 'Please, a definition: A hibernation is a covert preparation for a more overt action', and though by the novel's close, his own personal history has boomeranged ('the end was in the beginning', he muses, paraphrasing T. S. Eliot's 'East Coker'), he acknowledges it is time to 'come out'. 'Even hibernation can be overdone', he quips; 'perhaps that's my greatest social crime, I've overstayed my hibernation, since there's a possibility that even an invisible man has a socially responsible role to play' (p. 468).

---

* See Part Two: 'A Cultural Overview' for further information.

Civil Rights and the Black Arts Movement

By the late 1950s and early 1960s, the period of existential reflection on the black subject's position within society was, if not 'overdone', then certainly ready to transition. The invisible men were indeed 'coming out', as the Civil Rights Movement and associated campaigns gathered pace and urgency. From the mid-1950s on, mass sit-ins, protests and boycotts were organised in order to restart the national conversation about segregation, the colour line and the franchise. The Montgomery Bus Boycott, which lasted from December 1955 to December 1956, showed that through co-ordinated campaigns, white businesses could be severely imperilled by black protest. The boycott, which took place in the Southern state of Alabama, made a heroine of Rosa Parks (1913–2005), an African-American NAACP activist who refused to give up her bus seat to a white man, and was subsequently arrested. The boycott was led by a young reverend, Martin Luther King, Jr (1929–68), who soon became the most visible face of the Civil Rights Movement. Inspired by the example of Mohandas 'Mahatma' Gandhi during resistance to British rule in India, King advocated peaceful protest, and he combined this dedication to non-violent resistance with a gift for electrifying oratory; many of his speeches are themselves worthy entrants into the canon of great African-American literature.

The Civil Rights Movement had its own literary advocates too. The novelist and essayist James Baldwin (1924–87) was perhaps the most important African-American writer of the 1950s and 1960s. His novels, particularly *Go Tell It on the Mountain* (1953) and *Another Country* (1962), chronicle a multitude of divergent black experiences. *Go Tell It* is a semi-autobiographical exploration of 1930s Harlem; unlike the works of Wright and Ellison, it draws complex portraits of black people living with and despite each other. Likewise, *Another Country* is not interested in alienation so much as interaction, between blacks and whites, as well as within racial groups. Baldwin was sometimes accused of being a black writer consciously appealing to non-black readers; as Maya Angelou (1928–) recollects, some Africans thought him 'a creation of White America ... constructed by the establishment, for the establishment'.²² However, his experience was complicated; his potential social marginalisation was not only explained by his racial heritage. He was also predominantly homosexual, and as such was interested in bigotry and injustice of diverse forms; his fiction had to be capacious enough to deal with this, and thus did not always prioritise race issues. In any case, the Civil Rights Movement made direct appeals to the white population; its goal was equality and integration, the end of the 'double consciousness' once and for all.

In his influential essay 'Down at the Cross' (1963), Baldwin comments on another phenomenon, contemporaneous with the Civil Rights Movement but in many ways antithetical to it: the rise of African-American Islam. The organisations of Civil Rights often had a Christian basis, in the Baptist ministries of the South; however, a growing number of black Americans felt that Christianity was the religion of white oppression, carrying negative associations of colonial missionaries and cultural imperialism. The Nation of Islam, an organisation that came out of the ghettoes of Detroit, was founded in the 1930s, and led by Elijah Muhammad until his death in 1975. It proposed that Africans were the original human race, and that African Americans should turn away from westernisation and back towards the continent of their heritage. This 'black nationalism' did not share the integrationist ideals of the Civil Rights Movement, nor was it motivated by any belief in America as an ideal or Americanness as an identity. Much as the Civil Rights Movement had its hero in Martin Luther King, the Black Nationalist movement and its offshoots made an icon of Malcolm X (1925–65). Malcolm Little became Malcolm X because he refused to continue living under a slave name; all African Americans were forced to take the surnames of slave-owners and practice Christianity in the early days of bondage. In *The Autobiography of Malcolm X* (1964), a landmark testament written collaboratively with Alex Haley (1921–92), he rejects Martin Luther King's advocacy of non-violence, and argues that integration is a liberal sop, often hypocritical and unlikely to be of real or lasting advantage to the African-American. In 'Down at the Cross', James Baldwin is mindful of the attractiveness of Black Nationalism to many African Americans. He understands that 'in the United States, violence and heroism have been made synonymous except when it comes to blacks', though he then goes on to argue that Malcolm X's call for blacks to arm themselves against whites is potentially a grotesque mimicry of all the violent acts perpetrated in the past by whites in the name of 'glory'.[23] Baldwin's eloquent plea for black and white Americans to come together as Americans, 'to achieve our identity, our maturity, as men and women' (p. 83) is motivated by the fact that Black Nationalism only creates further divisions; after all, as he writes in another essay, 'the story of the Negro in America is the story of America',[24] an opinion that would not have been out of place in a work by W. E. B. Du Bois or Langston Hughes.

However, by the late 1960s, Baldwin's voice seemed anomalous in the wake of the Black Arts Movement, the literary expression of loosely affiliated 'black power' and black nationalist organisations. Black Arts was the brainchild of LeRoi Jones (1934–), a black American poet who in 1967 assumed the African name Imamu Amear Baraka, later shortened to Amiri Baraka. Baraka had been an associate of 'beat' writers such as Allen Ginsberg, but by the mid-1960s, he was spearheading his own literary revolution. The Black Arts Movement centred around avant-garde black theatre, yet again in Harlem, though Baraka is mostly known for his poetry. One piece in particular, 'Black Art' (1969), is the defining African-American poem of its era, a paramilitary assault in verse, calling explicitly for poems that 'kill'.[25] This is incendiary stuff, particularly at a time of almost unparalleled American military activity and civil disarray: the Vietnam War, the Detroit race riots of 1967 which resulted in President Lyndon B. Johnson mobilising the army to police the streets, the threat posed by the radical Black Panther terrorist organisation, the assassinations of Malcolm X (1965), Martin Luther King (1968) and the pro-civil rights Democratic politician Bobby Kennedy (also 1968) were all still fresh wounds in the body politic. Indeed, Amiri Baraka elsewhere declared the USA to be on its last legs, going through its decadent phase, or awaiting apocalypse as he prophesises in 'Poetry and Karma'.[26]

In this poem, the dropping of the initial 'A' of America, as if to indicate that the fall of the nation is already in progress, is a deliberate and politically resonant rhetorical device. During the late 1960s and early 1970s, many writers began to capitalise the adjective 'black' while reducing America to lower-case letters. A notable example can be found in the poem 'The American Cancer Society Or There Is More Than One Way To Skin A Coon' (1974) by Audre Lorde (1934–92), which protests against a barrage of tobacco advertising. In Lorde's poem America is figured as a decaying civilisation, caught in a downward spiral of cheap self-promotion, implicating black people in an increasingly redundant system of symbols.[27] As in the Baraka piece, Lorde cuts America down to size, graphically illustrating the demise predicted in the poem.

It seems that many African-American writers of the period were keen to dissociate themselves from American experience or identity, even those who had previously found value in it. The poet Gwendolyn Brooks (1917–2000), for example, discovered a new voice in the 1960s. Where previously she had called herself a 'Negro', she now spoke of black pride, and grew her hair into the Afro style, urging fellow black women to resist the straightening comb. The early phase of her career was notable for canonical non-African American influences as much as 'Negro' features. For example, her poem 'The Sundays of Satin-Legs Smith' (1945) is partly inspired by T. S. Eliot's 'The Love Song of J. Alfred Prufrock' (1915), and includes an echo of the repeated invitation in the earlier modernist poem, 'let us go'.[28] However, these white influences gradually disappear; by 1960, and the much-anthologised 'We Real Cool', Brooks was articulating black voices by using idiomatic rhythms and dialects, capturing the spirit of the pool hall and the dance club, and in 1968, she could add her voice to the many lamenting the passing of Malcolm X (p. 90). Even Maya Angelou, arguably one of the most 'establishment' African-American writers (she read a poem at the inauguration of President Bill Clinton in 1993) found herself downplaying her connection to Martin Luther King and foregrounding her 'black power' days on journeying to Africa in Part Five of her series of memoirs, All God's Children Need Travelling Shoes (1986): she describes her onetime belief in King's methods as 'deluded' and expresses scepticism about the success of the Civil Rights Movement.

African-American Diversities

In her 1976 novel *Meridian*, Alice Walker (1944–) proposes a middle ground. The protagonist, Meridian Hill, is a mediator, as her name suggests; she is involved in the Civil Rights Movement, and has some sympathy for more radical forms of black activism, but is sceptical about the role of violence, speculating that 'perhaps it will be my part to walk behind the real revolutionaries – those who know they must spill blood in order to help the poor and the black and therefore go right ahead'. She suggest that 'when they stop to wash off the blood and find their throats too choked with the smell of murdered flesh to sing, I will come forward and sing from memory songs they will need once more to hear.'[29] As discussed earlier in this chapter, the motif of singing has often been central to the struggle for black emancipation; here, Meridian draws on it to suggest that when the dust has settled on the upheavals of the 1960s, there might be a middle way for African-American experience that draws upon the past both good and bad. The conciliatory tone is characteristic of Walker's work, which prioritises the lives of African-American women working together against oppression. Her most read novel, *The Color Purple* (1982), is chiefly about black women initiating acts of connection; the novel centres around Celie's one-way correspondence to God, and her epistolary relationship with her sister Nettie, who is undertaking missionary work in Africa. Not only does the novel connect over continents, but it also introduces the possibility of fulfilling lesbian attachment among African-American women. Its final connection is a historical one: Walker sets the novel in Georgia in 1909. After a period in which books set in the segregated South were not politically expedient, the 1970s and 1980s saw a resurgence in black American writing that looked to reclaim or re-narrate aspects of African-American social history; the phenomenal success of Alex Haley's 1976 novel, *Roots: The Saga of an American Family*, and the subsequent television adaptation, proved that slavery too could now be revisited.

The diversity of African-American writing since the 1970s has been extraordinary. For example, Walker is only one of many female writers to consider what it means to be a woman of colour in postmodern America. It might be noted that much of the greatest African-American literature to have emerged in the last forty years or so has been by women. Maya Angelou's aforementioned five-part memoir, beginning with *I Know Why the Caged Bird Sings* (1969), is nothing less than a history of African Americans from the 1930s to the 1970s, told through the experiences of one woman. Other writers have renegotiated the past by discovering innate poetry within groundbreaking events. The title poem of *On the Bus with Rosa Parks* (1999) by Rita Dove (1952–) replicates some of Parks's interview statements since the Montgomery Bus Boycott almost verbatim: the implication is that her struggle is poetic enough already. Another poem in the collection, 'In the Lobby of the Warner Theatre, Washington, D.C.', recounts a public appearance by Parks, mapping her dignified 1950s protest onto her contemporary celebrity. Somewhat symbolically, attendants take great care in positioning her wheelchair correctly, referring to her as '*living* history'.[30]

Diversity has also been suggested by narrative experimentation in African-American writing. The postmodern novelist, poet and essayist Ishmael Reed (1938–) has carved his own distinct niche, arguing in his novels for a plurality of different African-American voices that are in many ways representative of the plurality of American voices at large in the great metropolises of the late twentieth century; meanwhile, his poetry anthology *From Totems to Hip-Hop* (2003) signposts where the writing and the study of poetry might be headed in the twenty-first century. Black gay male writing has flourished too. Though his life was cut tragically short by AIDS, the poet Essex Hemphill (1957–95) did much to increase the profile of black queer writers, both in the 1991 anthology he edited, *Brother to Brother*, and in his own poetry. There was enough of an African-American literary past for him to draw upon a 1950s classic in his poem ' Commitments', referring to himself as the 'invisible son'.[31] Where Ralph Ellison alluded to Dante and Homer, Hemphill invokes Ellison.

More recently, postmodern African-American writers have emphasised the performative nature of blackness; but often, the problems they encounter are the exact opposite of those of, say, Richard Wright. *Erasure* (2001), a novel by Percival Everett (1956–), satirises the vogue for all things black, ghetto or 'street' at the turn of the millennium. The protagonist is a writer called Thelonious Ellison; even his name suggests a kind of performed racial heritage, a conflation of the jazz pianist Thelonious Monk and the novelist Ralph Ellison. He is penning a novel, but his agent does not think it black enough; only when he changes its title to *Fuck* in an attempt to gain street-cred does he get his publisher's approval and a spot on a talk show (modelled on that of Oprah Winfrey, another huge influence on African-American culture in the late twentieth century). Everett's satire is drawn from personal experience; he is an African-American writer who does not always write about black characters or themes, something that would have been virtually unthinkable until the 1970s.

If this plurality of voices shows the diversity of African-American literature today, then the international esteem of the Nobel Prize-winning novelist Toni Morrison (1931–) proves that the mainstream canon can find space for the writing of black American women. Morrison's novels deal with the legacies of slavery, segregation and racism, which sometimes come back to haunt characters across different times and spaces, as in *Beloved* (1987). The last chapter of the novel repeats 'it was not a story to pass on', suggesting that the shame of Sethe killing her child rather than have her sold into slavery is too shameful or painful to retell. However, a transformation takes place on the page; the phrase becomes 'this is not a story to pass on', which suggests that the reader should not 'pass' on the message of the novel, but rather, absorb and claim it. Writing here is a form of exorcism, and also a way of taking the traumas of the past and letting the human spirit sing through them, by the magic of the pen and page. In this way, Morrison is the latest in a long line of African-American writers who have proved that literature can be a vital socio-political force, a force that can be both of its moment and generate the moments of the future.

Notes

1   W. E. B. Du Bois, *The Souls of Black Folk*, ed. Henry Louis Gates, Jr., and Terri Hume Oliver (New York: Norton, 1999), p. 17.
2   Quoted in 'Preface', in Du Bois, *The Souls of Black Folk*, p. xxi.
3   William H. Ferris, originally in *The African Abroad; or His Evolution in Western Civilization: Tracing his Development Under Caucasian Milieus* (1913), quoted in Gates and Oliver, Preface to *The Souls of Black Folk* (pp. ix–xxxv).
4   Dudley Randall, 'Booker T. and W. E. B.', in Margaret Danner and Dudley Randall, eds, *Poem Counterpoem* (Detroit: Broadside Press, 1966), p. 8.
5   James Weldon Johnson, Preface to *The Book of American Negro Poetry* (1921), reprinted in Henry Louis Gates Jr. and Nellie Y. Mackay, *The Norton Anthology of African American Literature* (New York: Norton, 1997), pp. 861–84 (861).
6   James Weldon Johnson, 'Race Prejudice and the Negro Artist', *Harper's* CLVII, November 1928, pp. 769–70 (769).
7   Langston Hughes, *The Big Sea* (New York: Hill and Wang, 1998), p. 223.
8   Langston Hughes, 'Lenox Avenue: Midnight', *The Collected Poems of Langston Hughes*, ed. Arnold Rampersad (New York: Vintage, 1994), p. 92.
9   Hughes, 'The Negro Artist and the Racial Mountain' (1926), reprinted in *The Norton Anthology of African American Literature*, pp. 1267–71 (1270).
10   See Paul McCartney, 'Blackbird', *Blackbird Singing: Poems and Lyrics 1965–1999* (London: Faber & Faber, 2002), p. vii.
11   C. W. E. Bigsby, *The Second Black Renaissance: Essays in Black Literature* (Westport, CN: Greenwood Press, 1980), p. 13. Matthew Arnold (1822–88) was a British poet and critic, notable especially for the essays of *Culture and Anarchy* (1869), in which he prescribes what 'culture' might be and outlines its civilising benefits.
12   Alain Locke, 'The New Negro' (1925), reprinted in *The Norton Anthology of African American Literature*, pp. 961–70 (963).
13   For studies of the links between the Harlem Renaissance and modernism, see Houston A. Baker, Jr., *Modernism and the Harlem Renaissance* (Chicago: University of Chicago Press, 1987); for a study of the influence of black art and literature on modernism in general, see Sieglinde Lemke, *Primitivist Modernism: Black Culture and the Origins of Transatlantic Modernism* (Oxford: Oxford University Press, 1998).
14   Quoted in Arna Bontemps, Introduction to Jean Toomer, *Cane* (1923. New York: Harper & Row, 1969), pp. vii–xvi (viii).

15   Toomer, *Cane*, p. 89.

16   Nella Larsen, *Passing* (1929. London: Serpent's Tail, 1995), pp. 157–8.

17   Zora Neale Hurston, 'How it Feels to Be Colored Me' (1928), *The Norton Anthology of African American Literature*, pp. 1008–11 (1010).

18   Richard Wright, *Black Boy: A Record of Childhood and Youth* (1945. London: Vintage, 2000), p. 198.

19   Hughes, 'Harlem (2)', *The Collected Poems of Langston Hughes*, p. 426.

20   See H. G. Wells, *The Invisible Man* (1897. London: Penguin, 2005).

21   Ralph Ellison, *Invisible Man* (1952. Harmondsworth: Penguin, 1987), p. 7.

22   Maya Angelou, *All God's Children Need Travelling Shoes* (1986. London: Virago, 1991), p. 120.

23   James Baldwin, 'Down at the Cross', *The Fire Next Time* (Harmondsworth: Penguin, 1965), p. 54.

24   Baldwin, 'Many Thousands Gone' (1951), *The Norton Anthology of African American Literature*, pp. 1659–70 (1659).

25   Amiri Baraka, 'Black Art', *The Norton Anthology of African American Literature*, pp. 1883–4 (1883).

26   Baraka, 'Poetry and Karma', *Raise Race Rays Raze: Essays Since 1965* (New York: Vintage, 1972), pp. 17–26 (18).

27   Audre Lorde, 'The American Cancer Society Or There Is More Than One Way To Skin A Coon', *The Collected Poems of Audre Lorde* (New York: Norton, 1997), pp. 107–8 (108).

28   Gwendolyn Brooks, 'The Sundays of Satin-Legs Smith' (1945), *The Essential Gwendolyn Brooks*, ed. Elizabeth Alexander (New York: Library of America, 2005), pp. 10–16 (12).

29   Alice Walker, *Meridian* (New York: Pocket Books, 1976), p. 13.

30   Rita Dove, 'In the Lobby of the Warner Theatre, Washington, D.C.', *On the Bus with Rosa Parks: Poems* (New York: Norton, 1999), pp. 86–7 (86).

31   Essex Hemphill, 'Commitments', *Brother to Brother: New Writings by Black Gay Men*, ed. Essex Hemphill (Boston: Alyson Publications, 1991), pp. 57–8 (58).

Part Five
References and Resources
Timeline

	Historical Events	Literary Events
1900	Hawaii becomes US territory	Theodore Dreiser, *Sister Carrie*
1901	President William McKinley assassinated; Philippine-American War ends; Booker T. Washington becomes first African American to dine at the White House	
1902	Cuba gains independence from the USA	
1903	Wright Brothers fly the first aeroplane	W. E. B. Du Bois, *The Souls of Black Folk*
1905		Edith Wharton, *The House of Mirth*
1906	San Francisco earthquake kills over 3,000	Upton Sinclair, *The Jungle*
1908	Henry Ford produces the first Model T. car; FBI established	
1909	National Association for the Advancement of Coloured People (NAACP) founded	Gertrude Stein, *Three Lives*
1911		Edith Wharton, *Ethan Frome*

Timeline

	Historical Events	Literary Events
1912	*Titanic* sinks on its way from UK to USA	Theodore Dreiser, *The Financier*
1913	Federal Reserve Act	Willa Cather, *O Pioneers!*; Edith Wharton, *The Custom of the Country*
1914	Congress establishes first federal income tax	
1915	US military occupies Haiti	Charlotte Perkins Gilman, *Herland*; Susan Glaspell, *Fidelity*; Willa Cather, *The Song of the Lark*
1916	First birth control clinic opens in New York	Robert Frost, 'The Road Not Taken'; John Dewey, *Democracy and Education*
1917	USA joins First World War	T. S. Eliot, *Prufrock and Other Observations*
1918	First World War ends; Wisconsin becomes first state to number its highways	Willa Cather, *My Antonia*
1919	Nineteenth Amendment passed, bringing suffrage to women; first 'Red Scare'; Seattle General Strike	Sherwood Anderson, *Winesburg, Ohio*
1920	Prohibition of alcohol begins	Edith Wharton, *The Age of Innocence*; John Dos Passos, *Three Soldiers*; F. Scott Fitzgerald, *This Side of Paradise*; Sinclair Lewis, *Main Street*
1921	President Warren G. Harding inaugurated; Tulsa race riots	
1922		T. S. Eliot, *The Waste Land*; F. Scott Fitzgerald, 'The Diamond as Big as the Ritz'; Sinclair Lewis *Babbitt*; E. E. Cummings, *The Enormous Room*

20th Century American Literature

	Historical Events	Literary Events
1923	*Time* magazine founded; Calvin Coolidge becomes president	Wallace Stevens, *Harmonium*; Jean Toomer, *Cane*; William Carlos Williams, *The Great American Novel*
1924	Ku Klux Klan membership reaches a peak; first performance of Gershwin's *Rhapsody in Blue*	Marianne Moore, *Observations*
1925	Scopes Trial outlaws anti-creationist teaching in Tennessee schools; first edition of *The New Yorker*	F. Scott Fitzgerald, *The Great Gatsby*; John Dos Passos, *Manhattan Transfer*; Langston Hughes, *I, Too, Sing America*; Alain Locke, *The New Negro*
1926	NBC becomes USA's first broadcast network	Hart Crane, *White Buildings*; Ernest Hemingway, *Fiesta: The Sun Also Rises*
1927	Charles Lindbergh flies across the Atlantic; first Academy Awards (Oscars) ceremony	
1928	Walt Disney's *Steamboat Willie* introduces Mickey Mouse	Nella Larsen, *Quicksand*; Eugene O'Neill, *Strange Interlude*
1929	Wall Street Crash; USA plunged into the Great Depression	William Faulkner, *The Sound and the Fury*; Ernest Hemingway, *A Farewell to Arms*; Thomas Wolfe, *Look Homeward, Angel*; Nella Larsen, *Passing*
1930	Dust Bowl begins in the Great Plains	William Faulkner, *As I Lay Dying*; Hart Crane, *The Bridge*
1931	Empire State Building completed	Eugene O'Neill, *Mourning Becomes Electra*
1932	Dow Jones Industrial Average reaches a record low	William Faulkner, *Light in August*; Erskine Caldwell, *Tobacco Road*

Timeline

Historical Events	Literary Events
1933 Franklin D. Roosevelt inaugurated as president; prohibition comes to an end; First New Deal; *Esquire* magazine launched	Gertrude Stein, *The Autobiography of Alice B Toklas*; Erskine Caldwell, *God's Little Acre*; Nathanael West, *Miss Lonelyhearts*
1934	F. Scott Fitzgerald, *Tender is the Night*; John O'Hara, *Appointment in Samarra*; Henry Roth, *Call It Sleep*; Malcolm Cowley, *Exile's Return*; Henry Miller, *Tropic of Cancer*
1935 Social Security Act introduced to provide pension system	Marianne Moore, *Selected Poems*; John O' Hara, *Butterfield 8*; Clifford Odets, *Waiting for Lefty*
1936 *Life* magazine founded; Jesse Owens wins four gold medals in Berlin Olympics	William Faulkner, *Absalom, Absalom!*; Djuna Barnes, *Nightwood*
1937 Hindenburg disaster as a German airship is destroyed in New Jersey; Golden Gate Bridge opens in San Francisco	John Steinbeck, *Of Mice and Men*; Zora Neale Hurston, *Their Eyes Were Watching God*; Margaret Mitchell, *Gone with the Wind*
1938 Superman first appears in DC comics	Thornton Wilder, *Our Town*
1939 *The Wizard of Oz* and *Gone with the Wind* are cinema box-office successes	John Steinbeck, *The Grapes of Wrath*
1940 Roosevelt is re-elected, the only president ever to serve more than two terms; the Macdonald brothers open their first fast-food restaurant in San Bernardino	Carson McCullers, *The Heart is a Lonely Hunter*; Ernest Hemingway, *For Whom the Bell Tolls*; Richard Wright, *Native Son*

Historical Events	Literary Events
1941 Pearl Harbour bombed; the USA joins Second World War	Eudora Welty, *A Curtain of Green*; F. Scott Fitzgerald, *The Last Tycoon*; James Agee, *Let Us Now Praise Famous Men*
1942 Manhattan Project to research atomic bomb begins	William Faulkner, *Go Down, Moses*
1943 Closure of the Works Progress Administration marks the official end of Great Depression	Ayn Rand, *The Fountainhead*; T. S. Eliot, *Four Quartets*
1944 D-Day landings in Normandy	Tennessee Williams, *The Glass Menagerie*
1945 Atomic bomb dropped on Hiroshima; end of Second World War; Death of President Roosevelt; United Nations founded in New York	Arthur Miller, *Focus*; John Steinbeck, *Cannery Row*; Richard Wright, *Black Boy*
1946 Nuclear bomb testing under the Pacific	Elizabeth Bishop, *North and South*; Eugene O'Neill, *The Iceman Cometh*; H. D., *Trilogy*; Carson McCullers, *The Member of the Wedding*; Robert Lowell, *Lord Weary's Castle*
1947 House Un-American Activities Committee (HUAC) begins investigating Hollywood Communist activity; Roswell UFO incident	Arthur Miller, *All My Sons*; John Cheever, 'The Enormous Radio'; Tennessee Williams, *A Streetcar Named Desire*
1948 President Truman begins Marshall Plan of aid to post-war Europe; the first Kinsey report into sexual behaviour published	Norman Mailer, *The Naked and the Dead*; Gore Vidal, *The City and the Pillar*
1949 NATO established	Arthur Miller, *Death of a Salesman*

Timeline

	Historical Events	Literary Events
1950	US troops embark on Korean War; McCarthyism begins	Lionel Trilling, *The Liberal Imagination*; Ray Bradbury, *The Martian Chronicles*
1951	Ninth Street Show introduces New Yorkers to avant-garde art	Carson McCullers, *The Ballad of the Sad Cafe*; J. D. Salinger, *The Catcher in the Rye*; James Jones, *From Here to Eternity*
1952	John Cage's avant-garde composition 4:33 premieres in New York; Lt. Ron Hubbard founds scientology	Ernest Hemingway, *The Old Man and the Sea*; Flannery O'Connor, *Wise Blood*; Ralph Ellison, *Invisible Man*; John Steinbeck, *East of Eden*; Bernard Malamud, *The Natural*
1953	Korean War ends; Hugh Hefner creates *Playboy* magazine; Rosenbergs sentenced to death for espionage; Dwight D. Eisenhower becomes president	William S. Burroughs, *Junky*; Arthur Miller, *The Crucible*; James Baldwin, *Go Tell It On the Mountain*; Saul Bellow, *The Adventures of Augie March*
1954	Supreme Court declares racial segregation in schools unlawful (*Brown* v. *Board of Education*); NBC airs the first late-night talk show, *The Tonight Show*	Randall Jarrell, *Pictures from an Institution*
1955	Rosa Parks refuses to give up her seat, leading to Montgomery bus boycott; Disneyland opens in California; 'Rock Around the Clock' becomes the first single to top the Billboard charts	Vladimir Nabokov, *Lolita*; Arthur Miller, *A View from the Bridge*; Flannery O'Connor, *A Good Man is Hard to Find*; Tennessee Williams, *Cat on a Hot Tin Roof*
1956	Interstate Highway Act	Allen Ginsberg, 'Howl'; Eugene O'Neill, *Long Day's Journey Into Night*; Saul Bellow, *Seize the Day*
1957	US Commission on Civil Rights formed	Jack Kerouac, *On the Road*; John Cheever, *The Wapshot Chronicle*

20th Century American Literature

Historical Events	Literary Events
1958 NASA established	Tennessee Williams, *Suddenly, Last Summer*; William Carlos Williams, *Paterson*
1959 Alaska and Hawaii become 49th and 50th states; Khrushchev and Nixon hold 'kitchen debates' at American National Exhibition in Moscow	Robert Lowell, *Life Studies*; Grace Paley, *The Little Disturbances of Man*; William S. Burroughs, *Naked Lunch*
1960 Contraceptive pill approved by US Food and Drug Administration	John Updike, *Rabbit, Run*; Flannery O'Connor, *The Violent Bear it Away*; Harper Lee, *To Kill a Mockingbird*; Leslie Fiedler, *Love and Death in the American Novel*; Anne Sexton, *To Bedlam and Part Way Back*
1961 President John F. Kennedy inaugurated	Joseph Heller, *Catch-22*; Richard Yates, *Revolutionary Road*
1962 Cuban Missile Crisis; Astronaut John Glenn becomes first American to orbit the earth; Bob Dylan releases first album; Andy Warhol moves into 'The Factory'	Edward Albee, *Who's Afraid of Virginia Woolf?*; James Baldwin, *Another Country*; Jack Kerouac, *Big Sur*; John Ashbery, *The Tennis Court Oath*
1963 President Kennedy assassinated; Martin Luther King delivers 'I have a dream' speech	James Baldwin, *The Fire Next Time*; Sylvia Plath, *The Bell Jar*; Mary McCarthy, *The Group*; Thomas Pynchon, *V*
1964 Civil Rights Act prohibits discrimination; Free Speech Movement begins at Berkeley; President Lyndon B. Johnson proposes the 'Great Society'	John Berryman, *77 Dream Songs*; Robert Lowell, *For the Union Dead*; John Cheever, 'The Swimmer'; Saul Bellow, *Herzog*
1965 American military begins ground war in Vietnam; Malcolm X assassinated; National Endowment for the Arts founded; Medicare and Medicaid established	Elizabeth Bishop, *Questions of Travel*; Malcolm X, *The Autobiography of Malcolm X*; Truman Capote, *In Cold Blood*

Timeline

Historical Events	Literary Events
1966 Troops in Vietnam reach 250,000; *Star Trek* premieres on NBC	Thomas Pynchon, *The Crying of Lot 49*
1967 Detroit race riots; first Super Bowl game of American football	Norman Mailer, *Why Are We in Vietnam?*
1968 Martin Luther King assassinated; Mai Lai Massacre in Vietnam; Robert Kennedy assassinated; continuing campus protests against Vietnam War	Richard Brautigan, *In Watermelon Sugar*; Donald Barthelme, *Unspeakable Practices, Unnatural Acts*; Joan Didion, *Slouching Towards Bethlehem*; Norman Mailer, *The Armies of the Night*
1969 Apollo 11 mission; Neil Armstrong becomes first man on the moon; President Richard Nixon inaugurated; Stonewall riots begin gay rights movement; Woodstock Festival; Charles Manson murders	Maya Angelou, *I Know Why the Caged Bird Sings*; Philip Roth, *Portnoy's Complaint*; Kurt Vonnegut, *Slaughterhouse-Five*; John Cheever, *Bullet Park*
1970 Kent State shootings as National Guard open fire on unarmed students	Kate Millett, *Sexual Politics*; Toni Morrison, *The Bluest Eye*
1971 Ban on TV cigarette advertising; Apollo 15 moon landings; first Starbucks cafe opens in Seattle	Don DeLillo, *Americana*; E. L. Doctorow, *The Book of Daniel*
1972 Nixon meets Chairman Mao in China; Watergate break-in	Ishmael Reed, *Mumbo Jumbo*; John Barth, *Chimera*
1973 US begins withdrawal from Vietnam; *Roe* v. *Wade* case invalidates anti-abortion laws; international oil crisis; *The Exorcist*, the most profitable horror movie of all time, is released	Thomas Pynchon, *Gravity's Rainbow*; Erica Jong, *Fear of Flying*; Tom Wolfe, *The New Journalism*

Historical Events	Literary Events
1974 Nixon resigns after Watergate scandal; US economy suffers 'stagflation'	Grace Paley, *Enormous Changes at the Last Minute*; Robert M. Pirsig, *Zen and the Art of Motorcycle Maintenance*
1975 Vietnam War officially ends; Microsoft founded; Sony Betamax becomes the first commercially available home videotape format	Maxine Hong Kingston, *The Woman Warrior*; E. L. Doctorow, *Ragtime*
1976 Viking II space probe lands on Mars	Elizabeth Bishop, *Geography III*; Raymond Carver, *Will You Please Be Quiet, Please?*
1977 President James Carter inaugurated; New York blackout results in arson and looting; death of Elvis Presley; first *Star Wars* film	Toni Morrison, *Song of Solomon*; Leslie Marmon Silko, *Ceremony*
1978 Harvey Milk assassinated	John Irving, *The World According to Garp*; Armistead Maupin, *Tales of the City*
1979 Iran hostage crisis; partial meltdown at Three Mile Island nuclear plant	William Styron, *Sophie's Choice*
1980 US boycotts Moscow Olympics; Mount St Helens eruption kills 57	Marilynne Robinson, *Housekeeping*; Sam Shepard, *True West*
1981 President Ronald Reagan inaugurated; AIDS first recognised by the Centres for Disease Control and Prevention; debut of MTV	Raymond Carver, *What We Talk About When We Talk About Love*
1982 Brief recession; Michael Jackson releases his bestselling album, *Thriller*	James Merrill, *The Changing Light at Sandover*; Alice Walker, *The Color Purple*

Timeline

	Historical Events	Literary Events
1983	US invades Grenada; Strategic Defence Initiative of space-based missiles (dubbed 'Star Wars')	Charles Olson, *The Maximus Poems*
1984	Apple Computer introduces the Macintosh PC; 'Crack epidemic' begins in Los Angeles	Jay McInerney, *Bright Lights, Big City*; Kathy Acker, *Blood and Guts in High School*; David Mamet, *Glengarry Glen Ross*
1985	President Reagan meets Mikhail Gorbachev	Don DeLillo, *White Noise*; Cormac McCarthy, *Blood Meridian*; Grace Paley, *Later the Same Day*; Lorrie Moore, *Self Help*
1986	Challenger space shuttle explodes; Contra controversy as US concedes selling weapons to guerrilla fighters in Nicaragua; first broadcast of *Oprah Winfrey Show*	Richard Ford, *The Sportswriter*
1987	Black Monday stock-market crash; Prozac antidepressants introduced	Paul Auster, *The New York Trilogy*; Toni Morrison, *Beloved*; Tom Wolfe, *The Bonfire of the Vanities*
1988	Mikhail Gorbachev visits the USA	Tama Janowitz, *A Cannibal in Manhattan*; Raymond Carver, *Elephant*
1989	Cold War ends with fall of Berlin Wall; George Bush Sr. becomes US president	John Irving, *A Prayer for Owen Meany*; Joyce Carol Oates, *American Appetites*; Amy Tan, *The Joy Luck Club*
1990	Hubble Space Telescope launched	Judith Butler, *Gender Trouble*; John Updike, *Rabbit at Rest*
1991	First Gulf War with Iraq; START 1 agreement with USSR, agreeing to eventually dismantle nuclear weapons	Bret Easton Ellis, *American Psycho*; Tony Kushner, *Angels in America*

20th Century American Literature

	Historical Events	Literary Events
1992	Riots in Los Angeles after the death of Rodney King	Toni Morrison, *Jazz*; Cormac McCarthy, *All the Pretty Horses*; Donna Tartt, *The Secret History*
1993	President Bill Clinton inaugurated; Waco Cult Siege	Jeffrey Eugenides, *The Virgin Suicides*; Annie Proulx, *The Shipping News*
1994	Investigations into Whitewater controversy begin	Cormac McCarthy, *The Crossing*; Rick Moody, *The Ice Storm*
1995	Oklahoma City bombing becomes worst domestic terrorist incident in US history; O. J. Simpson murder trial becomes worldwide television event; Chicago heat wave kills 750	T. Coraghessan Boyle, *The Tortilla Curtain*; James Merrill, *A Scattering of Salts*; Sherman Alexie, *Reservation Blues*
1996	Dot-com bubble	David Foster Wallace, *Infinite Jest*; Chuck Palahniuk, *Fight Club*; Annie Proulx, *Accordion Crimes*
1997	Clinton formally apologises for Tuskegee experiment (1932–72) on black males	Don DeLillo, *Underworld*; Philip Roth, *American Pastoral*; Thomas Pynchon, *Mason and Dixon*
1998	President Clinton impeached on charge of perjury relating to sex scandal; murder of Matthew Shepard causes debate about homophobia; Google founded	Philip Roth, *I Married a Communist*; Michael Cunningham, *The Hours*
1999	Columbine High School massacre	Jonathan Lethem, *Motherless Brooklyn*; Toni Morrison, *Paradise*
2000	Civil unions between same-sex couples legalised in Vermont	Philip Roth, *The Human Stain*; Michael Chabon, *The Amazing Adventures of Kavalier and Clay*

Timeline

	Historical Events	Literary Events
2001	President George W. Bush inaugurated; 9/11 terrorist attacks; Bush defies Kyoto Protocol on greenhouse gas emissions; US-led invasion of Afghanistan	Jonathan Franzen, *The Corrections*; Percival Everett, *Erasure*
2002	Homeland Security Act introduced	Edward Albee, *The Goat*; Jeffrey Eugenides, *Middlesex*; Jonathan Safran Foer, *Everything is Illuminated*
2003	Second Gulf War in Iraq	Don DeLillo, *Cosmopolis*; Siri Hustvedt, *What I Loved*
2004	Facebook launched; Abu Ghraib prisoner abuse footage shown on television	Marilynne Robinson, *Gilead*; Philip Roth, *The Plot Against America*
2005	Hurricane Katrina kills over 1,800 people in the Mississippi Delta	Cormac McCarthy, *No Country for Old Men*; Jonathan Safran Foer, *Extremely Loud and Incredibly Close*
2006	US housing bubble continues	Cormac McCarthy, *The Road*; Anne Tyler, *Digging to America*; Thomas Pynchon, *Against the Day*; John Updike, *Terrorist*
2007	Virginia Tech massacre; Bush vetoes congress decision to ease stem-cell research restrictions	Don DeLillo, *Falling Man*
2008	Global financial crisis necessitates government bailouts	Marilynne Robinson, *Home*
2009	Barack Obama becomes USA's first black president; 'tea-party' protests begin	Jonathan Lethem, *Chronic City*
2010	Deepwater Horizon oil rig explodes in Gulf of Mexico	Jonathan Franzen, *Freedom*

Further Reading

Social and Historical Context

Aaron, Daniel, *Writers on the Left: Episodes in American Literary Communism* (New York: Octagon, 1974)

> This study of the influence of the Left on American literature covers the period 1912–1940, taking in the first 'Red Scare' and the proletarian writers' movements of the 1920s and 1930s

Bayley, Sally, *Home on the Horizon: America's Search for Space from Emily Dickinson to Bob Dylan* (Oxford: Peter Lang, 2010)

> This engaging study of the spatial imagination and its relationship to American self-construction takes in a diverse range of texts and writers, from Frank L. Baum to Cormac McCarthy

Cobb, James C., *Away Down South: A History of Southern Identity* (New York: Oxford University Press, 2005)

> This stimulating study explores the shifting concept of Southernness, covering a breadth of issues including religion, politics, war and art

Cullen, Jim, *The American Dream: A Short History of an Idea That Shaped a Nation* (New York: Oxford University Press, 2003)

> This rewarding introduction rescues a much-discussed concept from cliché, examining the provenance and the current state of the national myth

Denning, Michael, *The Cultural Front: The Labouring of American Culture in the Twentieth Century* (New York: Verso, 2011)

> This highly recommendable study covers the 1930s and 1940s, arguing that this was in many ways the most 'progressive' time in US cultural history

Glickman, Lawrence B. (ed.), *Consumer Society in American History: A Reader* (Ithaca: Cornell University Press, 1999)

> This reader comprises various theoretical and historical studies of consumerism, from early America to the 1990s

Further Reading

Gray, Richard, *Writing the South: Ideas of an American Region* (Cambridge: Cambridge University Press, 1986)
> This landmark study details how Southern fiction responds to the collective trauma of the Civil War, and analyses its specific historical and cultural inheritance

Halliwell, Martin (series ed.), *Twentieth-Century American Culture* (9 vols. Edinburgh: Edinburgh University Press, 2007–10)
> These excellent introductions to the cultural context of the century run to nine volumes, each one dealing with a decade, and cover intellectual contexts and legacies as well as discussions of literature, music, television, film and the visual arts

Jackson, Kenneth T., *Crabgrass Frontier: The Suburbanization of America* (New York: Oxford University Press, 1985)
> This landmark study traces the history of the American suburb, and the reasons for its centrality in the American national imagination

May, Elaine Tyler, *Homeward Bound: American Families in the Cold War Era* (New York: Basic Books, 1988)
> This is an illuminative exploration of the impact of Cold War ideology on the domestic front

Ngai, Mae M., *Impossible Subjects: Illegal Aliens and the Making of Modern America* (Princeton: Princeton University Press, 2005)
> This book argues that illegal immigration has had as much of an effect on the nation as legal, and examines a wide array of different national and cultural identities

Susman, Warren, *Culture as History: The Transformation of American Society in the Twentieth Century* (New York: Pantheon, 1984)
> This collection of Susman's essays covers a broad range of topics, including mass production, the American city, and consumerism

Tallack, Douglas, *Twentieth-Century America: The Intellectual and Cultural Context* (London: Longman, 1991)
> This is a very helpful survey of the connections between different intellectual movements, covering cinema, architecture and painting as well as literature and literary theory

Genre and Form

Author-specific works on the eighteen writers explored in Part Three: 'Texts, Writers and Contexts' have been incorporated into this section under the appropriate headings.

Fiction

Arcana, Judith, *Grace Paley's Life Stories: A Critical Biography* (Urbana: University of Illinois Press, 1993)

> This is the only critical biography available at present, and features material from various conversations between Arcana and Paley

Bailey, Blake, *Cheever: A Life* (London: Picador, 2009)

> This is the definitive biography of John Cheever, rich in detail about both his life and work

Bell, Bernard W., *The Contemporary African-American Novel: Its Folk Roots and Modern Literary Branches* (Amherst: University of Massachusetts Press, 2004)

> This study of black American fiction traces its heritage from modernism to the postmodern and the present day

Bradbury, Malcolm, *The Modern American Novel* (Oxford: Oxford University Press, 1992)

> This is a very useful, chronologically organised overview of most of the major figures and trends in twentieth-century American fiction

Brooker, Peter, *New York Fictions: Modernity, Postmodernism, the New Modern* (London: Longman, 1996)

> This study of literary representations of the metropolis proceeds chronologically, from modernism to the Harlem Renaissance and the jazz age, on towards postmodernism

Brooks, Cleanth, *William Faulkner: Toward Yoknapatawpha and Beyond* (New Haven: Yale University Press, 1978)

> This is one of the classic studies of Faulkner's fiction, examining all of Faulkner's major works

Bruccoli, Matthew J., *Some Sort of Epic Grandeur: The Life of F. Scott Fitzgerald* (Columbia: University of South Carolina Press, 2002)
> This is the most comprehensive and useful biography of Fitzgerald, connecting life, work and socio-historical/literary context

Chandler, Marilyn R., *Dwelling in the Text: Houses in American Fiction* (Berkeley: University of California Press, 1991)
> This exploration of the theme of home in American fiction is an excellent 'next step' from Part Four: 'Home and Away' of this book, taking in discussions of Fitzgerald, Faulkner and Marilynne Robinson among others

Gelfant, Blanche H., *The Columbia Companion to the Twentieth-Century American Short Story* (New York: Columbia University Press, 2000)
> This comprehensive overview of the most American of literary forms includes a series of thematic essays, followed by an author-by-author encyclopaedia

Graham, Maryemma (ed.), *The Cambridge Companion to the African American Novel* (Cambridge: Cambridge University Press, 2004)
> This is a highly recommendable starting point for readers interested in the history and theory of African-American fiction, which includes essays on the legacies of slavery, the protest novel, and the relationship between literature and popular culture

Green, Jeremy, *Late Postmodernism: American Fiction at the Millennium* (New York: Palgrave Macmillan, 2005)
> This study analyses the current context of the American novel, discussing what might succeed postmodernism, and the place of social realism in the 2000s

Kennedy, J. Gerald (ed.), *Modern American Short-Story Sequences: Composite Fictions and Fictive Communities* (Cambridge: Cambridge University Press, 1995)
> This is a useful collection of essays covering writers from Sherwood Anderson to John Cheever and Raymond Carver

Killoran, Helen, *Edith Wharton: Art and Allusion* (Tuscaloosa: University of Alabama Press, 1996)
> This study goes beyond Wharton as a novelist of manners to consider her from a more psychological perspective

Kleppe, Sandra Lee and Miltner, Robert (eds), *New Paths to Raymond Carver: Critical Essays on His Life, Fiction, and Poetry* (Columbia: University of South Carolina Press, 2008)

> This is an excellent study of Carver's work, taking in his poems as well as thematic essays on the short fiction

Lee, Hermione, *Edith Wharton* (London: Vintage, 2008)

> This is the latest and most comprehensive critical biography of its subject

Millard, Kenneth, *Contemporary American Fiction* (Oxford: Oxford University Press, 2000)

> This collection of essays on individual authors covers many of the figures mentioned in Part Four of this book, including Roth, Morrison, Proulx, Walker, Alexie, DeLillo, Auster and Updike

Moreland, Richard C. (ed.), *A Companion to William Faulkner* (Oxford: Blackwell, 2007)

> This is a comprehensive and up-to-date introduction to the latest in Faulkner studies, including key critical approaches and discussions of publishing contexts

Prigozy, Ruth (ed.), *The Cambridge Companion to F. Scott Fitzgerald* (Cambridge: Cambridge University Press, 2002)

> This is a versatile collection of essays, covering women in Fitzgerald's fiction, his relationship with Hollywood, his short stories and the 1920s among other topics

Tuttleton, James W., *The Novel of Manners in America* (Chapel Hill: University of North Carolina Press, 1972)

> This study surveys the contexts of the novel of manners from Henry James through to John O'Hara, and their critical history

Wagner-Martin, Linda, *The Mid-Century American Novel 1935–1965: A Critical History* (New York: Twayne, 1997)

> This is a highly useful introduction to a very fertile time in American literary history, covering the key writers and movements of the period

Westling, Louise, *Sacred Groves and Ravaged Gardens: The Fiction of Eudora Welty, Carson McCullers, and Flannery O'Connor* (Athens: University of Georgia Press, 1985)

> This landmark study contextualises Welty, McCullers and O'Connor in terms of their southern heritage from a feminist perspective

Wolff, Geoffrey, *The Art of Burning Bridges: A Life of John O'Hara* (New York: Knopf, 2003)

> This is the only major biography of O'Hara; it also offers extensive interpretations of the novels

Woodhouse, Reed, *Unlimited Embrace: A Canon of Gay Fiction, 1945–1995* (Amherst: University of Massachusetts Press, 1998)

> This is a readable survey of American gay novels and novelists from the end of the war to the age of AIDS and beyond, which links debates about sexuality to wider American cultural history

Poetry

Beach, Christopher, *The Cambridge Introduction to Twentieth-Century American Poetry* (Cambridge: Cambridge University Press, 2003)

> This is a useful and readable introduction, taking in all the poets featured in Part Three of this book

Costello, Bonnie, *Elizabeth Bishop: Questions of Mastery* (Cambridge, MA: Harvard University Press, 1991)

> This examination of Bishop's poetry pays close attention to her visual imagination and explores additional aspects of her art

Erickson, Darlene Williams, *Illusion is More Precise than Precision: The Poetry of Marianne Moore* (Tuscaloosa: University of Alabama Press, 1992)

> This study is particularly good on questions of allusion and influence in Moore's poetry

Gabriel, Daniel, *Hart Crane and the Modernist Epic: Canon and Genre Formation in Crane, Pound, Eliot, and Williams* (New York: Palgrave, 2007)

> This study locates Crane within the modernist tradition, discussing his poetic form alongside that of key contemporaries

Gray, Richard, *American Poetry of the Twentieth Century* (London: Longman, 1990)

> This is an accessible and highly useful survey of the texts and contexts of twentieth-century American poetry

Holley, Margaret, *The Poetry of Marianne Moore: A Study in Voice and Value* (Cambridge: Cambridge University Press, 1997)

> This is an excellent study that traces the development of Moore's distinctive voice from early work to late

Hyde, Lewis (ed.), *On the Poetry of Allen Ginsberg* (Ann Arbor: University of Michigan Press, 1984)

> This book gathers reviews and articles and is a useful sourcebook for further reading on Ginsberg

Kalstone, David, *Becoming a Poet: Elizabeth Bishop with Marianne Moore and Robert Lowell* (Ann Arbor: University of Michigan Press, 2001)

> This now classic study, originally published in 1989, also contains an afterword by James Merrill

Keller, Lynn, *Re-making it New: Contemporary American Poetry and the Modernist Tradition* (Cambridge: Cambridge University Press, 2009)

> This study pairs post-war American poets with modernist predecessors, and features especially useful chapters on Moore's influence on Bishop, and W. H. Auden's influence on Merrill

Longenbach, James, *Modern Poetry After Modernism* (New York: Oxford University Press, 1997)

> This exploration of post-war American poetry considers the causes and consequences of postmodernism, covering Bishop and Ashbery among others

Further Reading

McGowan, Christopher, *Twentieth-Century American Poetry* (Malden: Blackwell, 2004)

> This comprehensive guide gives précis of individual poets, followed by commentaries on significant works, and thematic essays on the long poem, correspondences with other arts and war, amongst other topics

Nickowitz, Peter, *Rhetoric and Sexuality: The Poetry of Hart Crane, Elizabeth Bishop and James Merrill* (New York: Palgrave, 2006)

> This is a good study of how the three poets' homosexuality had an impact on their poetry, written from a psychoanalytical perspective

Parini, Jay (ed.), *The Columbia History of American Poetry* (New York: Columbia University Press, 1993)

> This history is an essential collection of essays covering the sweep of poetic history from the puritans up to the 1980s, including good introductions to the confessionals, Bishop, Merrill, Crane and African-American poetry

Sastri, Reena, *James Merrill: Knowing Innocence* (New York: Routledge, 2007)

> This is the latest book-length study of Merrill's work, and is particularly strong on close readings of his later poetry

Vendler, Helen, *Part of Nature, Part of Us* (Cambridge, MA: Harvard University Press, 1980)

> This is an indispensable collection of reviews and essays by one of the most important American poetry critics, covering Ginsberg, O'Hara, Bishop, Lowell, Merrill, Plath and Moore amongst others

Wheeler, Lesley, *The Poetics of Enclosure: American Women Poets from Dickinson to Dove* (Knoxville: University of Tennessee Press, 2002)

> This excellent study reads six poets (including Moore, Bishop and Gwendolyn Brooks) through their reconfiguration of the lyric voice, and how it interacts with issues of gender, sexuality and race

Drama

Bisgby, C. W. E., *A Critical Introduction to Twentieth-Century American Drama* (3 vols. Cambridge: Cambridge University Press, 1982–85)
> This is a landmark study of American drama, including all the major playwrights discussed in Part Three: 'The American Stage'

— *Modern American 1945–1990* (Cambridge: Cambridge University Press, 2000)
> This is an accessible and effective departure point for anyone interested in the sweep of post-war American theatre

Chothia, Jean, *Forging a Language: A Study of the Plays of Eugene O'Neill* (Cambridge: Cambridge University Press, 1979)
> This is an important study of O'Neill's plays from the Provincetown Players period to his later works, focusing especially on his use of language and form

Demastes, William W., *Realism and the American Dramatic Tradition* (Tuscaloosa: University of Alabama Press, 1996)
> This study examines how twentieth-century American theatre both welcomes and subverts realism, considering the experiments of O'Neill's and Williams's androgyny, amongst other subjects

Krasner, David (ed.), *A Companion to Twentieth-Century American Drama* (Malden: Blackwell, 2005)
> This collection of introductory essays contains excellent material on Williams, Miller and O'Neill, as well as Edward Albee, plays of the Harlem Renaissance and Asian-American theatre

Manheim, Michael (ed.), *The Cambridge Companion to Eugene O'Neill* (Cambridge: Cambridge University Press, 1998)
> This is a good starting point for anyone interested in O'Neill's plays, compiling thematic essays on gender, national identity and autobiography amongst other subjects

Murphy, Brenda (ed.), *Twentieth-Century American Drama: Critical Concepts in Literary and Cultural Studies* (4 vols. London: Routledge, 2006)

> This four-part study offers many different critical perspectives on the sweep of twentieth-century theatre, taking in key topics of debate such as race, feminism and form

Roudane, Matthew C. (ed.), *The Cambridge Companion to Tennessee Williams* (Cambridge: Cambridge University Press, 1997)

> This is an excellent point of departure for studies of Williams's work, with essays on genre, dramaturgy, gender and performance history

Savran, David, *Communists, Cowboys and Queers: The Politics of Masculinity in the Work of Arthur Miller and Tennessee Williams* (Minneapolis: University of Minnesota Press, 1992)

> This is a now classic study of Williams and Miller in their socio-historical context, discussing gender and politics in the major works

Theories and Methodologies

Baym, Nina, *Feminism and American Literary History: Essays* (New Brunswick: Rutgers University Press, 1992)

> This collection of Baym's essays suggests some useful ways of reading the scope of American literary history through a feminist lens

Gates Jr., Henry Louis (ed.), *Reading Black, Reading Feminist: A Critical Anthology* (New York: Penguin, 1990)

> This is a highly useful starting point for readers interested in how theories of race intersect with gender scholarship

Harper, Philip Brian, *Framing the Margins: The Social Logic of Postmodern Culture* (New York: Oxford University Press, 1994)

> This wide-ranging consideration of postmodernism includes chapters on black writing, marginalisation and questions of subjectivity

James, Joy and Sharpley-Whiting, T. Denean (eds), *The Black Feminist Reader* (Malden: Blackwell, 2000)

This readable anthology of critical and theoretical writing contextualises race within feminist theory, and includes essential essays by Toni Morrison and Bell Hooks among others

King, C. Richard, *Postcolonial America* (Urbana: University of Illinois Press, 2000)

This study considers American culture from a postcolonial standpoint, examining questions of American empire and race politics, and how they intersect with other social factors such as economics and religion

Messent, Peter, *New Readings of the American Novel: Narrative Theory and its Application* (Edinburgh: Edinburgh University Press, 1998)

This study makes the narrative theories of Barthes, Bakhtin and Genette accessible by applying them to eight classic novels, including *The House of Mirth* and *The Great Gatsby*

Singh, Amritjit and Schmidt, Peter (eds), *Postcolonial Theory and the United States: Race, Ethnicity, and Literature* (Jackson: University Press of Mississippi, 2000)

This is an excellent collection of essays on a wide variety of topics, including globalisation, race anxiety, masculinity and hybridity

Winchell, Mark Royden, *Cleanth Brooks and the Rise of Modern Criticism* (Charlottesville: University of Virginia Press, 1996)

This is an interesting study of American criticism in the mid century, examined through the life and work of one of the most significant of all 'new critics', Cleanth Brooks

Surveys and Reference Guides

Andrews, William L., Smith Foster, Frances and Harris, Trudier (eds), *The Concise Oxford Companion to African American Literature* (Oxford: Oxford University Press, 2001)

This is an alphabetical encyclopaedia, featuring entries on individual writers, texts, movements and characters, and appendices on African-American history

Bercovitch, Savcan (ed.), *The Cambridge History of American Literature* (8 vols. Cambridge: Cambridge University Press, 1994)

This is an exhaustive history up to 1990 in eight volumes, charting the key movements and trends from puritan literature of the 1590s to the plurality of American literatures in the late twentieth century

Champion, Laurie (ed.), *American Women Writers, 1900–1945: A Bio-Bibliographical Critical Sourcebook* (Westport: Greenwood Press, 2000)

This is a user-friendly encyclopaedia of major women writers in the first half of the twentieth century, covering many figures featured in this book (such as Moore, Wharton, O'Connor and Hurston)

Crow, Charles L., *A Companion to the Regional Literatures of America* (Malden: Blackwell, 2003)

This extensive guide to regionalism(s) in the United States includes essays on region and race, and region and realism, as well as discussion of individual geographies, such as the Midwest, the South, and California

Davidson, Cathy N. and Wagner-Martin, Linda (eds), *The Oxford Companion to Women's Writing in the U.S.* (New York: Oxford University Press, 1995)

This is an excellent encyclopaedia that covers women's writing and women writers through American literary history

Flora, Joseph M. and Mackethan, Lucinda H. (eds), *The Companion to Southern Literature: Themes, Genres, Places, People, Movements, and Motifs* (Baton Rouge: Louisiana State University Press, 2002)

This encyclopaedia organises its subject thematically rather than biographically or historically, itemising and assessing the different ways in which Southern literature responds to American literary history and culture more generally

Kalaidjian, Walter (ed.), *The Cambridge Companion to American Modernism* (Cambridge: Cambridge University Press, 2005)

This excellent collection of essays includes overviews of drama, fiction and poetry, as well as themed sections on African-American writing, nationalism, regionalism and critical contexts

McDonald, Gail, *American Literature and Culture 1900–1960* (Malden: Blackwell, 2007)

> This is an excellent introduction to the topic, broadly chronological though organised around themes such as freedom, novelty and affluence

Parini, Jay (ed.), *The Oxford Encyclopaedia of American Literature* (4 vols. Oxford: Oxford University Press, 2004)

> This is an exemplary four-volume compendium of essays on themes, authors, movements and historical contexts

Ruland, Richard and Bradbury, *Malcolm, From Puritanism to Postmodernism: A History of American Literature* (London: Penguin, 1992)

> This is a highly accessible and broad-ranging history of American literature from its beginnings to the 1990s, taking account of most major movements and writers

Websites

The Literary Encyclopedia: www.litencyc.com

> This is an online resource featuring indexes and bibliographies of major authors, a list of 4,000 internet resources for further study, and profiles of many key authors and individual works

Modern American Poetry: www.english.illinois.edu/maps/poets.htm

> This is a free-to-use site hosted by the University of Illinois. It is an essential resource for any student of twentieth-century American poetry, featuring critical materials and analyses of important individual poems

New York Review of Books: www.nybooks.com

> While the full texts are only available to subscribers, it is possible to browse the contents of the NYRB's impressive archive, and some of the featured articles, which go back to the 1960s

Index

Toomer, Jean, *Cane* 257
Trilling, Lionel 124, 125
　The Middle of the Journey 15
Turner, Frederick Jackson, 'The
　　Significance of the Frontier in
　　American History' 8
Twain, Mark 7, 83, 132
　Adventures of Huckleberry Finn 220

universities
　creative writing programmes 133
　protest movements 23
Updike, John 133, 149, 152, 221,
　　236, 244
　Rabbit, Run 213–14
　Terrorist 27, 199
urbanisation *see* cities

Van Vechten, Carl, *Parties* 121
Vanity Fair (magazine) 116
Veblen, Thorstein 108, 112, 120,
　　121, 127–8, 185
Vendler, Helen 45
Venturi, Robert 191–2
Vidal, Gore, *The City and the Pillar*
　　218–19
Vietnam War 21–2, 46, 221, 235,
　　265
Virgin Suicides, The (film) 235
Vonnegut, Kurt, *Slaughterhouse-Five*
　　16

Walker, Alice 267, 268
Wall Street (film) 221
Wall Street Crash (1929) 13–14, 186,
　　210, 231
Wallace, David Foster 26
Warhol, Andy 25
Warren, Robert Penn 9
Washington, Booker T., *Up From
　　Slavery* 252

Washington, DC 181, 257
Watergate scandal 21, 235
Weber, Max, *The Protestant Ethic and
　　the Spirit of Capitalism* 11, 185
Wells, H. G. 262
Welty, Eudora 84, 133
Wharton, Edith 9, 109–116, 121,
　　124, 125, 130, 133
　The Age of Innocence 114–15
　A Backward Glance 109, 110, 111
　'A Cup of Cold Water' 111
　The Custom of the Country 114
　The Glimpses of the Moon 114
　The House of Mirth 110, 111–13,
　　121
　Old New York 110, 114
White, Edmund 220
Whitman, Walt 20, 30–3, 34, 36–7,
　　38, 43, 44–5, 46, 48–50, 53,
　　56, 57–8, 190, 219, 255
Wilbur, Richard 72
Wild One, The (film) 21
Wilder, Thornton
　Our Town 14, 166
　The Skin of Our Teeth 166
Williams, Joy 133
Williams, Tennessee 19, 133, 165–70,
　　219, 239
　Camino Real 165
　Cat on a Hot Tin Roof 165, 170,
　　173
　The Glass Menagerie 165–7, 168,
　　170, 175
　A Streetcar Named Desire 18, 83,
　　168–70, 173, 178
　Suddenly Last Summer 175
Williams, William Carlos 37–8, 39,
　　41, 45, 57–8, 71
　Paterson 190–1, 199
Wilson, Sloan, *The Man in the Gray
　　Flannel Suit* 213

Acknowledgements

Reprinted by permission of Farrar, Straus and Giroux LLC:

Excerpts from 'Invitation to Miss Marianne Moore', 'The Man-Moth', 'The Fish', 'Roosters', 'The Moose', 'Poem', 'The Weed', 'Questions of Travel', 'The Map', 'North Haven', and 'In the Waiting Room' from THE COMPLETE POEMS 1927–1979 by Elizabeth Bishop. Copyright © 1979, 1983 by Alice Helen Methfessel.

Excerpt from 'As We Like It: Miss Moore and the Delight of Imitation' from PROSE by Elizabeth Bishop, edited by Lloyd Schwartz. Copyright © 2011 by the Alice H. Methfessel Trust

Excerpts from:

'Cathedral' from CATHEDRAL by Raymond Carver, published by Harvill Press, copyright © 1981, 1982, 1983 by Raymond Carver. Used by permission of Alfred A. Knopf, a division of Random House, Inc. and The Random House Group

'The Collectors' from WILL YOU PLEASE BE QUIET, PLEASE by Raymond Carver, published by Harvill Press. Reprinted by permission of The Random House Group Ltd

'The Collectors' and 'Cathedral' from *Where I'm Calling From*, 'The Collectors' copyright © 1976 by Raymond Carver. 'Cathedral' copyright © 1983 by Raymond Carver. Used by permission of Grove/Atlantic, Inc.

Acknowledgements

'A Terrestrial Cuckoo', 'Ode' and 'Invincibility' from *Meditations in an Emergency*, copyright © 1957 by Frank O'Hara. Used by permission of Grove/Atlantic, Inc.

APPOINTMENT IN SAMARRA by John O'Hara (published by Vintage Classics). Copyright © 1934 and renewed 1962 by John O'Hara. Used by permission of Random House, Inc. and The Random House Group Ltd

Strange Interlude and *Long Day's Journey into Night* by Eugene O'Neill, reproduced by kind permission of the Yale Committee on Literary Property

'A Pact' from *Personae: Collected Shorter Poems of Ezra Pound* by Ezra Pound. Reproduced by permission of Faber & Faber and New Directions Publishing

Reprinted with the permission of HarperCollins Publishers Ltd and Scribner, a Division of Simon & Schuster, Inc. from ACCORDION CRIMES by Annie Proulx. Copyright © 1996 by Dead Line, Ltd. All rights reserved

YORK NOTES **COMPANIONS**

Texts, Contexts and Connections from York Notes to help you through your literature degree ...

The best books ever written

20% discount on your essential reading from
Penguin Classics, only with *York Notes Companions*

The House of Mirth
Edith Wharton
Introduction and Notes by Cynthia Wolff
Paperback | 368 pages | ISBN 9780140187298 | 25 Nov 1993 | £7.99

Tender is the Night
F. Scott Fitzgerald
Edited by Arnold Goldman, with an Introduction and Notes by
Richard Godden
Paperback | 400 pages | ISBN 9780141183596 | 26 Apr 2001 | £8.99

Death of a Salesman
Arthur Miller
Paperback | 112 pages | ISBN 9780141182742 | 30 Mar 2000 | £8.99

Collected Poems 1947–1997
Allen Ginsberg
Paperback | 1216 pages | ISBN 9780141190181 | 26 Feb 2009 | £35.00

On the Road
Jack Kerouac
Introduction by Ann Charters
Paperback | 320 pages | ISBN 9780141182674 | 24 Feb 2000 | £8.99

The Heart is a Lonely Hunter
Carson McCullers
Introduction and Notes by Kasia Boddy
Paperback | 352 pages | ISBN 9780141185224 | 31 Aug 2000 | £9.99

To claim your 20% discount on any of these titles
visit **www.penguinclassics.co.uk** and use
discount code **YORK20**